Prentice Hall

GRAMMAR HANDBOOK

Grade 12

Upper Saddle River, New Jersey
Boston, Massachusetts
Chandler, Arizona
Glenview, Illinois

Prentice Hall Grammar Handbook Consulting Author

We wish to thank Jeff Anderson who guided the pedagogical approach to grammar instruction utilized in this handbook.

Grateful acknowledgment is made to the following for copyrighted material:

Dutton Signet

From *Beowulf*, translated by Burton Raffel, copyright © 1963 renewed copyright © 1991 by Burton Raffel.

Longman Publishing Group, A Division of Pearson Education, Inc.

"Writing in a Second Language" from *Writing: A Guide for College and Beyond (2nd Edition)* by Lester Faigley. Copyright © 2010 by Pearson Education, Inc.

Note: Every effort has been made to locate the copyright owner of material reproduced in this component. Omissions brought to our attention will be corrected in subsequent editions.

Credits

Cover

Photos provided by istockphoto.com

Illustrations

Maria Raymondsdotter

Photographs

All interior photos provided by Shutterstock, Inc.

ISBN-13: 978-0-13-363845-5
ISBN-10:   0-13-363845-6

2 3 4 5 6 7 8 9 10 VO64 13 12 11 10

GRAMMAR

USAGE

CHAPTER 8 Using Modifiers   195

CHAPTER 9 Miscellaneous Problems in Usage 207

MECHANICS

Numbered tags like this **EL1** are used on instruction pages of the Grammar Handbook to indicate where to find a related tip in the English Learner's Resource.

CHAPTER 1

THE PARTS *of* SPEECH

Use each part of speech to help you improve the quality and clarity of your writing.

WRITE GUY *Jeff Anderson, M.Ed.*

WHAT DO YOU NOTICE?

Spot different parts of speech as you zoom in on these lines from the poem "Sonnet 39" by Sir Philip Sidney.

MENTOR TEXT

> O make in me those civil wars to cease;
> I will good tribute pay, if thou do so.

Now, ask yourself the following questions:

- What is the subordinating conjunction in these lines?
- Does the subordinate clause in these lines come before or after the main, or independent, clause?

The subordinating conjunction in these lines is the word *if*. The subordinate clause *if thou do so* comes after the main clause *I will good tribute pay*. Conjunctions play an important role in starting clauses and in connecting related clauses.

Grammar for Writers A conjunction is an essential part of speech because it has a variety of functions. Based on the conjunction you choose, you can completely change the relationship between ideas in your sentences.

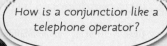

How is a conjunction like a telephone operator?

That's easy. Both make connections!

1

1.1 Nouns and Pronouns

Nouns and pronouns make it possible for people to label everything around them.

Nouns

The word *noun* comes from the Latin word *nomen*, which means "name."

RULE 1.1.1

> **A noun** is the part of speech that names a person, place, thing, or idea.

Nouns that name a *person* or *place* are easy to identify.

PERSON Uncle Mike, neighbor, girls, Bob, swimmer, Ms. Yang, Captain Smith

PLACE library, Dallas, garden, city, kitchen, James River, canyon, Oklahoma

The category *thing* includes visible things, ideas, actions, conditions, and qualities.

VISIBLE THINGS chair, pencil, school, duck, daffodil, fort

IDEAS independence, democracy, militarism, capitalism, recession, freedom

ACTIONS work, research, exploration, competition, exercise, labor

CONDITIONS sadness, illness, excitement, joy, health, happiness

QUALITIES kindness, patience, ability, compassion, intelligence, drive

Concrete and Abstract Nouns

Nouns can also be grouped as *concrete* or *abstract*. A **concrete noun** names something you can see, touch, taste, hear, or smell. An **abstract noun** names something you cannot perceive through any of your five senses.

CONCRETE NOUNS	person, cannon, road, city, music

See Practice 1.1A

ABSTRACT NOUNS	hope, improvement, independence, desperation, cooperation

Collective Nouns

A **collective noun** names a *group* of people or things. A collective noun looks singular, but its meaning may be singular or plural, depending on how it is used in a sentence.

COLLECTIVE NOUNS			
army	choir	troop	faculty
cast	class	crew	legislature

Do not confuse collective nouns—nouns that name a collection of people or things acting as a unit—with plural nouns.

Compound Nouns

A **compound noun** is a noun made up of two or more words acting as a single unit. Compound nouns may be written as separate words, hyphenated words, or combined words.

COMPOUND NOUNS	
Separate	life preserver coffee table bird dog
Hyphenated	sergeant-at-arms self-rule daughter-in-law
Combined	battlefield dreamland porthole

Check a dictionary if you are not sure how to write a compound noun.

Common and Proper Nouns

Any noun may be categorized as either *common* or *proper*.
A **common noun** names any one of a class of people, places,
or things. A **proper noun** names a specific person, place, or thing.
Proper nouns are capitalized, but common nouns are not.
(See Chapter 10 for rules of capitalization.)

COMMON
NOUNS
building, writer, nation, month, leader,

place, book, war

PROPER
NOUNS
Jones, Virginia, *Leaves of Grass,*

Revolutionary War, White House, Mark Twain,

France, June

A noun of direct address—the name of a person to whom you
are directly speaking—is always a proper noun, as is a family
title before a name. In the examples below, common nouns are
highlighted in yellow, and proper nouns are highlighted in orange.

COMMON
NOUNS
My **sister** is a **teacher** .

Our **doctor** always makes us wait.

My favorite person is my **brother** .

DIRECT
ADDRESS
Please, **Grandpa** , can you take us to the park?

Mom , can you get the check?

Analise , please bring your fruit cup when you come
to the party.

FAMILY
TITLE
Uncle Mike lived in **New York City** .

Grandma makes salad with marshmallows, a
favorite with the whole family.

My favorite person is **Aunt Emma** .

See Practice 1.1B

PRACTICE 1.1A ⟩ **Identifying and Labeling Nouns as Concrete or Abstract**

Read each item. Then label each item *concrete noun* or *abstract noun*, and write another similar abstract or concrete noun.

EXAMPLE   power

ANSWER   abstract noun, *authority*

1. timepiece
2. grace
3. maturity
4. petal
5. revenge
6. necklace
7. magazine
8. gallery
9. fear
10. restaurant

PRACTICE 1.1B ⟩ **Recognizing Kinds of Nouns (Collective, Compound, Proper)**

Read each sentence. Then, write whether the underlined nouns are *collective*, *compound*, or *proper*. Answer in the order the words appear.

EXAMPLE   <u>Marcia</u> can't wait to rejoin her <u>team</u>.

ANSWER   *proper, collective*

11. Janice's car had a <u>tune-up</u> on <u>Friday</u>.
12. I think <u>Scrappy</u> is the best-behaved dog in the litter.
13. I hope <u>Captain Martin</u> makes me a part of his <u>crew</u>.
14. My <u>mother-in-law</u> just arrived from <u>Greece</u>.
15. There are some poisonous snakes in <u>Arizona</u>.
16. Some professionals believe <u>fingerpainting</u> is an art.
17. I watched a <u>busload</u> of tourists enter the <u>Natural History Museum</u>.
18. Her favorite <u>radio station</u> plays jazz.
19. There is a <u>host</u> of sparrows in the tree.
20. <u>Sam</u> tells me there is good fishing in <u>Lake Superior</u>.

SPEAKING APPLICATION

Take turns with a partner. Describe a country you would like to visit and tell why. Include at least three abstract nouns in your response. Your partner should listen for and name the abstract nouns.

WRITING APPLICATION

Write a paragraph about what you plan to do during your next summer vacation. Include at least one common, one collective, one compound, and one proper noun.

Pronouns

Pronouns help writers and speakers avoid awkward repetition of nouns.

> **Pronouns** are words that stand for nouns or for words that take the place of nouns.

Antecedents of Pronouns Pronouns get their meaning from the words they stand for. These words are called **antecedents.**

> **Antecedents** are nouns or words that take the place of nouns to which pronouns refer.

The arrows point from pronouns to their antecedents.

EXAMPLES   **Dad** said that **he** had left **his** book at home.

When my **grandparents** moved, **they** gave **their** books to me.

Attending the senior prom was tiring, but **it** was fun!

Antecedents do not always appear before their pronouns, however. Sometimes an antecedent follows its pronoun.

EXAMPLE   Because of **its** weather, **San Diego**, California, is my favorite city.

There are several kinds of pronouns. Most of them have specific antecedents, but a few do not.

See Practice 1.1C

Personal Pronouns The most common pronouns are the **personal pronouns.**

> **Personal pronouns** refer to the person speaking (first person), the person spoken to (second person), or the person, place, or thing spoken about (third person).

1.1.4 RULE

PERSONAL PRONOUNS		
	SINGULAR	PLURAL
First Person	I, me my, mine	we, us our, ours
Second Person	you your, yours	you your, yours
Third Person	he, him, his she, her, hers it, its	they, them their, theirs

In the first example below, the antecedent of the personal pronoun is the person speaking. In the second, the antecedent of the personal pronoun is the person being spoken to. In the last example, the antecedent of the personal pronoun is the thing spoken about.

FIRST PERSON   **My** name is not Bonnie.

SECOND PERSON   When **you** left, **you** forgot **your** briefcase.

THIRD PERSON   The carpet is new, and **its** padding is soft.

Reflexive and Intensive Pronouns These two types of pronouns look the same, but they function differently in sentences.

> A **reflexive pronoun** ends in *-self* or *-selves* and indicates that someone or something in the sentence acts for or on itself. A reflexive pronoun is essential to the meaning of a sentence. An **intensive pronoun** ends in *-self* or *-selves* and simply adds emphasis to a noun or pronoun in the sentence.

1.1.5 RULE

REFLEXIVE AND INTENSIVE PRONOUNS		
	SINGULAR	PLURAL
First Person	myself	ourselves
Second Person	yourself	yourselves
Third Person	himself, herself, itself	themselves

REFLEXIVE The restaurant chefs prepared **themselves** for the dinner rush.

INTENSIVE Joshua David **himself** wrote an account of what had taken place.

See Practice 1.1D

Reciprocal Pronouns **Reciprocal pronouns** show a mutual action or relationship.

RULE

1.1.6

> The **reciprocal pronouns** *each other* and *one another* refer to a plural antecedent. They express a mutual action or relationship.

EXAMPLES The two teachers shared the papers with **each other**.

The teachers shared their evaluations with **one another**.

See Practice 1.1E

Demonstrative Pronouns **Demonstrative pronouns** are used to point out one or more nouns.

RULE

1.1.7

> A **demonstrative pronoun** directs attention to a specific person, place, or thing.

There are four demonstrative pronouns.

DEMONSTRATIVE PRONOUNS	
SINGULAR	PLURAL
this, that	these, those

Demonstrative pronouns may come before or after their antecedents.

BEFORE   **That** is the **car** I would like to purchase.

AFTER   I hope to visit **Greece** and **Italy** . **Those** are my first choices.

One of the demonstrative pronouns, *that*, can also be used as a relative pronoun.

Relative Pronouns

Relative pronouns are used to relate one idea in a sentence to another. There are five relative pronouns.

A **relative pronoun** introduces an adjective clause and connects it to the word that the clause modifies.

1.1.8 RULE

RELATIVE PRONOUNS				
that	which	who	whom	whose

EXAMPLES   We read a **biography that** contained an account of the officer's life.

The **soldier who** had written it described his experiences.

The hiking **trip** , **which** they knew would be long, was last weekend.

See Practice 1.1F

Read each sentence. Then, write an appropriate pronoun to complete the sentence and write the antecedent.

EXAMPLE   I am planning a big party for _____ parents.

ANSWER   *my, I*

1. Patrick is someone who spends _____ money wisely.

2. The sauce was so spicy that _____ made my eyes water.

3. Neither Samantha nor Jacinta had any difficulty selecting _____ college.

4. The professor and her teaching aide have posted _____ research online.

5. Phillip hopes _____ submission will get to the magazine on time.

6. Lucas is watching _____ brother's basketball team play.

7. Several subscribers are voicing _____ opinions on the matter.

8. Mrs. Johnson, _____ dinner is now ready.

9. Cora has started babysitting to help with _____ car payments.

10. Either Frank or Nathaniel will offer _____ services as a volunteer.

Read each sentence. Then, identify the pronoun and label it *personal, reflexive,* or *intensive.*

EXAMPLE   Stacy played with the dog and gave him a biscuit.

ANSWER   *him — personal*

11. Please remember to bring all the equipment yourself.

12. I told him about the plans for the picnic.

13. They will wear costumes during the play.

14. Colin gave himself plenty of time to finish.

15. Who besides yourself can finish the project?

16. I have only myself to blame for the ruined plans.

17. I won, and the gold medal was mine!

18. The audience entered and found seats themselves.

19. They couldn't fasten their seat belts.

20. The monkeys looked at themselves in the mirror and started howling.

SPEAKING APPLICATION

Take turns with a partner. Describe your ideal employer. Include three or more pronouns that refer to him or her. Your partner should listen for and name the pronouns and their antecedents.

WRITING APPLICATION

Write a paragraph about a memorable event that you have attended. Use personal, reflexive, and intensive pronouns.

PRACTICE 1.1E > **Identifying Reciprocal Pronouns**

Read each sentence. Then, write the reciprocal pronoun in each sentence.

EXAMPLE The tennis partners were proud of each other.

ANSWER *each other*

1. Tina and Bruce will never forget each other.
2. They write each other every month.
3. Alana, Stacey, and Rachel sent letters to one another.
4. Ben and Mei completely respect each other.
5. David, Miguel, and Sarah definitely care a lot for one another.
6. The group drew closer to one another.
7. It is understood that we like each other.
8. We are expected to like one another.
9. John and Ashley certainly cared for each other.
10. They talk to one another about current events.

PRACTICE 1.1F > **Recognizing Demonstrative and Relative Pronouns**

Read each sentence. Then, write each underlined pronoun and label it *demonstrative* or *relative*.

EXAMPLE That is the best part of the album.

ANSWER *That* — demonstrative

11. The shirt that Daryl bought has a stain on the collar.
12. These belong to Kara and Jim.
13. The man who is standing near the entrance is a lawyer.
14. Those are the games I am going to buy.
15. It is hard to believe that he said it so loudly.
16. This tastes just like it did in the restaurant.
17. The chef who won the contest studied overseas.
18. The man, whose son is the band, is clapping along with the music.
19. The house, which was bright green, was very noticeable.
20. Have you found the map that was missing?

SPEAKING APPLICATION

Describe to a partner a good friend of yours. Use reciprocal pronouns in your description. Your partner should listen for and name the reciprocal pronouns.

WRITING APPLICATION

Write a paragraph about your favorite movie. Use demonstrative and relative pronouns in your paragraph.

Interrogative Pronouns

Interrogative pronouns are used to ask questions.

RULE 1.1.9

> An **interrogative pronoun** is used to begin a question.

The five interrogative pronouns are *what, which, who, whom,* and *whose.* Sometimes the antecedent of an interrogative pronoun is not known.

EXAMPLE | **Which** team finished first?

See Practice 1.1G

Indefinite Pronouns

Indefinite pronouns sometimes lack specific antecedents.

RULE 1.1.10

> An **indefinite pronoun** refers to a person, place, or thing that may or may not be specifically named.

INDEFINITE PRONOUNS				
SINGULAR			**PLURAL**	**BOTH**
another	everyone	nothing	both	all
anybody	everything	one	few	any
anyone	little	other	many	more
anything	much	somebody	others	most
each	neither	someone	several	none
either	nobody	something		some
everybody	no one			

Indefinite pronouns sometimes have specific antecedents.

NO SPECIFIC ANTECEDENT | **Both** wore the same dress.

SPECIFIC ANTECEDENTS | **All** of the **employees** left early.

Indefinite pronouns can also function as adjectives.

ADJECTIVE | **Few** painters are as famous as this one.

See Practice 1.1H

PRACTICE 1.1G > Recognizing Interrogative Pronouns

Read each sentence. Then, write the interrogative pronoun needed to complete the sentence.

EXAMPLE _____ wants my help?

ANSWER *Who*

1. _____ of the two books was easier to understand?

2. _____ family brought all this terrific food?

3. With _____ are you going to the concert?

4. _____ of the tournaments do you plan to enter?

5. _____ inspired you to write this book?

6. To _____ did you deliver the package?

7. _____ found out about the surprise party?

8. _____ was the total price of the entertainment system?

9. _____ idea was it to show up late?

10. _____ have you encountered that is a problem?

PRACTICE 1.1H > Identifying Personal and Indefinite Pronouns

Read each sentence. Write the appropriate personal pronoun to complete the sentence. Then, write the indefinite pronoun used in the sentence.

EXAMPLE Few of my friends have sold _____ raffle tickets.

ANSWER *their, Few*

11. Many of the contestants brought noisemakers with _____.

12. Several of my colleagues turned in _____ reports before the meeting.

13. No one on the boys' soccer team wears _____ uniform during practice.

14. Everyone in the girl's choir brings _____ own style to the group.

15. Few of my classmates changed _____ minds after the council speeches.

16. Some of the tourists carried travel books with _____.

17. All of the drivers are revving _____ engines.

18. None of our luggage has scratches on _____.

19. Most of the students like _____ new teacher.

20. Each of the men raised _____ trophy to the spectators.

SPEAKING APPLICATION

Imagine you are applying for a job. Take turns with a partner interviewing each other. Use interrogative pronouns in your questions. Your partner should listen for and name the interrogative pronouns.

WRITING APPLICATION

Using three of the completed sentences above, replace the indefinite pronouns with your own. Make sure that the new sentences still make sense.

1.2 Verbs

Every complete sentence must have at least one **verb**, which may consist of as many as four words.

RULE 1.2.1

A **verb** is a word or group of words that expresses time while showing an action, a condition, or the fact that something exists.

EL5

Action Verbs and Linking Verbs

Action verbs express action. They are used to tell what someone or something does, did, or will do. **Linking verbs** express a condition or show that something exists.

RULE 1.2.2

An **action verb** tells what action someone or something is performing.

ACTION VERBS

Ricky **learned** about hockey rules.

The radio **blared** the broadcast from the weather station.

We **chose** two books about former presidents.

I **remember** the play about Dr. Jekyll.

The action expressed by a verb does not have to be visible. Words expressing mental activities—such as *learn*, *think*, or *decide*—are also considered action verbs.

The person or thing that performs the action is called the *subject* of the verb. In the examples above, *Ricky*, *radio*, *we*, and *I* are the subjects of *learned*, *blared*, *chose*, and *remember*.

> A **linking verb** is a verb that connects its subject with a noun, pronoun, or adjective that identifies or describes the subject.

LINKING
VERBS

That man **is** a famous author.

The window **seems** to sparkle.

EL6

The verb *be* is the most common linking verb.

THE FORMS OF *BE*			
am	am being	can be	have been
are	are being	could be	has been
is	is being	may be	had been
was	was being	might be	could have been
were	were being	must be	may have been
		shall be	might have been
		should be	shall have been
		will be	should have been
		would be	will have been
			would have been

Most often, the forms of *be* that function as linking verbs express the condition of the subject. Occasionally, however, they may merely express existence, usually by showing, with other words, where the subject is located.

EXAMPLE   The yogurt **is** in the freezer.

Other Linking Verbs A few other verbs can also serve as linking verbs.

OTHER LINKING VERBS		
appear	look	sound
become	remain	stay
feel	seem	taste
grow	smell	turn

EXAMPLES

The lasagna **smelled** like garlic and tomatoes.

The music **sounds** too loud.

The house **smelled** delicious when we were done.

The situation at the school **remained** tense.

The drivers **grew** tired.

Some of these verbs may also act as action—not linking—verbs. To determine whether the word is functioning as an action verb or as a linking verb, insert *am*, *are*, or *is* in place of the verb. If the substitute makes sense while connecting two words, then the original verb is a linking verb.

LINKING VERB The air **felt** damp. (The air **is** damp.)

ACTION VERB The climbers **felt** the snowflakes.

LINKING VERB The horseradish **tastes** bitter. (The horseradish **is** bitter.)

ACTION VERB I **taste** the chili pepper.

See Practice 1.2A
See Practice 1.2B

PRACTICE 1.2A > Identifying Action and Linking Verbs

Read each sentence. Write the action verb in each sentence.

EXAMPLE   The speeding train raced through the station.

ANSWER   *raced*

1. Olivia negotiated extra time for her project.
2. The owls hooted all night.
3. Gloria represents her high school on the city volleyball team.
4. She thought about the problem.
5. For a science project, Duane constructed a sundial.

Read each sentence. Write the linking verb in each sentence.

EXAMPLE   It felt humid earlier this morning.

ANSWER   *felt*

6. David Beckham is a soccer player.
7. The children remained quiet.
8. Amy looked very pale and sick.
9. Some dog breeds are extremely active.
10. Everyone felt sorry about the misunderstanding.

PRACTICE 1.2B > Distinguishing Between Action and Linking Verbs

Read each sentence. Then, write the verb in each sentence, and label it *action* or *linking*.

EXAMPLE   Emma Grace seems unusually quiet.

ANSWER   *seems* — linking

11. The freighter sailed away in the morning.
12. The capital of Texas is Austin.
13. My sister grew tall in a short time.
14. The magician's assistant reached into the bag.
15. The speaker was extremely late for the assembly.
16. We slipped out the door unnoticed.
17. The blueberry cobbler smells delicious.
18. The trail was dangerous for hikers.
19. The coyote appeared from behind the bushes.
20. I tasted lots of garlic in the soup.

SPEAKING APPLICATION

Take turns with a partner. Describe the plot of your favorite movie. Your partner should listen for and identify the action and linking verbs that you use.

WRITING APPLICATION

Write three sentences with action verbs and underline the action verbs. Then, write three sentences with linking verbs and underline the linking verbs.

Transitive and Intransitive Verbs

All verbs are either **transitive** or **intransitive,** depending on whether or not they transfer action to another word in a sentence.

RULE 1.2.4

A **transitive verb** directs action toward someone or something named in the same sentence. An **intransitive verb** does not direct action toward anyone or anything named in the same sentence.

The word toward which a transitive verb directs its action is called the *object* of the verb. Intransitive verbs never have objects. You can determine whether a verb has an object by asking *whom* or *what* after the verb.

TRANSITIVE   Mark **threw** the basketball.
(Threw what? basketball)

The lion **ate** the prey.
(Ate what? prey)

INTRANSITIVE   The graduates **practiced** on the field.
(Practiced what? [no answer])

The kids **shouted** loudly.
(Shouted what? [no answer])

RULE 1.2.5

Because linking verbs do not express action, they are always intransitive. Most action verbs can be either transitive or intransitive, depending on the sentence. However, some action verbs can only be transitive, and others can only be intransitive.

TRANSITIVE   I **wrote** a letter from Washington, D.C.

INTRANSITIVE   The author **wrote** quickly.

ALWAYS TRANSITIVE	The Capulets **rival** the Montagues.
ALWAYS INTRANSITIVE	They **winced** at the sound of the gong.

See Practice 1.2C

EL5

Verb Phrases

A verb that has more than one word is a **verb phrase.**

> A **verb phrase** consists of a main verb and one or more helping verbs.

1.2.6 RULE

Helping verbs are often called auxiliary verbs. One or more helping verbs may precede the main verb in a verb phrase.

VERB PHRASES

I **will be taking** my car to the shop.

I **should have been watching** when I tripped on the curb.

All the forms of *be* listed in this chapter can be used as helping verbs. The following verbs can also be helping verbs.

OTHER HELPING VERBS			
do	have	shall	can
does	has	should	could
did	had	will	may
		would	might
			must

A verb phrase is often interrupted by other words in a sentence.

INTERRUPTED VERB PHRASES

I **will** definitely **be taking** my car to the shop.

See Practice 1.2D

Should I **take** my car to the shop?

PRACTICE 1.2C > **Distinguishing Between Transitive and Intransitive Verbs**

Read each sentence. Identify each underlined verb as *transitive* or *intransitive*.

EXAMPLE   Derrick <u>greeted</u> the visitors.

ANSWER   *transitive*

1. When <u>will</u> Felicia <u>paint</u> her room?
2. The train <u>stopped</u> at the station.
3. The children <u>play</u> checkers.
4. Mr. Lopez <u>baked</u> bread.
5. Last night, we <u>ate</u> on the patio.
6. Alex <u>wrote</u> a research report.
7. Both Roland and Tracy <u>ran</u> in the race.
8. The kite <u>flew</u> overhead.
9. Sharika <u>returns</u> from her trip tomorrow.
10. Gabriel <u>drives</u> a minivan.

PRACTICE 1.2D > **Recognizing Verb Phrases**

Read each sentence. Then, write the verb phrase in each sentence.

EXAMPLE   The astronauts are working in space.

ANSWER   *are working*

11. A tiny kitten was wandering around the yard.
12. His favorite movie is playing tonight.
13. The new computer chip is not recommended.
14. A funny costume will always make children laugh.
15. Fairy tales are sometimes called folktales.
16. We have used computers in math class before.
17. The magician is thinking of a number.
18. The firefighters had appeared uninjured.
19. We had heard the new song on the radio.
20. The refreshments will be welcomed after the game.

SPEAKING APPLICATION

Take turns with a partner. Tell about your favorite school trip, using transitive and intransitive verbs. Your partner should listen for and name each type of verb.

WRITING APPLICATION

Write three sentences with verb phrases. Underline the verb phrases in your sentences.

1.3 Adjectives and Adverbs

Adjectives and **adverbs** are the two parts of speech known as *modifiers*—that is, they slightly change the meaning of other words by adding description or making them more precise.

Adjectives

An **adjective** clarifies the meaning of a noun or pronoun by providing information about its appearance, location, and so on.

> An **adjective** is a word used to describe a noun or pronoun or to give it a more specific meaning.

An adjective answers one of four questions about a noun or pronoun: *What kind? Which one? How many? How much?*

EXAMPLES   **snow** boots (What kind of boots?)

          that shoe (Which shoe?)

          four pairs of shoes (How many pairs?)

          six gallons of water (How much water?)

When an adjective modifies a noun, it usually precedes the noun. Occasionally, the adjective may follow the noun.

EXAMPLES   The student was **calm** about her low grade.

          I considered the student **calm**.

An adjective that modifies a pronoun usually follows it. Sometimes, however, the adjective precedes the pronoun as it does in the example on the next page.

AFTER   She was **ashamed** when she didn't pass.

BEFORE   **Ashamed** that he broke the glass, he handed her a towel.

More than one adjective may modify a single noun or pronoun.

EXAMPLE   The school hired a **creative, experienced** art teacher.

Articles Three common adjectives—*a, an,* and *the*—are known as **articles.** *A* and *an* are called **indefinite articles** because they refer to any one of a class of nouns. *The* refers to a specific noun and, therefore, is called the **definite article.**

INDEFINITE EXAMPLES	DEFINITE EXAMPLES
a daisy	the stem
an orchid	the mask

Remember that *an* is used before a vowel sound; *a* is used before a consonant sound.

EXAMPLES   **a** once-clean house (*w* sound)

a unicycle (*y* sound)

an honest politician (no *h* sound)

See Practice 1.3A

Nouns Used as Adjectives Words that are usually nouns sometimes act as adjectives. In this case, the noun answers the questions *What kind?* or *Which one?* about another noun.

NOUNS USED AS ADJECTIVES	
flower	flower garden
lawn	lawn mower

See Practice 1.3B

Proper Adjectives Adjectives can also be proper. **Proper adjectives** are proper nouns used as adjectives or adjectives formed from proper nouns. They usually begin with capital letters.

PROPER NOUNS	PROPER ADJECTIVES
Monday	Monday morning
San Francisco	San Francisco streets
Europe	European roses
Rome	Roman hyacinth

Compound Adjectives Adjectives can be compound. Most are hyphenated; others are combined or are separate words.

HYPHENATED **rain-forest** plants

water-soluble pigments

COMBINED **airborne** pollen

evergreen shrubs

See Practice 1.3C SEPARATE **North American** rhododendrons

Pronouns Used as Adjectives Certain pronouns can also function as adjectives. The seven personal pronouns, known as either **possessive adjectives** or **possessive pronouns,** do double duty in a sentence. They act as pronouns because they have antecedents. They also act as adjectives because they modify nouns by answering *Which one?* The other pronouns become adjectives instead of pronouns when they stand before nouns and answer the question *Which one?*

> **A pronoun is used as an adjective if it modifies a noun.**

RULE 1.3.2

Possessive pronouns, demonstrative pronouns, interrogative pronouns, and indefinite pronouns can all function as adjectives when they modify nouns.

PRONOUNS USED AS ADJECTIVES	
POSSESSIVE PRONOUNS OR ADJECTIVES	
my, your, his, her, its, our, their	The baby girl threw her ball.
DEMONSTRATIVE ADJECTIVES	
this, that, these, those	This book and these papers are mine.
INTERROGATIVE ADJECTIVES	
which, what, whose	Which color do you like best?
INDEFINITE ADJECTIVES	
Singular nouns: another, each, either, little, much, neither, one	Each mug has a handle.
Plural nouns: both, few, many, several	Both students read the book.
Singular or plural nouns: all, any, more, most, other, some	We would appreciate any help.

Verb Forms Used as Adjectives Verb forms used as adjectives usually end in -*ing* or -*ed* and are called **participles.**

EXAMPLE   I picked the **growing** vegetables.

Nouns, pronouns, and verb forms function as adjectives only when they modify other nouns or pronouns. The following examples show how their function in a sentence can change.

	REGULAR FUNCTION	AS AN ADJECTIVE
Noun	The road was curved.	The road surface was bumpy.
Pronoun	This was a fun party.	This party was fun.
Verb	I plant flowers in the garden.	The planted flowers needed sun.

See Practice 1.3D

PRACTICE 1.3A Recognizing Adjectives and Articles

Read each sentence. Then, write the adjective(s) and the article(s) in each sentence.

EXAMPLE   A fish swam around a small reef.

ANSWER   *small; A, a*

1. Maya picked the perfect spot for the garden.
2. The Indian restaurant has delicious food.
3. In late spring, we see the beautiful flowers.
4. The story is funny and has a positive message.
5. The city has a dry climate.
6. Please set these bowls on the round table.
7. The explorers went to the frigid Alaskan wilderness.
8. Please bring me a blue shirt.
9. A beach ball bobbed up and down in the lake.
10. In many Japanese homes, the people sleep on futons.

PRACTICE 1.3B Identifying Nouns Used as Adjectives

Read each sentence. Then, write the noun that is used as an adjective in each sentence.

EXAMPLE   The puppy slept on a feather pillow.

ANSWER   *feather*

11. She offered us some spinach casserole.
12. The baseball practice lasted until after dark.
13. The vegetable farmers planted corn.
14. Old photographs and a diamond ring filled her keepsake box.
15. I set my radio alarm for 7:00 A.M.
16. We went to the shore during our school holiday.
17. She donated the entire cash reward from the settlement.
18. The club organized a Sunday picnic.
19. Air bubbles give the fish oxygen.
20. The fisherman threw crab nets into the ocean.

SPEAKING APPLICATION

Take turns with a partner. Tell about a special holiday that you have spent with your family. Your partner should listen for and name the adjectives and articles that you use.

WRITING APPLICATION

Write three sentences that contain nouns used as adjectives.

PRACTICE 1.3C ▷ **Recognizing Proper and Compound Adjectives**

Read each sentence. Then, write the adjective in each sentence, and label it *proper* or *compound*.

EXAMPLE   The meal began with a French soup.

ANSWER   *French* — proper

1. Do you enjoy Chinese food?
2. My dad built a four-foot table.
3. I am a part-time worker at the restaurant.
4. The speaker was a Buddhist priest.
5. Sean listens to Celtic music.
6. My grandmother is a kind-hearted person.
7. Anne speaks with a British accent.
8. She lives in an area called the Old South neighborhood.
9. Ours is a densely-populated continent.
10. That's an Irish lullaby.

PRACTICE 1.3D ▷ **Recognizing Pronouns and Verbs Used as Adjectives**

Read each sentence. Then, write the pronoun or verb used as an adjective in each sentence and the noun it modifies.

EXAMPLE   This drawing is mine.

ANSWER   *this, drawing*

11. That laptop is his.
12. These shoes are very comfortable.
13. The swaying trees moved gracefully.
14. Both squirrels disappeared behind a tree.
15. The last step is to trim those edges.
16. The bouncing kangaroo was everyone's favorite.
17. My wilting flowers could use water.
18. Each person wanted something different.
19. Which court will we play on?
20. This food is the best I have tasted in a long time.

SPEAKING APPLICATION

With a partner, name four adjectives that are proper or compound. Then, use these adjectives in a brief paragraph that tells how people can help others in their community.

WRITING APPLICATION

Write four sentences about your town. Include pronouns used as adjectives and verbs used as adjectives in your sentences.

Adverbs

Adverbs, like adjectives, describe other words or make other words more specific.

> An **adverb** is a word that modifies a verb, an adjective, or another adverb.

When an adverb modifies a verb, it will answer any of the following questions: *Where? When? In what way? To what extent?*

An adverb answers only one question when modifying an adjective or another adverb: *To what extent?* Because it specifies the degree or intensity of the modified adjective or adverb, such an adverb is often called an **intensifier.**

The position of an adverb in relation to the word it modifies can vary in a sentence. If the adverb modifies a verb, it may precede or follow it or even interrupt a verb phrase. Normally, adverbs modifying adjectives and adverbs will immediately precede the words they modify.

ADVERBS MODIFYING VERBS	
Where?	**When?**
The children ran outside.	She never picked the flowers.
The children ran there.	Later, we toured the flower show.
The boy ran around.	She waters the flowers daily in the yard.
In what way?	**To what extent?**
She officially sold flowers in the shop.	The puppy was still playing energetically.
She graciously made any kind of bouquet.	He always made the right choice.
Jane left quickly after the presentation.	Be sure to wash completely after gardening.

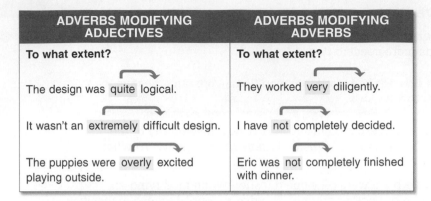

ADVERBS MODIFYING ADJECTIVES	ADVERBS MODIFYING ADVERBS
To what extent? The design was quite logical. It wasn't an extremely difficult design. The puppies were overly excited playing outside.	**To what extent?** They worked very diligently. I have not completely decided. Eric was not completely finished with dinner.

Adverbs as Parts of Verbs Some verbs require an adverb to complete their meaning. Adverbs used this way are considered part of the verb. An adverb functioning as part of a verb does not answer the usual questions for adverbs.

EXAMPLES   The garbage truck **backed up** along the side of the street.

Please **point out** which ship model is yours.

Daniel had to **run out** to pick up dinner for the team.

See Practice 1.3E

Nouns Functioning as Adverbs
Several nouns can function as adverbs that answer the questions *Where?* or *When?* Some of these words are *home, yesterday, today, tomorrow, mornings, afternoons, evenings, nights, week, month,* and *year.*

NOUNS USED AS ADVERBS	
NOUNS	**AS ADVERBS**
Nights seems to fly by.	I work out at night.
My year in Italy seems like so long ago.	Let's go on vacation this year.
Tomorrow will be a sunny day.	I am sure I will finish my book by tomorrow.

Adverb or Adjective?

Adverbs usually have different forms from adjectives and thus are easily identified. Many adverbs are formed by the addition of -*ly* to an adjective.

ADJECTIVES   The forest was **beautiful**.

The baby looked through the **open** door.

ADVERBS   The forest was cared for **beautifully**.

The students discussed the test **openly**.

Some adjectives, however, also end in -*ly*. Therefore, you cannot assume that every word ending in -*ly* is an adverb.

ADJECTIVES   a **weekly** magazine

a **monthly** payment

a **stately** mansion

smelly socks

Some adjectives and adverbs share the same form. You can determine the part of speech of such words by checking their function in the sentence. An adverb will modify a verb, adjective, or adverb; an adjective will modify a noun or pronoun.

ADVERB   The presentation ran **late**.

ADJECTIVE   We enjoyed the **late** brunches on vacation.

ADVERB   The surfer glided **straight** through the wave.

See Practice 1.3F   ADJECTIVE   The horizon was **straight**.

PRACTICE 1.3E > Recognizing Adverbs

Read each sentence. Then, write the adverb or adverbs in each sentence, and tell whether each one modifies a *verb*, an *adjective*, or an *adverb*.

EXAMPLE   My sister draws well.

ANSWER   *well* — verb

1. Is your dog still sick?
2. Our neighbor drives cautiously.
3. The parade route ended there.
4. Suze thinks they returned yesterday.
5. The goalie blocked every shot perfectly.
6. We already wrote our thank-you e-mails.
7. Seth always completes his assignments.
8. The mail is quite obviously late.
9. Mom speaks glowingly about her garden.
10. Our dog is very friendly.

PRACTICE 1.3F > Identifying Adverbs and the Words They Modify

Read each sentence. Then, write the adverb or adverbs in each sentence and the word they modify.

EXAMPLE   We will be riding home on the bus.

ANSWER   *home, riding*

11. I am really sorry that I missed the party.
12. She gets up early to go to school.
13. Carla expects her team to finish first in the tournament.
14. Our new car arrived yesterday from the factory.
15. Serena rode fast, and we could not catch up with her.
16. The soup seems rather salty to me.
17. The plane will be landing very soon.
18. My sister works weekday afternoons at the college.
19. To the end, the warrior fought bravely.
20. He bought a car that was almost new.

SPEAKING APPLICATION

Take turns with a partner. Tell about something that you enjoy doing. Your partner should name adverbs that you use and whether each one modifies a verb, an adjective, or another adverb.

WRITING APPLICATION

Use sentence 16 as a model to write three similar sentences. Replace the adverb in sentence 16 with other adverbs.

1.4 Prepositions, Conjunctions, and Interjections

Prepositions and conjunctions function in sentences as connectors. **Prepositions** express relationships between words or ideas, whereas **conjunctions** join words, groups of words, or even entire sentences. **Interjections** function by themselves and are independent of other words in a sentence.

Prepositions and Prepositional Phrases

Prepositions make it possible to show relationships between words. The relationships may involve, for example, location, direction, time, cause, or possession. A preposition may consist of one word or multiple words. (See the chart on the next page.)

> **A preposition** relates the noun or pronoun that appears with it to another word in the sentence.

RULE 1.4.1

Notice how the prepositions below, highlighted in pink, relate to the words highlighted in yellow.

LOCATION   Jewelry **is made around** the **world**.

TIME   Classical music will **last for centuries**.

CAUSE   Kim is **late because of** the **traffic**.

> **A prepositional phrase** is a group of words that includes a preposition and a noun or pronoun.

RULE 1.4.2

The noun or pronoun with a preposition is called the **object of the preposition.** Objects may have one or more modifiers. A prepositional phrase may also have more than one object. In the example below, the objects of the prepositions are highlighted in blue, and the prepositions are in pink.

EXAMPLE   Thomas and Nick waited **on** the **corner for** a **bus**.

PREPOSITIONS			
aboard	before	in front of	over
about	behind	in place of	owing to
above	below	in regard to	past
according to	beneath	inside	prior to
across	beside	in spite of	regarding
across from	besides	instead of	round
after	between	into	since
against	beyond	in view of	through
ahead of	but	like	throughout
along	by	near	till
alongside	by means of	nearby	to
along with	concerning	next to	together with
amid	considering	of	toward
among	despite	off	under
apart from	down	on	underneath
around	during	on account of	until
aside from	except	onto	unto
as of	for	on top of	up
as	from	opposite	upon
atop	in	out	with
barring	in addition to	out of	within
because of	in back of	outside	without

See Practice 1.4A

Preposition or Adverb?
Many words may be used either as prepositions or adverbs.
Words that can function in either role include *around*, *before*,
behind, *down*, *in*, *off*, *on*, *out*, *over*, and *up*. If an object
accompanies the word, the word is used as a preposition.

PREPOSITION   The committee meets **around** a huge table.

ADVERB   The discussion about the topic went **around
and around** .

See Practice 1.4B

PRACTICE 1.4A > **Identifying Prepositions and Prepositional Phrases**

Read each sentence. Then, write each prepositional phrase and underline each preposition.

EXAMPLE   In the evening, we went to the opera.

ANSWER *In the evening, to the opera*

1. The girls asked for tickets to the play.
2. Please keep the information between you and me.
3. Their plane arrived from New York at midnight.
4. Across the lake is a village with a hotel.
5. We talked for hours about the past.
6. The price of this car is below its market value.
7. Enter through those doors and into the station.
8. With much nervousness, I walked across the bridge.
9. The singer received a standing ovation from the audience.
10. Your keys are under the mat near the front door.

PRACTICE 1.4B > **Distinguishing Between Prepositions and Adverbs**

Read each sentence. Then, label each underlined word as a *preposition* or an *adverb*.

EXAMPLE   I will wait <u>near</u> the entrance.

ANSWER *preposition*

11. A squirrel scurried <u>up</u> the tree.
12. The moon rose <u>up</u> above the clouds.
13. Someone left the radio <u>on</u> all day.
14. When Marty moved <u>away</u>, I wanted to go with him.
15. Becca turned <u>around</u> and waved at me.
16. Chuck stayed <u>behind</u> after the game ended.
17. A tassel on my parasol fell <u>off</u>.
18. A creek runs <u>below</u> the fields.
19. My grandfather is <u>in</u> good health again.
20. They went <u>out</u> and took a long walk in the garden.

SPEAKING APPLICATION

Take turns with a partner. Describe the locations of objects in the room. Your partner should listen for and identify the prepositional phrases that you use and the preposition in each phrase.

WRITING APPLICATION

Write a sentence using the word *down* as a preposition. Then, write a sentence using *down* as an adverb.

Conjunctions

There are three main kinds of conjunctions: **coordinating, correlative,** and **subordinating.** Sometimes a type of adverb, the **conjunctive adverb,** is also considered a conjunction.

> A **conjunction** is a word used to connect other words or groups of words.

Coordinating Conjunctions The seven coordinating conjunctions are used to connect similar parts of speech or groups of words of equal grammatical weight.

COORDINATING CONJUNCTIONS						
and	but	for	nor	or	so	yet

EXAMPLES   Linda **and** Margaret ran the editorial meeting.

Linda left early, **so** Margaret left with her.

Correlative Conjunctions The five paired correlative conjunctions join elements of equal grammatical weight.

CORRELATIVE CONJUNCTIONS		
both . . . and	either . . . or	neither . . . nor
not only . . . but also	whether . . . or	

EXAMPLES   She made **both** pasta **and** eggplant.

Neither Beth **nor** Fred liked the eggplant.

I don't know **whether** to meet them for brunch **or** dinner.

Subordinating Conjunctions Subordinating conjunctions join two complete ideas by making one of the ideas subordinate to, or dependent upon, the other.

SUBORDINATING CONJUNCTIONS			
after	because	lest	till
although	before	now that	unless
as	even if	provided	until
as if	even though	since	when
as long as	how	so that	whenever
as much as	if	than	where
as soon as	inasmuch as	that	wherever
as though	in order that	though	while

The subordinate idea in a sentence always begins with a subordinating conjunction and makes up what is known as a subordinate clause. A subordinate clause may either follow or precede the main idea in a sentence.

EXAMPLES   I lived in my parents' house **because** I was saving money.

After the rain ends, the flowers in the desert bloom.

Conjunctive Adverbs Conjunctive adverbs act as transitions between complete ideas by indicating comparisons, contrasts, results, and other relationships. The chart below lists the most common conjunctive adverbs.

CONJUNCTIVE ADVERBS		
accordingly	finally	nevertheless
again	furthermore	otherwise
also	however	then
besides	indeed	therefore
consequently	moreover	thus

Punctuation With Conjunctive Adverbs Punctuation is usually required both before and after conjunctive adverbs.

EXAMPLES   There was almost two feet of snow this weekend. **Therefore** , we shoveled our way out.

Felix was a very persuasive speaker; **indeed** , he could convince you to do almost anything.

We arrived on time; **otherwise** , the reservation would be canceled.

See Practice 1.4C

Interjections

Interjections express emotion. Unlike most words, they have no grammatical connection to other words in a sentence.

An **interjection** is a word that expresses feeling or emotion and functions independently of a sentence.

Interjections can express a variety of sentiments, such as happiness, fear, anger, pain, surprise, sorrow, exhaustion, or hesitation.

SOME COMMON INTERJECTIONS				
ah	dear	hey	ouch	well
aha	goodness	hurray	psst	whew
alas	gracious	oh	tsk	wow

EXAMPLES   **Ouch** ! That knife is very sharp.

Wow ! I can't believe that!

Oh ! I can't go.

Whew ! We worked hard at the gym.

See Practice 1.4D

PRACTICE 1.4C > Identifying Different Conjunctions

Read each sentence. Then, write the conjunction in each sentence, and label it *coordinating*, *correlative*, *subordinating*, or *conjunctive*.

EXAMPLE   Either you can visit me, or I will visit you.

ANSWER   *Either ... or* — correlative

1. We are going skiing even though there is not much snow.

2. The applause was deafening; therefore, the speaker paused.

3. Not only is Max smart, but also he is a good watchdog.

4. Dad said we can have pasta or chicken for dinner.

5. Tricia and Maria are my closest friends.

6. Whether it rains or not, we will have fun.

7. I had planned to have a party, but I got sick.

8. Both Jill and Nguyen are having dinner with us.

9. We did our best; indeed, we practiced every day.

10. As soon as the mayor arrived, the speeches began.

PRACTICE 1.4D > Supplying Interjections

Read each sentence. Then, write an interjection that shows the feeling expressed in the sentence.

EXAMPLE   _____, I spilled my drink!

ANSWER   *Oops*

11. _____, what have you done now?

12. _____! I hit my thumb with the hammer!

13. _____, the prince would never see the princess again.

14. _____, I don't know what else to do.

15. _____! That's a beautiful sunset!

16. _____! Want to buy a used stereo?

17. _____, where do you think you're going?

18. _____! We are the champions!

19. _____, I can't find the map.

20. _____! I'm so glad that's over!

SPEAKING APPLICATION

Take turns with a partner. Tell about something that you did with a friend. Your partner should name conjunctions that you use and tell what kind of conjunction each one is.

WRITING APPLICATION

Write three sentences with interjections.

1.5 Words as Different Parts of Speech

Words are flexible, often serving as one part of speech in one sentence and as another part of speech in another.

Identifying Parts of Speech

To *function* means "to serve in a particular capacity." The function of a word may change from one sentence to another.

The way a word is used in a sentence determines its part of speech.

The word *well* has different meanings in the following sentences.

As a Noun	The well in the yard is made of stone.
As a Verb	During the graduation ceremony, tears welled in their eyes.
As an Adjective	Alia didn't feel well before class.

Nouns, Pronouns, and Verbs A **noun** names a person, place, or thing. A **pronoun** stands for a noun. A **verb** shows action, condition, or existence.

The chart below reviews the definition of each part of speech.

PARTS OF SPEECH	QUESTIONS TO ASK YOURSELF	EXAMPLES
Noun	Does the word name a person, place, or thing?	His visit to the Statue of Liberty awakened Mark's curiosity.
Pronoun	Does the word stand for a noun?	They shared some samples with her.

PARTS OF SPEECH	QUESTIONS TO ASK YOURSELF	EXAMPLES
Verb	Does the word tell what someone or something did? Does the word link one word with another word that identifies or describes it? Does the word show that something exists?	I played piano. That woman was a pianist. The soloist appeared nervous. The audience is getting impatient.

See Practice 1.5A

The Other Parts of Speech An **adjective** modifies a noun or pronoun. An **adverb** modifies a verb, an adjective, or another adverb. A **preposition** relates a noun or pronoun that appears with it to another word. A **conjunction** connects words or groups of words. An **interjection** expresses emotion.

PARTS OF SPEECH	QUESTIONS TO ASK YOURSELF	EXAMPLES
Adjective	Does the word tell *what kind, which one, how many, or how much?*	Those four muffins are an unusual texture.
Adverb	Does the word tell *where, when, in what way,* or *to what extent?*	Please go back. Run now. Sing very quietly. I am extremely overwhelmed.
Preposition	Is the word part of a phrase that includes a noun or pronoun?	Inside the library, the students were on the computers.
Conjunction	Does the word connect other words in the sentence or connect clauses?	Both Laura and I will bake because they need snacks; besides, it will be fun!
Interjection	Does the word express feeling or emotion and function independently of the sentence?	Hey, hold onto that. Wow! That's exciting!

See Practice 1.5B

PRACTICE 1.5A > **Identifying Nouns, Pronouns, and Verbs**

Read each sentence. Then, label the underlined word *noun*, *pronoun*, or *verb*.

EXAMPLE   I showed the <u>group</u> my outline.

ANSWER   *noun*

1. Sally <u>groups</u> the flowers in her garden by color.
2. <u>He</u> is learning to play a guitar.
3. The photographer <u>said</u>, "Please smile."
4. Liam always has a big <u>smile</u> on his face.
5. We <u>left</u> the store in a hurry.
6. <u>Dad</u> pulled out of the driveway and made a left turn.
7. <u>They</u> are coming over, and we will paint the house.
8. Bill, will <u>you</u> and Scarlet come here, please?
9. You must be careful about what you <u>post</u> online.
10. I helped Mom put up a new <u>post</u> for the fence.

PRACTICE 1.5B > **Recognizing All the Parts of Speech**

Read each sentence. Then, write which part of speech each underlined word is in the sentence.

EXAMPLE   I did my homework <u>before</u> dinner.

ANSWER   *preposition*

11. <u>She</u> had warned us <u>before</u> the storm hit.
12. Certain people <u>do</u> their chores too <u>fast</u>.
13. Theo made a <u>quick</u> trip to the grocery store.
14. <u>Many</u> of us voted to have school uniforms.
15. <u>Well</u>, I have <u>nothing</u> more to say.
16. Jake eats a <u>light</u> snack before a track <u>meet</u>.
17. <u>After</u> staying up all night, I was <u>exhausted</u>.
18. Charles <u>threw</u> the ball <u>low</u>, and I missed it.
19. Why are you sitting there <u>in</u> the dark?
20. They are leaving, <u>and</u> so am <u>I</u>.

SPEAKING APPLICATION

Take turns with a partner. Tell about something that you did earlier today. Your partner should identify some nouns, pronouns, and verbs that you use.

WRITING APPLICATION

Write the part of speech of each word in sentence 18.

CHAPTER 2

BASIC SENTENCE PARTS

Write high-quality sentences by pairing strong subjects and verbs in your writing and using complements and clauses to add description.

WRITE GUY *Jeff Anderson, M.Ed.*

WHAT DO YOU NOTICE?

Focus on different sentence parts as you zoom in on these lines from the poem "The Lake Isle of Innisfree" by William Butler Yeats.

MENTOR TEXT

> There midnight's all a glimmer, and noon a purple glow,
> And evening full of the linnet's wings.

Now, ask yourself the following questions:

- What is the subject and the verb in the clause *There midnight's all a glimmer*?
- How does recognizing subjects and verbs help you understand the poem?

The subject and verb in the clause *There midnight's all a glimmer* are *midnight's (midnight is)*. Recognizing subjects and verbs in the poem helps you group ideas, so you know who or what is giving or receiving action or being described. In the clause *There midnight's all a glimmer*, Yeats is describing how the night looks in Innisfree.

Grammar for Writers Poets use the special forms and devices of poetry, but they also depend on their understanding of subjects and verbs and other sentence parts to create lines that readers can follow. As you write, ask yourself questions like, *Will the subject of this sentence (or this line) be clear to my readers?*

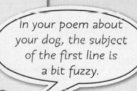

In your poem about your dog, the subject of the first line is a bit fuzzy.

I agree. That dog needs a haircut!

2.1 Subjects and Predicates

A **sentence** is a group of words that expresses a complete unit of thought. *The cereal in the bowl* is not a complete unit of thought because you probably wonder what the writer wanted to say about the cereal. *The cereal in the bowl is soggy,* however, does express a complete unit of thought.

RULE 2.1.1

A **sentence** is a group of words that has two main parts: a complete subject and a complete predicate. Together, these parts express a complete thought or paint a complete picture.

EL9

The **complete subject** contains a noun, pronoun, or group of words acting as a noun, plus its modifiers. These words tell *who* or *what* the sentence is about. The **complete predicate** consists of the verb or verb phrase, plus its modifiers. These words tell what the complete subject is or does.

COMPLETE SUBJECTS	COMPLETE PREDICATES
Snakes	slither.
A bell-clanging streetcar	moved through the turn.
Wood or cellulose	makes a delicious meal for a termite.
The candidate's approach to fiscal problems	impressed the voters attending the rally.

Sometimes, part of the predicate precedes the complete subject.

EXAMPLES

At noon , the cluster of waiters
complete   complete subject

served tea .
predicate

Tonight my English class
complete   complete subject

visited a theater .
predicate

See Practice 2.1A

42   **Basic Sentence Parts**

Simple Subjects and Predicates

The most essential parts of a sentence are the **simple subject** and the **simple predicate.** These words tell you the basics of what you need to know about the topic of the sentence. All of the other words in the sentence give you information about the simple subject and simple predicate.

> The **simple subject** is the essential noun, pronoun, or group of words that acts as a noun in a complete subject. The **simple predicate** is the essential verb or verb phrase in a complete predicate.

Note: When sentences are discussed in this chapter, the term *subject* will refer to a simple subject, and the term *verb* will refer to a simple predicate.

SUBJECTS	VERBS
Small feet	fit nicely into ballet slippers.
Many schoolteachers	have used films in their lessons.
Jars of beads	were sitting on the craft table.
A colorful painting	covered the wall.
The student's counselor	reviewed all of her college applications.
Studies of other cultures	have certainly revealed much about their traditions.

In the last example, the simple subject is *studies,* not *cultures; cultures* is the object of the preposition *of.* Objects of prepositions never function as simple subjects. In this same example, the simple predicate is a verb phrase. In addition, the word *certainly* is not part of the simple predicate because it does not provide essential information.

See Practice 2.1B

PRACTICE 2.1A > Recognizing Complete Subjects and Predicates

Read each sentence. Then, rewrite the sentence, and draw a vertical line between the complete subject and the complete predicate.

EXAMPLE   The man with the leash is looking for his dog.

ANSWER   *The man with the leash | is looking for his dog.*

1. The campground in New Mexico is close to Texas.

2. Spaghetti with meatballs is Dad's favorite dish.

3. The teacher responded enthusiastically to our suggestion.

4. Gathering up their books, the students left.

5. The twelve-person jury reached a unanimous verdict.

6. The classic holiday songs have been recorded in many arrangements and styles.

7. My uncle Jack has a secret recipe for barbeque sauce.

8. The field trips to the museum and the television station have been postponed.

9. The principal, a friendly, outgoing woman, began to converse with the students.

10. Many different kinds of tea are now available in stores.

PRACTICE 2.1B > Identifying Simple Subjects and Predicates

Read each sentence. The complete subject is underlined. The rest of the sentence is the complete predicate. Write the simple subject and simple predicate.

EXAMPLE   The road to the cabin was blocked by snow.

ANSWER   *road, was blocked*

11. A basket of seasonal fruits makes a delightful gift.

12. The package had obviously been carefully addressed.

13. At eighteen, my sister got a part-time job.

14. Uncle Bill's movie collection is limited to westerns and mysteries.

15. The ancient coins at the museum are rare and valuable.

16. The entire city came to a halt during the power outage.

17. We talked to our old teacher at the library.

18. That old vacant warehouse may be renovated.

19. An increasing number of students are volunteering in the community.

20. Telltale pawprints on the floor pointed to our dog as the guilty party.

SPEAKING APPLICATION

Take turns with a partner. Tell about something interesting that has happened to you. Your partner should name the complete subject and complete predicate in each of your sentences.

WRITING APPLICATION

Write a paragraph about your favorite place to visit. In each sentence, underline the simple subject, and double underline the simple predicate.

Fragments

A **fragment** is a group of words that does not contain either a complete subject or a complete predicate, or both. Fragments are usually not used in formal writing. You can correct a fragment by adding the parts needed to complete the thought.

A **fragment** is a group of words that lacks a subject or a predicate, or both. It does not express a complete unit of thought.

FRAGMENTS	COMPLETE SENTENCES
glass of water (complete predicate missing)	The glass of water was cold and delicious. (complete predicate added)
swim in the ocean (complete subject missing)	Sharks swim in the ocean. (complete subject added)
from the pot (complete subject and predicate missing)	Pasta from the pot was poured into the bowl. (subject and complete predicate added)

In conversations, fragments usually do not present a problem because tone of voice, gestures, and facial expressions can add the missing information. A reader, however, cannot ask a writer for clarification.

Fragments are sometimes acceptable in writing that represents speech, such as the dialogue in a play or short story. Fragments are also sometimes acceptable in elliptical sentences.

An **elliptical sentence** is one in which the missing word or words can be easily understood.

EXAMPLES   Until tonight.

Why such a scared face?

Please don't yell!

Locating Subjects and Verbs

To avoid writing a fragment, look for the subject and verb in a sentence. To find the subject, ask, "Which word tells *what* or *who* this sentence is about?" Once you have the answer (the subject), then ask, "What does the subject do?" or "What is being done to the subject?" This will help you locate the verb.

In some sentences, it's easier to find the verb first. In this case, ask, "Which word states the action or condition in this sentence?" This question should help you locate the verb. Then ask, "*Who* or *what* is involved in the action of the verb?" The resulting word or words will be the subject.

EXAMPLE   Birds often feed on insects and seeds.

To find the subject first, ask, "Which word or words tell what or whom this sentence is about?"

ANSWER   Birds (*Birds* is the subject.)

Then ask, "What do birds do?"

ANSWER   feed (*Feed* is the verb.)

To find the verb first, ask, "Which word or words state the action or condition in the sentence?"

ANSWER   feed (*Feed* states the action, so it is the verb.)

Then ask, "Who or what feeds?"

ANSWER   Birds (*Birds* is the subject.)

To easily locate the subject and verb, mentally cross out any adjectives, adverbs, and prepositional phrases you see. These words add information, but they are usually less important than the simple subject and verb.

EXAMPLE   The **vegetables** **should grow** rapidly
                          simple subject   verb phrase
             in the next three weeks.

Sentences With More Than One Subject or Verb

Some sentences contain a **compound subject** or a **compound verb,** or a subject or verb with more than one part.

> A **compound subject** consists of two or more subjects. These subjects may be joined by a conjunction such as *and* or *or*.

RULE 2.1.5

EXAMPLES   The **campers** and **hikers** found their way with a compass.

Sandals, towels, and **pails** are always found around the beach house.

Neither the **host** nor the **guests** were tired.

> A **compound verb** consists of two or more verbs. These verbs may be joined by a conjunction such as *and, but, or,* or *nor*.

RULE 2.1.6

EXAMPLES   I neither **saw** the movie nor **read** the book.

Laura **left** class and **ran** to the movies.

They **cried** and **laughed** throughout the entire movie.

Some sentences contain both a compound subject and a compound verb.

EXAMPLES   My **dad** and **uncle** **chased** after the squirrels but **ran** into each other instead.

The **mom** and **dad** eyed each other, **turned** warily, and then **jumped** in the pool.

See Practice 2.1C
See Practice 2.1D

PRACTICE 2.1C > Locating Subjects and Verbs

Read each sentence. Then, write the subject and the verb in each sentence. Underline the subject.

EXAMPLE   The state with the best weather is Hawaii.

ANSWER   *state, is*

1. We hiked uphill for more than an hour and then took a break.
2. Some trained birds have large vocabularies.
3. Serena Zambrano was the first girl from our school to win the state championship.
4. Students and teachers enjoyed competing on the softball field.
5. Both Roger and Ling wrote and performed original songs.
6. We built and painted our own bookshelves.
7. Both bats and owls are active at night.
8. Many of today's television shows feature real people, not actors.
9. Members of the community took the trash away from the waterfront.
10. People in unfamiliar surroundings may feel anxious and uncertain.

PRACTICE 2.1D > Fixing Sentence Errors

Read each group of words. Decide if it is a sentence or a fragment. If it is a sentence, write *sentence*. If it is a fragment, rewrite it to make it a sentence.

EXAMPLE   In spite of not feeling well.

ANSWER   *Rosita continued in spite of not feeling well.*

11. His sister, a funny yet shy girl.
12. Stepped off the plane after a grueling flight.
13. She organized her locker before going to class.
14. Onto a street, lined with shops and restaurants.
15. The metal tabletop extremely cold after the freezing night.
16. Our class was winning the recycling contest.
17. Were playing happily in the snow fort.
18. Riding the subway to work that morning, Mr. Green.
19. I typed steadily from early in the morning until lunchtime.
20. On the bank of the creek sat.

SPEAKING APPLICATION

Take turns with a partner. Tell about your favorite possessions. Your partner should name the subject and the verb in each of your sentences.

WRITING APPLICATION

Write a fragment of your own. Use the fragment in three different sentences.

2.2 Hard-to-Find Subjects

While most sentences have subjects that are easy to find, some present a challenge.

Subjects in Declarative Sentences Beginning With *Here* or *There*

When the word *here* or *there* begins a declarative sentence, it is often mistaken for the subject.

> **_Here_ and _there_ are never the subject of a sentence.**

RULE 2.2.1

Here and *there* are usually adverbs that modify the verb by pointing out *where* something is located. However, *there* may occasionally begin a sentence simply as an introductory word.

In some sentences beginning with *here* or *there*, the subject appears before the verb. However, many sentences beginning with *here* or *there* are **inverted.** In an inverted sentence, the subject follows the verb. If you rearrange such a sentence in subject–verb order, you can identify the subject more easily.

INVERTED   There **are** the **tickets** . (verb–subject order)

REARRANGED   The **tickets** **are** there. (subject–verb order)

SENTENCES BEGINNING WITH *HERE* OR *THERE*	SENTENCES REARRANGED IN SUBJECT–VERB ORDER
There are the company's office buildings .	The company's office buildings are there.
Here is the ticket to get in.	The ticket to get in is here.
There is money stuck in the machine.	Money is stuck in the machine there.

> **In some declarative sentences, the subject is placed after the verb in order to give the subject greater emphasis.**

RULE 2.2.2

Because most sentences are written in subject–verb order, changing that order makes readers stop and think. Inverted sentences often begin with prepositional phrases.

SENTENCES INVERTED FOR EMPHASIS	SENTENCES REARRANGED IN SUBJECT–VERB ORDER
Toward the waiting taxi raced the anxious tourists .	The anxious tourists raced toward the waiting taxi.
Around the corner sped the police car .	The police car sped around the corner.

Subjects in Interrogative Sentences

Some interrogative sentences use subject–verb order. Often, however, the word order of an interrogative sentence is verb–subject.

EXAMPLES   Which **breeder** **has** the best puppies?
(subject–verb order)

Are we going there?
(verb–subject order)

RULE 2.2.3

> In interrogative sentences, the subject often follows the verb.

An inverted interrogative sentence can begin with an action verb, a helping verb, or one of the following words: *how, what, when, where, which, who, whose,* or *why.* Some interrogative sentences divide the helping verb from the main verb. To help locate the subject, mentally rearrange the sentence into subject–verb order.

INTERROGATIVE SENTENCES	REARRANGED IN SUBJECT–VERB ORDER
Is the Seattle Space Needle open at night?	The Seattle Space Needle is open at night.
Do they own those puppies?	They do own those puppies.
Where will the game be held?	The game will be held where?

Subjects in Imperative Sentences

EL9

The subject of an imperative sentence is usually implied rather than specifically stated.

> **In imperative sentences, the subject is understood to be *you*.**

2.2.4 RULE

IMPERATIVE SENTENCES	SENTENCES WITH *YOU* ADDED
First, visit the Space Needle.	First, [you] visit the Space Needle.
After the tour, come back here.	After the tour, [you] come back here.
Jane, introduce me to the tour guide.	Jane, [you] introduce me to the tour guide.

In the last example, the name of the person being addressed, *Jane*, is not the subject of the imperative sentence. Instead, the subject is still understood to be *you*.

Subjects in Exclamatory Sentences

In some **exclamatory sentences**, the subject appears before the verb. In others, the verb appears first. To find the subject, rearrange the sentence in subject–verb order.

> **In exclamatory sentences, the subject often appears after the verb, or it may be understood.**

2.2.5 RULE

EXAMPLES   What **do I know**!
(**I do know** what.)

Run now!
(Subject understood: **[You]** run now!)

In other exclamatory sentences, both the subject and verb may be unstated.

EXAMPLES   Tree! ([**You watch** out for the] tree!)

See Practice 2.2A
See Practice 2.2B

Smoke! ([**I see**] smoke!)

PRACTICE 2.2A > Identifying Hard-to-Find Subjects

Read each sentence. Then, write the subject of each sentence.

EXAMPLE   There are many paths in the woods.

ANSWER   *paths*

1. Here is my phone number.
2. Where is the rest of your report?
3. What did you get for lunch?
4. Just outside of town is a little park.
5. There have been a number of questions about the schedule.
6. Between the gym and the locker rooms are some storage rooms.
7. Tell me in great detail about your wonderful trip.
8. There are three fascinating art classes for the seniors.
9. When did the accident occur?
10. Behind the garage are some chicken coops.

PRACTICE 2.2B > Locating Hard-to-Find Verbs

Read each sentence. Then, write the verb in each sentence.

EXAMPLE   High in the sky soared the eagle.

ANSWER   *soared*

11. Can you believe what that man just donated?
12. Why not taste a new type of food?
13. Outside the window gathered a noisy crowd.
14. Before the concert, play your favorite song for me.
15. In the warm water swam the graceful dolphin.
16. As a last resort, tug lightly on the dog's leash.
17. Hey, get our luggage out of the rain!
18. Where are the keys to the back door?
19. To whom did you give the book?
20. Please take your foot off the pedal.

SPEAKING APPLICATION

Take turns with a partner. Say sentences that describe someone doing something. Your partner should name the subject in each of your sentences.

WRITING APPLICATION

Write three imperative sentences. Underline the verb in each sentence.

2.3 Complements

Some sentences are complete with just a subject and a verb or with a subject, verb, and modifiers: *The crowd cheered.* Other sentences need more information to be complete.

The meaning of many sentences, however, depends on additional words that add information to the subject and verb. For example, although *The satellite continually sends* has a subject and verb, it is an incomplete sentence. To complete the meaning of the predicate—in this case, to tell *what* a satellite sends—a writer must add a **complement.**

> **A complement is a word or group of words that completes the meaning of the predicate of a sentence.**

There are five kinds of complements in English: **direct objects, indirect objects, object complements, predicate nominatives,** and **predicate adjectives.** The first three occur in sentences that have transitive verbs. The last two are often called **subject complements.** Subject complements are found only with linking verbs. (See Chapter 1 for more information about action and linking verbs.)

Direct Objects

Direct objects are the most common of the five types of complements. They complete the meaning of action verbs by telling *who* or *what* receives the action.

> **A direct object is a noun, pronoun, or group of words acting as a noun that receives the action of a transitive verb.**

EXAMPLES   I **visited** the **Metropolitan Museum of Art**.
                                         direct object

Snow and **sleet** **covered** the **driveway**.
                                    direct object

Direct Objects and Action Verbs The direct object answers the question *Whom?* or *What?* about the action verb. If you cannot answer the question *Whom?* or *What?* the verb may be intransitive, and there is no direct object in the sentence.

EXAMPLES

Dogs **can see** in black and white.
(Ask, "Dogs can see *what*?" No answer; the verb is intransitive.)

The girl **spun** in a circle.
(Ask, "The girl spun *what*?" No answer; the verb is intransitive.)

In some inverted questions, the direct object may appear before the verb. To find the direct object easily, rearrange inverted questions in subject–verb order.

INVERTED
QUESTION

Which **newspapers did they read**?
    direct object

REARRANGED
IN SUBJECT–
VERB ORDER

They did read which **newspapers**?
                            direct object

Some sentences have more than one direct object, known as a **compound direct object.** If a sentence contains a compound direct object, asking *Whom?* or *What?* after the action verb will yield two or more answers.

EXAMPLES

The surgeons **wore masks** and
              direct object
gloves.
direct object

The team **has played** at **stadiums** and
                          direct object
arenas during the last six months.
direct object

In the last example, *months* is the object of the preposition *during*. The object of a preposition is never a direct object.

54   Basic Sentence Parts

Indirect Objects

Indirect objects appear only in sentences that contain transitive verbs and direct objects. Indirect objects are common with such verbs as *ask, bring, buy, give, lend, make, show, teach, tell,* and *write.* Some sentences may contain a compound indirect object.

> An **indirect object** is a noun or pronoun that appears with a direct object. It often names the person or thing that something is given to or done for.

2.3.4 RULE

EXAMPLES The **editor gave** the **author** a manuscript
indirect object
correction .
direct object

I **showed** my **mom** and **sister** the party
compound indirect object
invitation .
direct object

To locate an indirect object, make sure the sentence contains a direct object. Then, ask one of these questions after the verb and direct object: *To* or *for whom?* or *To* or *for what?*

EXAMPLES The **coach taught** our **team** a new **play** .
(The coach taught a play *to whom*? ANSWER: our team)

We **made** our **mother** a **jewelry box** .
(Made a jewelry box *for whom*? ANSWER: our mother)

An indirect object almost always appears between the verb and the direct object. In a sentence with subject–verb order, the indirect object never follows the direct object, nor will it ever be the object of the preposition *to* or *for.*

EXAMPLES **Jane sent** the **shoes** to me .
direct object object of preposition

Tina sent me the **book** .
indirect object direct object

Tina gave Jon a **critique** of the book.
indirect object direct object

See Practice 2.3A

Object Complements

While an indirect object almost always comes *before* a direct object, an **object complement** almost always *follows* a direct object. The object complement completes the meaning of the direct object.

RULE 2.3.5

> An **object complement** is an adjective or noun that appears with a direct object and describes or renames it.

A sentence that contains an object complement may seem to have two direct objects. However, object complements occur only with such verbs as *appoint, call, consider, declare, elect, judge, label, make, name, select,* and *think.* The words *to be* are often understood before an object complement.

EXAMPLES   The **organizers** of the concert **declared** **it** a
                                                            direct object
successful **benefit**.
       object complement

The **president** **appointed** **her** **chair**
                           direct   object
over the organization.   object complement

I **consider** **Christina** a caring **mother** and
              direct object   object complement
compassionate **sister**.
       object complement

Subject Complements

Linking verbs require **subject complements** to complete their meaning.

RULE 2.3.6

> A **subject complement** is a noun, pronoun, or adjective that appears with a linking verb and gives more information about the subject.

There are two kinds of subject complements: **predicate nominatives** and **predicate adjectives**.

Predicate Nominatives
The **predicate nominative** refers to the same person, place, or thing as the subject of the sentence.

> A **predicate nominative** is a noun or pronoun that appears with a linking verb and renames, identifies, or explains the subject. Some sentences may contain a compound predicate nominative.

RULE 2.3.7

EXAMPLES **Kevin Charles** **is** an **officer** with the navy.
predicate nominative

The **winner** **will be** **Kelly**.
predicate nominative

Mark Cullen **was** a **teacher** and former **coach**.
compound predicate nominative

Predicate Adjectives
A **predicate adjective** is an adjective that appears with a linking verb. It describes the subject in much the same way that an adjective modifies a noun or pronoun. Some sentences may contain a compound predicate adjective.

> A **predicate adjective** is an adjective that appears with a linking verb and describes the subject of the sentence.

RULE 2.3.8

EXAMPLES Your **action** **seems** **vindictive**.
predicate adjective

The **football player** **was** **strong**.
predicate adjective

The **sun** **felt** **warm** and **comforting**.
compound predicate adjective

The band **uniforms** **are** **green** and **black**.
compound predicate adjective

See Practice 2.3B

PRACTICE 2.3A ▶ Identifying Direct and Indirect Objects

Read each sentence. Then, write and label each direct object and indirect object.

EXAMPLE   The mail carrier delivered a letter to my father.

ANSWER   *letter* — direct object

1. The neighbors planned a surprise party.
2. Mix the raisins into your oatmeal.
3. I wrote the city council a letter.
4. You can rent DVDs through the mail.
5. Nonfiction books give readers an alternative to novels.
6. Chase needs a knife and fork.
7. Mom's clothing designs may bring her fame and fortune.
8. I sent Alia a package.
9. Stores have sold customers thousands of these gadgets.
10. Sheila plans to ask the singer for his autograph.

PRACTICE 2.3B ▶ Locating Object and Subject Complements

Read each sentence. Then, write the complement and label it *object complement* or *subject complement*.

EXAMPLE   Our club named Vanessa president.

ANSWER   *president* — object complement

11. These shoes used to be tight.
12. We all declared the experiment a success.
13. Jen's best stroke is the butterfly.
14. Sanjay considers his music teacher brilliant.
15. This part of the country is rich in oil and gas.
16. With hard work, you can make your goals attainable.
17. My great-grandfather was famous for his photographs.
18. Most of that restaurant's food is too spicy for me.
19. Dad calls his new car The Chariot.
20. The students voted Lee Ann the most popular student.

SPEAKING APPLICATION

Take turns with a partner. Tell about a family event. Your partner should name the direct object and indirect object, if any, in each of your sentences.

WRITING APPLICATION

Use sentences 11 and 12 as models to write similar sentences. Underline and label the complement in each sentence.

CHAPTER 3

PHRASES *and* CLAUSES

Use phrases and clauses to add important detail and dimension to your writing.

WRITE GUY *Jeff Anderson, M.Ed.*

WHAT DO YOU NOTICE?

Spot the clauses as you zoom in on these sentences from Act V of the play *Macbeth* by William Shakespeare.

MENTOR TEXT

> **Doctor:** This disease is beyond my practice. Yet I have known those which have walked in their sleep who have died holily in their beds.

Now, ask yourself the following questions:

- What is the first adjectival clause in the doctor's speech, and what noun or pronoun does it modify?
- What is the second adjectival clause in the speech, and what noun or pronoun does it modify?

The first adjectival clause is *which have walked in their sleep,* and the second adjectival clause is *who have died holily in their beds.* Both clauses modify the demonstrative pronoun *those.* Commas are not used to set off either of these restrictive clauses because each one adds essential meaning to the sentence.

Grammar for Writers Writers can use adjectival and adverbial clauses to add significant details to their sentences. Choose your words carefully so that they add to your writing in the way you intend.

What's a good adjectival phrase for the hamburger I ate for lunch?

Let's see. How about a burger with fries?

3.1 Phrases

When one adjective or adverb cannot convey enough information, a phrase can contribute more detail to a sentence. A **phrase** is a group of words that does not include a subject and verb and cannot stand alone as a sentence.

There are several kinds of phrases, including **prepositional phrases, appositive phrases, participial phrases, gerund phrases,** and **infinitive phrases.**

Prepositional Phrases

A **prepositional phrase** consists of a preposition and a noun or pronoun, called the object of the preposition. *Over their heads, until dark,* and *after the baseball game* are all prepositional phrases. Prepositional phrases often modify other words by functioning as adjectives or adverbs.

Sometimes, a single prepositional phrase may include two or more objects joined by a conjunction.

EXAMPLES   between the **chair** and the **desk**
            preposition   object   object

            with the **moon** and the **stars**
            preposition   object   object

            beside the **car** and **bike**
            preposition   object   object

See Practice 3.1A

Adjectival Phrases
A prepositional phrase that acts as an adjective is called an **adjectival phrase.**

> An **adjectival phrase** is a prepositional phrase that modifies a noun or pronoun by telling *what kind* or *which one.*

ADJECTIVES	ADJECTIVAL PHRASES
A beautiful mural hung in the library.	A mural of great beauty hung in the library. (*What kind of mural?*)
I sent my college friend a photograph of the team.	I sent my friend at college a photograph of the team. (*Which friend?*)

Like one-word adjectives, adjectival phrases can modify subjects, direct objects, indirect objects, or predicate nominatives.

MODIFYING A SUBJECT	The school **across the road** has been convenient.
MODIFYING A DIRECT OBJECT	Let's take a picture **of the Statue of Liberty**.
MODIFYING AN INDIRECT OBJECT	I gave the people **at the gardens** a tour.
MODIFYING A PREDICATE NOMINATIVE	Rome is a city **with many buildings**.

A sentence may contain two or more **adjectival phrases.** In some cases, one phrase may modify the preceding phrase. In others, two phrases may modify the same word.

EXAMPLES	We bought tickets **for the game** **at Central**.
	The mural **in the hallway** **of the dance** was wonderful.

Adverbial Phrases

RULE

3.1.2

> An **adverbial phrase** is a prepositional phrase that modifies a verb, an adjective, or an adverb by pointing out *where, why, when, in what way,* or *to what extent.*

ADVERBS	ADVERBIAL PHRASES
We worked quickly. (Worked *in what way?*)	We worked with great speed .
I was happy then. (Happy *when?*)	I was happy at the dance .
The helicopter flew overhead. (Flew *where?*)	The helicopter flew over the garden .

Adverbial phrases can modify verbs, adjectives, or adverbs.

MODIFYING
A VERB

The apples fell and rolled **across the barn** .

MODIFYING
AN ADJECTIVE

Tom was excited **beyond belief** .

MODIFYING
AN ADVERB

Her fear showed deep **in her eyes** .

An adverbial phrase may either follow the word it modifies or be located elsewhere in the sentence. Often, two adverbs in different parts of a sentence can modify the same word.

EXAMPLES

The beautiful flowers appeared **along the river** .

Along the river , beautiful flowers appeared.

After breakfast , we gathered **in the garden** .   See Practice 3.1B

PRACTICE 3.1A	**Identifying Prepositional Phrases**

Read each sentence. Write the prepositional phrase or phrases in each sentence. Then, write the word each phrase modifies.

EXAMPLE   She wanted tickets for the baseball game.

ANSWER   *for the baseball game, tickets*

1. In the afternoon they traveled to the country.
2. They arrived at about nine in the morning.
3. This secret is between you and me.
4. There is a gas station over the hill.
5. We planned our class reunion for months.
6. We clapped our hands with great joy.
7. The room is filled with antiques.
8. The flower shop is not far from the library.
9. I received recognition from the panel.
10. I walked to the store in about two hours.

PRACTICE 3.1B	**Identifying Adjectival and Adverbial Phrases**

Read each sentence. Write the adjectival or adverbial phrase. Then, label the phrase *adjectival* or *adverbial*.

EXAMPLE   A seat on an airplane is inexpensive right now.

ANSWER   *on an airplane* — adjectival

11. After dinner Jody and I went to the beach.
12. The baseball coach was happy after the win.
13. We will tell you the story at a later time.
14. Which subway train will take me into Manhattan?
15. A team of professional actors visited the school today.
16. He spoke politely to the teacher.
17. The food in the cafeteria tasted good today.
18. The latch on the fence needs repair.
19. The potholes in the road worried drivers.
20. Will sat near Monisha.

SPEAKING APPLICATION

Take turns with a partner. Describe the location of an object in the room. Your partner should listen for and name three prepositions that you use.

WRITING APPLICATION

Show that you understand the function of adjectival and adverbial clauses. Write sentences using the adjectival and adverbial clauses in any four sentences from Practice 3.1B. Read your sentences to a partner who should identify the clauses as you speak.

Appositives and Appositive Phrases

The term *appositive* comes from a Latin verb that means "to put near or next to."

Appositives Using **appositives** in your writing is an easy way to give additional meaning to a noun or pronoun.

RULE 3.1.3

> An **appositive** is a group of words that identifies, renames, or explains a noun or pronoun.

As the examples below show, appositives usually follow immediately after the words they explain.

EXAMPLES   The breakfast staff, **Jerome and Mia**, cleared the dishes.

Janice's band, **Falling Leaves**, played at the charity event.

Notice that commas are used in the examples above because these appositives are **nonessential.** In other words, the appositives could be omitted from the sentences without altering the basic meaning of the sentences.

Some appositives, however, are not set off by any punctuation because they are **essential** to the meaning of the sentence.

EXAMPLES   The artist **Picasso** was a famous Spanish painter.
(The appositive is essential because it identifies which specific artist.)

My friend **Kris** is an excellent sketch artist.
(The appositive is essential because you might have several friends.)

Note About Terms: Sometimes, the terms *nonrestrictive* and *restrictive* are used in place of *nonessential* and *essential.*

Appositive Phrases When an appositive is accompanied by its own modifiers, it is called an **appositive phrase.**

> An **appositive phrase** is a noun or pronoun with modifiers that adds information by identifying, renaming, or explaining a noun or pronoun.

3.1.4 RULE

Appositives and appositive phrases may follow nouns or pronouns used in almost any role within a sentence. The modifiers within an appositive phrase can be adjectives, adjective phrases, or other groups of words functioning as adjectives.

EXAMPLES Mr. Reid, **my gym teacher**, had us run laps around the field.

Bon explained horticulture, **the study of cultivating plants**.

ROLES OF APPOSITIVE PHRASES IN SENTENCES	
Identifying a Subject	Louis Pasteur, a famous scientist, conducted many experiments.
Identifying a Direct Object	The holistic nutritionist prepared a salad, a vegetarian meal.
Identifying an Indirect Object	I bought my friend, a girl of seventeen, a camera.
Identifying an Object Complement	I chose yellow, an unusual color for shoes.
Identifying a Predicate Nominative	My favorite sound is summer rain, a relaxing sound.
Identifying the Object of a Preposition	Plant the vegetables in the garden, a warm, sunny place.

Compound Appositives Appositives and appositive phrases can also be compound.

EXAMPLES   The entire family—**grandparents**, **parents**, and **children**—went together.

All nuts, **shelled** and **unshelled**, are on sale at the store today.

I used three herbs, **basil**, **oregano**, and **marjoram**, to flavor my stew.

See Practice 3.1C

Grammar and Style Tip When **appositives** or **appositive phrases** are used to combine sentences, they help to eliminate unnecessary words. One way to streamline your writing is to combine sentences by using an appositive phrase.

TWO SENTENCES	COMBINED SENTENCE
New York City is located on the Hudson River. It is an important U.S. seaport.	New York City, an important U.S. seaport, is located on the Hudson River.
Soccer is one of my favorite sports. It is a sport that is played all over the world.	Soccer, one of my favorite sports, is played all over the world.
Bordering Mexico, Texas is one of our largest states. It is also one of our richest oil states.	Texas, which borders Mexico, is one of our largest and richest oil states.

Read aloud the pairs of sentences in the chart. Notice how the combined sentences, which began as two choppy sentences, include the same information. However, they flow much more smoothly once the information in both sentences is clearly linked.

See Practice 3.1D

PRACTICE 3.1C > **Identifying Appositives and Appositive Phrases**

Read each sentence. Then, write the appositive or appositive phrase in each sentence.

EXAMPLE   I read a good book, *Twilight*, by Stephenie Meyer.

ANSWER   *Twilight*

1. Brad has an unusual hobby, ventriloquism.
2. Playing her instrument, a cello, takes great concentration and skill.
3. I visited my sister's class, a group of four-year-olds.
4. I made my special dessert, a strawberry tart.
5. Have you spoken to your sister Josanna today?
6. Meryl Streep, a talented actress, is my pick to win the award.
7. My mom loves her job, writing children's books.
8. Leigh Leggett, a doctor, lives in Washington.
9. I planted my favorite tree, a crape myrtle.
10. Football, one of my favorite sports, is fun to watch.

PRACTICE 3.1D > **Using Appositive and Appositive Phrases**

Read each pair of sentences. Then, combine the sentences using an appositive or an appositive phrase.

EXAMPLE   The dog ran into the culvert. A culvert is a type of drainage ditch.

ANSWER   *The dog ran into the culvert, a type of drainage ditch.*

11. Greenland is a country. It is a Danish territory.
12. Richard I was Robin Hood's hero. Richard I was king of England.
13. Will you let me borrow your skirt? It is the one with the white flowers.
14. Deena drank chai. Chai is a black tea.
15. The schnauzer is a sturdy and active dog. It is my favorite.
16. He lives in a yurt. A yurt is a type of tent.
17. Alaska is the nation's forty-ninth state. It entered the Union in January 1959.
18. Surtsey is an island. It is uninhabited.
19. Sam is my friend. He lives in Portland.
20. The graduates were part of the Class of 1991. They discussed having a reunion.

SPEAKING APPLICATION

Take turns with a partner. Tell about three different family members. Use three appositives or appositive phrases in your sentences. Your partner should identify the appositives or appositive phrases.

WRITING APPLICATION

Write two sentences about the same subject. Then, combine the sentences with an appositive or an appositive phrase.

Verbal Phrases

When a verb is used as a noun, an adjective, or an adverb, it is called a **verbal.** Although a verbal does not function as a verb, it retains two characteristics of verbs: It can be modified in different ways, and it can have one or more complements. A verbal with modifiers or complements is called a **verbal phrase.**

Participles

Many of the adjectives you use are actually verbals known as **participles.**

RULE 3.1.5

> A **participle** is a form of a verb that can act as an adjective.

The most common kinds of participles are **present participles** and **past participles.** These two participles can be distinguished from one another by their endings. Present participles usually end in *-ing (frightening, entertaining)*. Past participles usually end in *-ed (frightened, entertained)*, but many have irregular endings, such as *-t* or *-en (burnt, written)*.

PRESENT PARTICIPLES	PAST PARTICIPLES
The limping runner favored her aching leg.	Confused, they returned to their interrupted dinner.

Like other adjectives, participles answer the question *What kind?* or *Which one?* about the nouns or pronouns they modify.

EXAMPLES   Joe's **tearing** eyes betrayed the pain of his injury.
(*What kind* of eyes? Answer: *tearing* eyes)

The **splintered** floorboard needs to be replaced.
(*Which* floorboard? Answer: *splintered* floorboard)

Participles may also have a **present perfect** form.

EXAMPLES   **Having decided**, Joe jumped into the water.

Being greeted by the staff, the couple

checked in.

Verb or Participle? Because **verbs** often have endings such as *-ing* and *-ed,* you may confuse them with **participles.** If a word ending in *-ed* or *-ing* expresses the action of the sentence, it is a verb or part of a verb phrase. If it describes a noun or pronoun, it is a participle.

> A **verb** shows an action, a condition, or the fact that something exists. A **participle** acting as an adjective modifies a noun or a pronoun.

3.1.6 RULE

ACTING AS VERBS	ACTING AS ADJECTIVES
The baby is crying at the loud noise. (What is the baby doing?)	The crying baby sat in her crib. (Which baby?)
The doctor delighted the new parents. (What did the doctor do?)	Delighted, the new parents thanked the doctor. (What kind of parents?)

See Practice 3.1E

Participial Phrases

A participle can be expanded by adding modifiers and complements to form a **participial phrase.**

> A **participial phrase** is a participle modified by an adverb or adverbial phrase or accompanied by a complement. The entire participial phrase acts as an adjective.

3.1.7 RULE

The following examples show different ways that participles may be expanded into phrases.

WITH AN ADVERB

Traveling quickly, we made it in time for the delivery.

WITH AN ADVERB PHRASE

Traveling at breakneck speed, we made it in time for the delivery.

WITH A COMPLEMENT

Avoiding stops, we made it in time for the delivery.

A participial phrase that is nonessential to the basic meaning of a sentence is set off by commas or other forms of punctuation. A participial phrase that is essential is not set off by punctuation.

NONESSENTIAL PHRASES	ESSENTIAL PHRASES
There is Tim, waiting in the car.	The man waiting in the car is Tim.
Built in 1901, the building was innovative.	The building built in 1901 was innovative.

In the first sentence on the left side of the chart above, *waiting in the car* merely adds information about Tim, so it is nonessential. In the sentence on the right, however, the same phrase is essential because many different men might be in view.

In the second sentence on the left, *Built in 1901* is an additional description of *building,* so it is nonessential. In the sentence on the right, however, the phrase is essential because it identifies the specific building that is being discussed.

Participial phrases can often be used to combine information from two sentences into one.

TWO SENTENCES
We were exhausted from the flight to Greece. We rested at the airport.

COMBINED
Exhausted from the flight to Greece, we rested at the airport.

TWO SENTENCES
We ate brunch. We shared stories from our past.

COMBINED
Eating brunch, we shared stories from our past.

Notice how part of the verb in one sentence is changed into a participle in the combined sentence.

See Practice 3.1F

PRACTICE 3.1E ▷ Identifying Participles

Read each sentence. Then, identify the underlined word as *present participle* or *past participle*, and write the word that is modified.

EXAMPLE   Elated, he phoned his parents.

ANSWER   *past participle,* **he**

1. Grinning, my cousin accepted her prize.

2. The old man, moving slowly, inched his way across the street.

3. Confused, the performer stopped the performance.

4. The lead actress, overwhelmed, took another bow.

5. Disturbed by her decision, Tisha lay awake.

6. The participant, exhausted, finished first in the race.

7. Inspired, she began to write her speech.

8. The river, swollen, began to overflow.

9. The relieved climber finally got back down.

10. Her shining eyes showed her pride in her son's achievement.

PRACTICE 3.1F ▷ Recognizing Participial Phrases

Read each sentence. Write the participial phrase in each sentence. Then, write *E* for *essential* or *N* for *nonessential*.

EXAMPLE   The wheat swaying in the wind was like waves.

ANSWER   *swaying in the wind* — E

11. The shoreline eroded by the waves will be reinforced.

12. A balloon blowing back and forth rose slowly into the sky.

13. I listened to the mockingbirds imitating calls of other birds.

14. Boyd's expression, beaming with excitement, showed his enthusiasm.

15. The water, evaporating quickly, was soon at a very low level.

16. The document, crinkled with age, was sealed in a glass container.

17. Led by the coach, the team ran onto the field.

18. The parade participants, dancing in the streets, soon grew tired.

19. The boat sailing at top speed reached the shore quickly.

20. Overjoyed by the triumphant win, the crowd began cheering.

SPEAKING APPLICATION

Take turns with a partner. Describe your plans for the future. Your partner should listen for and identify the participles that you use.

WRITING APPLICATION

Write two sentences using the participial phrase: *spending time with friends.* In the first sentence, the participial phrase should be essential. In the second sentence, the participial phrase should be nonessential.

Gerunds

Many nouns that end in *-ing* are actually **verbals** known as **gerunds.** Gerunds are not difficult to recognize: They always end in *-ing,* and they always function as **nouns.**

RULE 3.1.9

> A **gerund** is a form of a verb that ends in *-ing* and acts as a **noun.**

FUNCTIONS OF GERUNDS	
Subject	Painting is my favorite pastime.
Direct Object	The wonderful food makes visiting Italy a pleasure.
Indirect Object	Mrs. Kim's recipes give home cooking a good name.
Predicate Nominative	My brother's favorite activity is swimming.
Object of a Preposition	The pilot's smooth flight showed signs of his extensive training.
Appositive	Tim's hobby, climbing, is very strenuous.

Verb, Participle, or Gerund? Words ending in *-ing* may be parts of verb phrases, participles acting as adjectives, or gerunds.

RULE 3.1.10

> Words ending in *-ing* that act as **nouns** are called **gerunds.** Unlike verbs ending in *-ing,* gerunds do not have helping verbs. Unlike participles ending in *-ing,* they do not act as adjectives.

VERB	Angela is **dancing** in the studio.
PARTICIPLE	The **dancing** girl is very good.
GERUND	**Dancing** is very exciting.
VERB	The class was **yawning**, and that distracted the teacher.
PARTICIPLE	**Yawning**, the class distracted the teacher.
GERUND	The class's **yawning** distracted the teacher.

Gerund Phrases Like participles, gerunds may be joined by other words to make **gerund phrases.**

> A **gerund phrase** consists of a gerund and one or more modifiers or a complement. These phrases act together as a noun.

GERUND PHRASES	
With Adjectives	Her constant, happy smiling made everyone around her joyful.
With an Adverb	Writing quickly does not always help.
With a Prepositional Phrase	Many hotels in the city prohibit pets sleeping in the beds.
With a Direct Object	Owen was incapable of remembering the list.
With an Indirect and a Direct Object	The history teacher tried giving her students praise.

Note About Gerunds and Possessive Pronouns: Always use the possessive form of a personal pronoun in front of a gerund.

INCORRECT   We never listen to **him** bragging.

CORRECT   We never listen to **his** bragging.

INCORRECT   **Them** refusing to drive slowly is dangerous.

See Practice 3.1G   CORRECT   **Their** refusing to drive slowly is dangerous.

Infinitives

The third kind of verbal is the **infinitive.** Infinitives have many different uses. They can act as nouns, adjectives, or adverbs.

> An **infinitive** is a form of a verb that generally appears with the word *to* in front of it and acts as a noun, an adjective, or an adverb.

The police officer asked them **to drive slowly** .

INFINITIVES USED AS NOUNS	
Subject	To appreciate music requires careful listening.
Direct Object	The villagers decided to rebel .
Predicate Nominative	The couple's only option was to wait .
Object of a Preposition	The plane to Canada was about to leave .
Appositive	There is only one choice, to leave !

Unlike gerunds, infinitives can also act as adjectives and adverbs.

INFINITIVES USED AS MODIFIERS	
Adjective	The teacher told the students to cooperate .
Adverb	The soldier was too tired to fight .

Prepositional Phrase or Infinitive? Although both **prepositional phrases** and **infinitives** often begin with *to*, you can tell the difference between them by analyzing the words that follow *to*.

RULE 3.1.13

> A **prepositional phrase** always ends with a noun or pronoun that acts as the object of the preposition. An **infinitive** always ends with a verb.

PREPOSITIONAL PHRASE	INFINITIVE
The pilot listened to the command .	The president's purpose is to command .
We were told to go to the back of the house.	Please make sure to back up the supply list.

Note About Infinitives Without *to*: Sometimes infinitives do not include the word *to*. When an infinitive follows one of the eight verbs listed below, the *to* is generally omitted. However, it may be understood.

VERBS THAT PRECEDE INFINITIVES WITHOUT *TO*			
dare	help	make	see
hear	let	please	watch

EXAMPLES   He won't dare **[to] go** without a map.

Please help me **[to] find** the destination.

Spencer helped Alan **[to] climb** up the hill.

Infinitive Phrases Infinitives also can be joined with other words to form phrases.

> An **infinitive phrase** consists of an infinitive and its modifiers, complements, or subject, all acting together as a single part of speech.

INFINITIVE PHRASES	
With an Adverb	Kate's family likes to run early.
With an Adverb Phrase	To walk in high heels is not easy.
With a Direct Object	Quinn hated to leave Houston.
With an Indirect and a Direct Object	He promised to show us the slides from direct indirect direct his hiking trip. object object object
With a Subject and a Complement	I want him to decide to go on his own. subject complement

See Practice 3.1H

PRACTICE 3.1G > Identifying Gerunds and Gerund Phrases

Read each sentence. Then, write the gerund or gerund phrase in each sentence.

EXAMPLE   Skateboarding is not allowed in certain areas of the park.

ANSWER   *Skateboarding*

1. He spoke about gardening.
2. Cracking your knuckles is a bad habit.
3. My father doesn't recommend driving fast.
4. Collecting teapots is her favorite hobby.
5. He enjoys playing golf.
6. Olivia tried riding her bicycle for the first time.
7. Traveling is a big part of her job.
8. My fear, flying in an airplane, is shared by others.
9. She was praised for helping her sister.
10. My great joy is reading.

PRACTICE 3.1H > Identifying Infinitives and Infinitive Phrases

Read each sentence. Write the infinitive or infinitive phrase in each sentence.

EXAMPLE   Everyone wants to go swimming.

ANSWER   *to go swimming*

11. Amy tries to eat healthy foods everyday.
12. To graduate from college is her main priority.
13. This is necessary information to know.
14. We hiked for three miles to reach the campsite.
15. The banker had money to invest.
16. The manager that you need to talk to about your account is at lunch.
17. His goal was to earn one million dollars before he retired.
18. To take the picture was proving difficult.
19. During the test, we were allowed to use our dictionaries.
20. The trail to take is about three miles from here.

SPEAKING APPLICATION

Take turns with a partner. Say sentences with the following gerunds: *running, climbing, reading, studying,* and *searching*.

WRITING APPLICATION

Write three sentences with infinitive phrases. Underline each infinitive phrase.

3.2 Clauses

Every **clause** contains a subject and a verb. However, not every clause can stand by itself as a complete thought.

A **clause** is a group of words that contains a subject and a verb.

Independent and Subordinate Clauses

The two basic kinds of clauses are **independent** or **main clauses** and **subordinate clauses.**

An **independent** or **main clause** can stand by itself as a complete sentence.

Every sentence must contain an independent clause. The independent clause can either stand by itself or be connected to other independent or subordinate clauses.

STANDING
ALONE

Dr. Onevi teaches biology .
               independent clause

WITH
ANOTHER
INDEPENDENT
CLAUSE

Dr. Onevi teaches biology , and
           independent clause

his wife teaches chemistry .
          independent clause

WITH A
SUBORDINATE
CLAUSE

Dr. Onevi teaches biology , **while his wife**
        independent clause   subordinate clause

teaches chemistry .

When you subordinate something, you give it less importance.

A **subordinate clause,** although it has a subject and verb, cannot stand by itself as a complete sentence.

Subordinate clauses can appear before or after an independent clause in a sentence or can even split an independent clause.

LOCATIONS OF SUBORDINATE CLAUSES	
In the Middle of an Independent Clause	The man to whom I introduced you teaches technology courses.
Preceding an Independent Clause	Unless the ice melts soon, the road will be too slick.
Following an Independent Clause	Mike asked that he be excused.

See Practice 3.2A

Like phrases, subordinate clauses can function as adjectives, adverbs, or nouns in sentences.

Adjectival Clauses

One way to add description and detail to a sentence is by adding an **adjectival clause.**

> An **adjectival clause** is a subordinate clause that modifies a noun or pronoun in another clause by telling *what kind* or *which one.*

An adjectival clause usually begins with one of the relative pronouns: *that, which, who, whom,* or *whose.* Sometimes, it begins with a relative adverb, such as *before, since, when, where,* or *why.* Each of these words connects the clause to the word it modifies.

> An **adjectival clause** often begins with a **relative pronoun** or a **relative adverb** that links the clause to a noun or pronoun in another clause.

The adjectival clauses in the examples on the next page answer the questions *What kind?* and *Which one?* Each modifies the noun in the independent clause that comes right before the adjectival clause. Notice also that the first two clauses begin with relative pronouns and the last one begins with a relative adverb.

EXAMPLES   I finished listening to the CD **that you had loaned me** .

We gave eating salad, **which we thought was healthful** , a second try.

In Germany, we visited the town **where my grandfather was born** .

Adjectival clauses can often be used to combine information from two sentences into one. Using adjectival clauses to combine sentences can indicate the relationship between ideas as well as add detail to a sentence.

TWO SENTENCES	COMBINED SENTENCES
The architect is ready to design the building. He is well known for unusual designs.	The architect, who is ready to design the building , is well known for unusual designs.
My sister swam a mile and broke the school record. She is a freshman in college.	My sister, who is a freshman in college , swam a mile and broke the school record.

Essential and Nonessential Adjectival Clauses Adjectival clauses, like appositives and participial phrases, are set off by punctuation only when they are not essential to the meaning of a sentence. Commas are used to indicate information that is not essential to the meaning of the sentence. When information in an adjectival clause is essential to the sentence, no commas are used.

NONESSENTIAL CLAUSES	ESSENTIAL CLAUSES
One of Shakespeare's best characters is Romeo, who is the main character in *Romeo and Juliet* .	The program that everyone must watch tonight promises to be very informative.
Bill Johnson, who trained day and night for a year , won the state championship.	An athlete who trains faithfully usually finds winning to be easy.

See Practice 3.2B

PRACTICE 3.2A Identifying Independent and Subordinate Clauses

Read each sentence. Identify the underlined clause in each sentence as *independent* or *subordinate*.

EXAMPLE   We didn't make plans <u>because we don't know the outcome</u>.

ANSWER   *subordinate*

1. Her plan, <u>that we improve the environment</u>, received much support.
2. Bill's reply, <u>that we remain firm</u>, upset us all.
3. <u>Even though he wondered about his choice</u>, he went ahead with the decision.
4. When the school won an award, <u>everyone was elated</u>.
5. <u>Whenever I am in Chicago</u>, I like to visit the Sears Tower.
6. The child <u>who plays the tambourine</u> is my niece.
7. <u>After I pay the bill</u>, I will drop it by the office.
8. Leaving the safety of the shore, <u>we swam out to sea</u>.
9. <u>For a person who dislikes dancing</u>, you certainly attend a lot of dance classes.
10. If you leave food out, <u>the food will attract bugs</u>.

PRACTICE 3.2B Identifying Adjectival Clauses

Read each sentence. Write the adjectival clause in each sentence. Then, write *E* if it is essential or *N* if it is nonessential.

EXAMPLE   The ability to speak to others, which is Greg's greatest strength, helped him win support easily.

ANSWER   *which is Greg's greatest strength — N*

11. CD Warehouse, which is the best music store in town, is having a sale.
12. The office manager to whom we had written has not yet replied.
13. The movie, which I saw last night, was very long.
14. Hope McVey, whose father is in the military, has lived all over the world.
15. The song that I wanted to hear was playing on the radio.
16. This is the necklace that my mother wants.
17. The clown, who is in the parade, is funny.
18. The sweater that I am wearing is too heavy.
19. Our mayor, who is very powerful, lives in a large house.
20. My brother collects stamps that portray different presidents.

SPEAKING APPLICATION

With a partner, take turns saying sentences that have independent and subordinate clauses. Your partner should identify the clauses as either independent or subordinate.

WRITING APPLICATION

Write four sentences using adjectival clauses. Exchange papers with a partner and underline the adjectival clauses in each sentence.

Relative Pronouns **Relative pronouns** help link a subordinate clause to another part of a sentence. They also have a function in the subordinate clause.

> **Relative pronouns** connect adjectival clauses to the words they modify and act as subjects, direct objects, objects of prepositions, or adjectives in the subordinate clauses.

3.2.6 RULE

To tell how a relative pronoun is used within a clause, separate the clause from the rest of the sentence, and find the subject and verb in the clause.

FUNCTIONS OF RELATIVE PRONOUNS IN CLAUSES	
As a Subject	The plane that is engineered correctly is sure to stay subject in the air.
As a Direct Object	Pier, whom my sister met in France , is a good friend. direct object (Reworded clause: my sister met *whom* in France)
As an Object of a Preposition	This is the car about which I heard rave reviews . object of preposition (Reworded clause: I heard rave reviews about *which*)
As an Adjective	The child whose behavior was questionable spoke to adjective his parents.

Sometimes in writing and in speech, a relative pronoun is left out of an adjectival clause. However, the missing word, though simply understood, still functions in the sentence.

EXAMPLES   The heroes [**whom**] we studied were great leaders.

The suggestions [**that**] they made were implemented.

See Practice 3.2C

Relative Adverbs Like relative pronouns, **relative adverbs** help link the subordinate clause to another part of a sentence. However, they have only one use within a subordinate clause.

Relative adverbs connect adjectival clauses to the words they modify and act as adverbs in the clauses.

EXAMPLE   Tom couldn't wait for the day **when** he could go on vacation.

In the example, the adjectival clause is *when he could go on vacation.* Reword the clause this way to see that *when* functions as an adverb: *he could go on vacation when.*

Adverbial Clauses

Subordinate clauses may also serve as adverbs in sentences. They are introduced by subordinating conjunctions. Like adverbs, **adverbial clauses** modify verbs, adjectives, or other adverbs.

Subordinate **adverbial clauses** modify verbs, adjectives, adverbs, or verbals by telling *where, when, in what way, to what extent, under what condition,* or *why.*

An adverbial clause begins with a subordinating conjunction and contains a subject and a verb, although they are not the main subject and verb in the sentence. In the chart that follows, the adverbial clauses are highlighted in orange. Arrows point to the words they modify.

ADVERBIAL CLAUSES	
Modifying a Verb	After you've been in Italy, you should begin your cooking class. (Begin *when?*)
Modifying an Adjective	Angela seemed delighted wherever she was. (Delighted *where?*)
Modifying a Gerund	Chicago is interesting because of the different cultures and communities. (Interesting *under what condition?*)

Adverbial clauses begin with **subordinating conjunctions** and contain subjects and verbs.

EXAMPLE   **Even though** it rained, we still had a picnic.
           subordinating
           conjunction

Recognizing the subordinating conjunctions will help you identify adverbial clauses. The following chart shows some of the most common subordinating conjunctions.

SUBORDINATING CONJUNCTIONS			
after	because	so that	when
although	before	than	whenever
as	even though	though	where
as if	if	unless	wherever
as long as	since	until	while

Whether an adverbial clause appears at the beginning, middle, or end of a sentence can sometimes affect the sentence meaning.

EXAMPLES   **Before she moved**, Anne planned to visit Rome.

            Anne planned to visit Rome **before she moved**.

Like adjectival clauses, adverbial clauses can be used to combine the information from two sentences into one. The combined sentence shows a close relationship between the ideas.

TWO   **It was icy**. They did not drive home.
SENTENCES

COMBINED   **Because** it was icy, they did not drive home.
            subordinating
            conjunction

See Practice 3.2D

PRACTICE 3.2C **Identifying Relative Pronouns and Adjectival Clauses**

Read each sentence. Then, write the adjectival clause in each sentence, and underline the relative pronoun that introduces the clause.

EXAMPLE   The book, which you requested, is unavailable.

ANSWER   <u>which</u> you requested

1. This is the play that was reviewed in the newspaper.

2. The story that he told is unbelievable.

3. It is Sarah whose watch was stolen.

4. Is this the moment that we have been waiting for?

5. A team that doesn't play well together should be reorganized.

6. Here are the concert tickets that we ordered.

7. He applied to the university that his father graduated from.

8. We visited the coastline, which was spectacular.

9. My brother, who arrived during the game, won't be leaving soon.

10. The low-pressure system that is approaching could produce tornadoes.

PRACTICE 3.2D **Recognizing Adverbial Clauses**

Read each sentence. Then, write the adverbial clause in each sentence.

EXAMPLE   She developed a cough whenever she caught a cold.

ANSWER   *whenever she caught a cold*

11. Your hair looks better since you had it cut.

12. We had hoped to put in a pool when the weather became warmer.

13. Talking on the phone while cooking dinner is hard for my mother.

14. She is happier today than she was yesterday.

15. Nia didn't have her purse when we left the restaurant.

16. The meeting ended much earlier than we expected.

17. When I start my project, my father will help me buy the materials.

18. I am unable to join you while I am on vacation.

19. Faster than predicted, the storm descended upon us.

20. We decided to take action when we heard the news.

SPEAKING APPLICATION

Take turns with a partner. Tell about something funny that happened to you, using relative pronouns to introduce the adjectival clauses. Your partner should listen for and identify the relative pronouns that you use.

WRITING APPLICATION

Write sentences using the relative adverbs *when, while,* and *than.*

Elliptical Adverbial Clauses Sometimes, words are omitted in adverbial clauses, especially in those clauses that begin with *as* or *than* and are used to express comparisons. Such clauses are said to be *elliptical*.

> An **elliptical clause** is a clause in which the verb or the subject and verb are understood but not actually stated.

3.2.10 RULE

Even though the subject or the verb (or both) may not appear in an elliptical clause, they make the clause express a complete thought.

In the following examples, the understood words appear in brackets. The sentences are alike, except for the words *he* and *him*. In the first sentence, *he* is a subject of the adverbial clause. In the second sentence, *him* functions as a direct object of the adverbial clause.

VERB UNDERSTOOD — She resembles their aunt more **than he [does]**.

SUBJECT AND VERB UNDERSTOOD — She resembles their aunt more **than [she resembles] him**.

See Practice 3.2E

When you read or write elliptical clauses, mentally include the omitted words to clarify the intended meaning.

Noun Clauses

Subordinate clauses can also act as nouns in sentences.

> A **noun clause** is a subordinate clause that acts as a noun.

3.2.11 RULE

A noun clause acts in almost the same way a one-word noun does in a sentence: It tells what or whom the sentence is about.

In a sentence, a noun clause may act as a subject, direct object, indirect object, predicate nominative, object of a preposition, or appositive.

EXAMPLES   **Whatever you lost** can be found in your
                        subject
messy room!

My grandparents remembered **what food I liked
when I visited** .
                                    direct object

The chart on the next page contains more examples of the functions of noun clauses.

Introductory Words

Noun clauses frequently begin with the words *that, which, who, whom,* or *whose*—the same words that are used to begin adjective clauses. *Whichever, whoever,* or *whomever* may also be used as introductory words in noun clauses. Other noun clauses begin with the words *how, if, what, whatever, where, when, whether,* or *why.*

Introductory words may act as subjects, direct objects, objects of prepositions, adjectives, or adverbs in noun clauses, or they may simply introduce the clauses.

SOME USES OF INTRODUCTORY WORDS IN NOUN CLAUSES	
FUNCTIONS IN CLAUSES	EXAMPLES
Adjective	He could not determine which puppy he wanted most.
Adverb	They wanted to know how to order in French.
Subject	I want the design from whoever built their house .
Direct Object	Whatever my parents advised , I obeyed.
No Function	The doctor determined that he had broken his arm .

Note that in the following chart the introductory word *that* in the last example has no function except to introduce the clause.

FUNCTIONS OF NOUN CLAUSES IN SENTENCES	
Acting as a Subject	Whoever leaves last must close the garage.
Acting as a Direct Object	Please tell whomever you want about the reunion.
Acting as an Indirect Object	His terse manner made whomever worked for him nervous.
Acting as a Predicate Nominative	Our choice is whether to buy a cat or dog.
Acting as an Object of a Preposition	As long as you clean, you can use the house for whatever you like.
Acting as an Appositive	The team embraced the offer that they receive new uniforms before the game.

Some words that introduce noun clauses also introduce adjectival and adverbial clauses. It is necessary to check the function of the clause in the sentence to determine its type. To check the function, try substituting the words *it, you, fact,* or *thing* for the clause. If the sentence retains its smoothness, you probably replaced a noun clause.

NOUN CLAUSE	I knew **that they wouldn't bring it** .
SUBSTITUTION	I knew it.

In the following examples, all three subordinating clauses begin with *where,* but only the first is a noun clause because it functions in the sentence as a direct object.

NOUN CLAUSE	Mr. Santos told the students **where they would be during the fire drill** .
	(Told the students *what?*)
ADJECTIVAL CLAUSE	They took the tiger out of the cage, **where the lock was broken** .
	(*Which* cage?)
ADVERBIAL CLAUSE	They live **where the weather is cold all year** .
	(Live *where?*)

Note About Introductory Words: The introductory word *that* is often omitted from a noun clause. In the following examples, the understood word *that* is in brackets.

EXAMPLES	The manager suggested **[that] you leave the application** .
	After the band had chosen him for the show, Ben knew **[that] he was going to have a very busy month** .
	They remembered **[that] you wanted to use the black guitar** .

See Practice 3.2F

PRACTICE 3.2E	**Identifying Elliptical Adverbial Clauses**

Read each sentence. Then, write the adverbial clause in each sentence. For the adverbial clauses that are elliptical, add the understood words in parentheses.

EXAMPLE   My report received a higher grade than Mike's report.

ANSWER   *than Mike's report (did)*

1. Eric knows my brother better than I.

2. Lydia's outfit is as colorful as Carolyn's outfit.

3. George's cousin is as tall as George.

4. The train station is closer to my house than to Jeff's.

5. The oak tree is taller than the house.

6. Lousia can run faster than Joe.

7. My desserts taste better than Maria's desserts.

8. The cat ran as fast as the dog.

9. Claude's hair is as short as Ron's hair.

10. My errors are worse than Timmy's errors.

PRACTICE 3.2F	**Recognizing Noun Clauses**

Read each sentence. Then, write the noun clause and label it *subject, direct object, indirect object, predicate nominative, object of a preposition,* or *appositive.*

EXAMPLE   A good quality, affordable education is what everyone wants.

ANSWER   *what everyone wants* — predicate nominative

11. The new rules curbed whatever freedom I had.

12. We gave whoever stopped by a free meal.

13. Our petition, that the team be reinstated, needed signatures.

14. We decided that his stubborness could no longer be ignored.

15. Whoever fails this test must quit the team.

16. My brother asked someone about what time the shuttle was launched.

17. The factory sent whoever had pending business an invoice.

18. His fear is that he will have to give an acceptance speech.

19. Whatever friends Sandy invites to our home will be welcomed.

20. Hand this receipt to whoever is behind the counter.

SPEAKING APPLICATION

Take turns with a partner. Say sentences that include adverbial clauses. Your partner should listen for and identify what each adverbial clause modifies.

WRITING APPLICATION

Show that you understand the function of noun clauses. Write four sentences with noun clauses. Then, read your sentences to a partner. Your partner should identify the noun clauses as you speak your sentences.

3.3 The Four Structures of Sentences

Independent and subordinate clauses are the building blocks of sentences. These clauses can be combined in an endless number of ways to form the four basic sentence structures: **simple, compound, complex,** and **compound-complex.**

RULE 3.3.1

A **simple sentence** contains a single independent or main clause.

Although a simple sentence contains only one main or independent clause, its subject, verb, or both may be compound. A simple sentence may also have modifying phrases and complements. However, it cannot have a subordinate clause.

In the following simple sentences, the subjects are highlighted in yellow, and the verbs are highlighted in orange.

ONE SUBJECT AND VERB	The **ballerina danced**.
COMPOUND SUBJECT	**Trish** and **Faith cooked** Thanksgiving dinner.
COMPOUND VERB	The **bonfire crackled** and **burned**.
COMPOUND SUBJECT AND VERB	Neither the **pilot** nor the **passengers saw** or **heard** the engine fire.

RULE 3.3.2

A **compound sentence** contains two or more main clauses.

The main clauses in a compound sentence can be joined by a comma and a coordinating conjunction *(and, but, for, nor, or, so, yet)* or by a semicolon (;). Like a simple sentence, a compound sentence contains no subordinate clauses.

EXAMPLE   The **student carried** books to class, and **she started** taking notes in her notebook.   See Practice 3.3A

> A **complex sentence** consists of one independent or main clause and one or more subordinate clauses.

RULE 3.3.3

The independent clause in a complex sentence is often called the main clause to distinguish it from the subordinate clause or clauses. The subject and verb in the independent clause are called the subject of the sentence and the main verb. The second example shows that a subordinate clause may fall between the parts of a main clause. In the examples below, the main clauses are highlighted in blue, and the subordinate clauses are highlighted in pink.

EXAMPLES **No one reacted to the pager when it vibrated**.

The garden that she waters daily was full of flowers.

Note on Complex Sentences With Noun Clauses: The subject of the main clause may sometimes be the subordinate clause itself.

EXAMPLE **That they were very late upset them**.

> A **compound-complex sentence** consists of two or more independent clauses and one or more subordinate clauses.

RULE 3.3.4

In the example below, the independent clauses are highlighted in blue, and the subordinate clause is highlighted in pink.

EXAMPLE **Sparky barked when he saw a cat, and he ran through the park chasing it**.

See Practice 3.3B

The Four Structures of Sentences   **91**

PRACTICE 3.3A > **Distinguishing Between
Simple and Compound
Sentences**

Read each sentence. Then, label each sentence
simple or *compound*.

EXAMPLE   His speech was both short and
poignant.

ANSWER   *simple*

1. Either Laurel plays, or we forfeit the game.

2. At this juncture, there are several good routes
that are accessible.

3. Tito's in Cleveland is known for its
sandwiches.

4. The playoff victory was the Panthers' last
impressive showing of the season.

5. Neither did the brush fire die, nor did the
strong winds calm.

6. The waiter wrapped our leftovers, and then
he gave us our bill.

7. We found the exit to the museum easily, but
it was locked.

8. The cows wandered out to pasture and
munched on the grass.

9. Either Kyle or Marcus will arrive at noon.

10. The police car arrived at the scene, and it left
within one hour.

PRACTICE 3.3B > **Identifying the Four
Structures of Sentences**

Read each sentence. Then, label each
sentence *simple, compound, complex,* or
compound-complex.

EXAMPLE   At this time, there are many
dates available.

ANSWER   *simple*

11. The bluff was covered with hanging vines.

12. Though the partners worked tirelessly, they
could not finish the project.

13. After the actors performed the play, the
audience gave them a standing ovation.

14. The quarterly meeting was held on Thursday,
and those in attendance, the shareholders,
asked many questions about the company's
future.

15. Ruby bought decorative stationery and spent
all day writing letters.

16. If you leave lights on, you're wasting energy.

17. The dogs were barking, so Clarence stopped
cleaning his room and fed them.

18. Would you rather see a movie or a play?

19. As soon as I have some free time, I will take
down the tent and store it in the attic.

20. For a girl who doesn't like sports, you go to
a lot of football games.

SPEAKING APPLICATION

Take turns with a partner. Tell about
something fun that you did with a family
member. Use both simple and compound
sentences. Your partner should listen for and
identify each sentence as simple or compound.

WRITING APPLICATION

Write a paragraph about what you think you
will be doing twenty years from now. Your
paragraph should include a variety of correctly
structured sentences: simple, compound,
complex, and compound-complex.

Cumulative Review Chapters 1–3

PRACTICE 1 ▷ Identifying Nouns

Read the sentences. Then, label each underlined noun *concrete* or *abstract*. If the noun is concrete, label it *collective*, *compound*, *common*, or *proper*.

1. The crew team stayed after practice to work on their strategy for the next meet.
2. My mother told me that she left my geometry book on the coffee table.
3. People often asked if we were sisters because we looked so much alike.
4. Lauren did not like physics class because the theories were difficult to understand.
5. The train is departing for Wyoming in half an hour.

PRACTICE 2 ▷ Identifying Pronouns

Read the sentences. Then, label each underlined pronoun *reciprocal*, *demonstrative*, *relative*, *interrogative*, or *indefinite*.

1. These people generally don't agree on much.
2. The contest, which we knew would be challenging, was in March.
3. Most of the students dissected a frog last year in biology class.
4. Whose turn is it to read aloud?
5. The children enjoyed playing with one another.

PRACTICE 3 ▷ Classifying Verbs and Verb Phrases

Read the sentences. Then, write the verb or verb phrase in each sentence. Label each *action* or *linking verb*, and *transitive* or *intransitive*.

1. The crowd cheered the band on with thunderous applause.

2. Eric's singing sounds magnificent in the empty auditorium.
3. Rebecca left the game begrudgingly.
4. Every spring, Matthew cleans the garage.
5. This chicken tastes delicious.

PRACTICE 4 ▷ Identifying Adjectives and Adverbs

Read the sentences. Then, label the underlined word as an *adverb* or *adjective*. Write the word that is modified.

1. She felt sincere gratitude for the help.
2. The flowers on the table smelled divine.
3. I was immensely happy to see such a turnout.
4. Conrad was the oldest player on the squad.
5. We greatly appreciated her kindness.

PRACTICE 5 ▷ Using Prepositions, Conjunctions, and Interjections

Read the sentences. Then, write the preposition, conjunction, or interjection. Label conjunctions *coordinating*, *correlative*, or *subordinating*.

1. Wow! The stars are brilliant tonight.
2. Before we can leave the house, Sarah needs to put her shoes on.
3. Both Randy and Jorge wanted to win the competition.
4. Stop! Don't sit on the bench with the wet paint sign on it!
5. Erin wanted to meet early, so I had to make sure that I left on time.

Continued on next page ▶

Recognizing Direct and Indirect Objects and Object of a Preposition

Identify the underlined items as *direct object*, *indirect object*, or *object of a preposition*.

1. My mother gave <u>us</u> another <u>chance</u> to tell the truth.

2. Was Matilda running into the <u>school</u>?

3. Before leaving, Molly told us the <u>itinerary</u> for her <u>trip</u>.

4. The soldiers walked up <u>hills</u> and along <u>riverbeds</u>.

5. Dad promised <u>Irene</u> and <u>me</u> that he would take us to the planetarium next Wednesday.

6. The principal proposed new <u>hours</u> to the <u>faculty</u>.

7. Across from my <u>house</u> sat two stray cats.

8. Caroline recalled how calm the town looked before it was hit by the <u>hurricane</u>.

9. During the <u>play</u>, the students remained quiet.

10. Have you commended <u>Walt</u> and <u>Brian</u> for their excellent behavior?

PRACTICE 7 **Identifying Phrases**

Read the sentences. Then, write the phrases, and label them *prepositional, appositive, participial, gerund,* or *infinitive*.

1. Over the course of three months, we studied twentieth-century U.S. history.

2. The teacher decided to postpone the exam for one week.

3. The howling wind blew the windows in the front rooms shut.

4. My dog, a German shepherd, has lived with us for nine years.

5. Running every day after school allowed him to gain energy and stamina.

6. It is important to stand up for your beliefs.

7. Theodore Roosevelt, a dedicated Progressive, fought to lessen the power of big business.

8. We stayed until midnight, when the game was officially over.

9. Thinking it over, Jaime decided to take decisive action.

10. Reading aloud is a good way to understand difficult texts.

PRACTICE 8 **Recognizing Clauses**

Label the underlined clauses in the following sentences *independent* or *subordinate*. Identify any subordinate clause as *adjectival, adverbial,* or *noun clause.* Then, label any adjectival clauses *essential* or *nonessential.*

1. We will go to the beach <u>if it is warm enough</u>.

2. My mom, <u>who was born in Florida</u>, has never seen snow.

3. <u>Even though I can't come to your birthday party</u>, I would like to help you set up for it.

4. <u>When the next storm will hit</u> has not yet been forecasted.

5. <u>I think of my grandmother</u> whenever I hear this song.

6. Sammy, <u>who traveled the farthest to get here</u>, set up her exhibit next to mine.

7. <u>Danielle walked up and down the aisles</u>, searching for the earring she lost.

8. You can set up the display <u>wherever you can find room</u>.

9. The real problem is <u>how to settle this dispute</u>.

10. My aunt <u>who never talks much</u> is coming to visit us next week.

EFFECTIVE SENTENCES

Vary your sentence length and structure to add interest and surprise to your writing.

WRITE GUY *Jeff Anderson, M.Ed.*

WHAT DO YOU NOTICE?

Analyze phrasing as you zoom in on this sentence from the story "The Lady in the Looking Glass: A Reflection" by Virginia Woolf.

MENTOR TEXT

> She was thinking, perhaps, that she must order a new net for the strawberries; that she must send flowers to Johnson's widow; that it was time she drove over to see the Hippesleys in their new house.

Now, ask yourself the following questions:

- How does the author use parallel, or similar, phrasing in the sentence?
- In addition to words and punctuation, what else is parallel?

The author repeats the relative pronoun *that* at the start of each of the three subordinate clauses in the series. She also uses semicolons to separate them. Beyond words and punctuation, the author repeats similar ideas in each clause to help create a sense of how the character's thoughts flow from one proposed action to the next.

Grammar for Writers Parallel structure does more than clarify ideas. Writers can also use it to create a sense of lively, repetitive rhythm in their prose—much like meter in poetry.

We listened carefully, studied hard, and learned well.

You're right. We came, we saw, we conquered parallel structure.

4.1 The Four Functions of a Sentence

Sentences can be classified according to what they do—that is, whether they state ideas, ask questions, give orders, or express strong emotions.

Declarative sentences are used to declare, or state, facts.

RULE 4.1.1

> A **declarative sentence** states an idea and ends with a period.

DECLARATIVE   Paris is a city in France.

To *interrogate* means "to ask." An **interrogative sentence** is a question.

RULE 4.1.2

> An **interrogative sentence** asks a question and ends with a question mark.

INTERROGATIVE   In which country are people the healthiest?

Imperative sentences give commands or directions.

RULE 4.1.3

> An **imperative sentence** gives an order or a direction and ends with either a period or an exclamation mark.

Most imperative sentences start with a verb. In this type of imperative sentence, the subject is understood to be *you.*

IMPERATIVE   Follow my instructions word for word.

Exclamatory sentences are used to express emotions.

RULE 4.1.4

> An **exclamatory sentence** conveys strong emotion and ends with an exclamation mark.

EXCLAMATORY   Congratulations on your acceptance!

See Practice 4.1A
See Practice 4.1B

Identifying the Four Types of Sentences

Read each sentence. Then, label each sentence *declarative, interrogative, imperative,* or *exclamatory.*

EXAMPLE   How much did the ticket cost?

ANSWER   *interrogative*

1. My favorite pizza topping is mushrooms.
2. Who knows where I can find a locksmith?
3. Take all the tools out of the truck.
4. What an absolutely wonderful occasion!
5. The game this weekend should be competitive.
6. Do you remember how many paintings we sold last year?
7. Make certain that you proofread your essay thoroughly.
8. What a strange coincidence!
9. Which movie would you recommend?
10. Watch out!

Punctuating the Four Types of Sentences

Read each sentence. Label each sentence *declarative, interrogative, imperative,* or *exclamatory.* Then, in parentheses, write the correct end mark.

EXAMPLE   There are many pieces to this puzzle

ANSWER   *declarative (.)*

11. What a frightful mess
12. Is there a way out of this cave
13. Please deliver these to your brother
14. I always considered myself to be independent
15. Are you sure he went that way
16. Close all the windows before you leave
17. Beware
18. Which car do you prefer to drive
19. This visit will more than likely be a different experience
20. How many times do we have to go over this scene

SPEAKING APPLICATION

Take turns with a partner. Say declarative, interrogative, imperative, and exclamatory sentences. Your partner should identify each type of sentence.

WRITING APPLICATION

Write an intriguing first paragraph to a mystery novel, using at least one declarative, interrogative, imperative, and exclamatory sentence in your paragraph.

4.2 Sentence Combining

Too many short sentences can make your writing choppy and disconnected.

One way to avoid the excessive use of short sentences and to achieve variety is to combine sentences.

Sentences can be combined by using a compound subject, a compound verb, or a compound object.

TWO SENTENCES	Tara enjoyed the vacation to Mexico. Heather enjoyed the vacation to Mexico.
COMPOUND SUBJECT	Tara and Heather enjoyed the vacation to Mexico.
TWO SENTENCES	Mike worked hard. Mike was promoted.
COMPOUND VERB	Mike worked hard and was promoted.
TWO SENTENCES	Kelly saw the college. Kelly saw the professor.
COMPOUND OBJECT	Kelly saw the college and the professor.

See Practice 4.2A

Sentences can be combined by joining two main or independent clauses to create a compound sentence.

Use a compound sentence when combining ideas that are related but independent. To join main clauses, use a comma and a coordinating conjunction (*for, and, but, or, nor, yet,* or *so*) or a semicolon.

EXAMPLE	The boy looked for his books. He did not notice them under the bed.
COMPOUND SENTENCE	The boy looked for his books, but he did not notice them under the bed.

> **Sentences can be combined by changing one into a subordinate clause to create a complex sentence.**

To show the relationship between ideas in which one depends on the other, use a **complex sentence.** The subordinating conjunction will help readers understand the relationship. Some common subordinating conjunctions are *after, although, because, if, since, when,* and *while.*

EXAMPLE   We were excited. We thought the trip to Florida would be fun.

COMBINED WITH A SUBORDINATE CLAUSE   We were excited **because we thought the trip to Florida would be fun**.

> **Sentences can be combined by changing one of them into a phrase.**

EXAMPLE   My team plays softball today. We play on the new field.

COMBINED WITH PREPOSITIONAL PHRASE   My team plays softball **on the new field** today.

EXAMPLE   My mom will leave for Florida today. She is staying for a week.

See Practice 4.2B
See Practice 4.2C

COMBINED WITH APPOSITIVE PHRASE   My mom will leave for Florida today, **staying for a week**.

Combining Sentences Using Compound Subjects, Verbs, and Objects

Read each set of sentences. Then, write one sentence that combines them.

EXAMPLE   Tanya is a good sister. She is also a model student.

ANSWER   *Tanya is a good sister and a model student.*

1. Cara is a gifted tennis player. Alan also plays tennis very well.

2. The performers picked up their instruments. The performers picked up their sheet music.

3. Heath Farnsworth is an army captain. He is a career military officer.

4. Jermaine Collins is an accomplished actor. He is also a volunteer firefighter.

5. The university's lacrosse team won their division. The basketball team won their division, too.

Combining Sentences Using Phrases

Read each set of sentences. Combine each set by turning one sentence into a phrase that adds detail to the other.

EXAMPLE   Luke easily passed the exam. It was a biology test.

ANSWER   *Luke easily passed the exam, a biology test.*

6. The homecoming dance took place this weekend. It was attended by all the juniors and seniors.

7. Thyme is a flavorful herb. It is often used in gourmet cooking.

8. She had trouble tying the knot. Her name is Ellen Stewart.

9. Our team captains were Viktor Shah and Kenneth Mooney. They were seniors.

10. The tourists noticed a taxi as it appeared near the intersection. The intersection is a busy corner.

SPEAKING APPLICATION

Take turns with a partner. Say two related sentences about graduating high school. Your partner should combine these two sentences into one.

WRITING APPLICATION

Write two sentences about your school that relate to each other. Then, combine the sentences by turning one into a phrase. Repeat with two new related sentences.

| PRACTICE 4.2C | **Combining Sentences** |

Read each pair of sentences. Then, combine the sentences, using a coordinating or subordinating conjunction and indicate which kind of conjunction you have used.

EXAMPLE   Dave was thirsty. He went to the water fountain.

ANSWER   *Dave was thirsty, so he went to the water fountain.*; coordinating

1. Fresh gumbo simmered in the pot. Rion set the table for dinner.
2. There was a terrible storm brewing. I decided to take an umbrella.
3. John is considering taking a job in Houston. His wife has family where they live now.
4. Thalia was eating her lunch. Her friend stopped by.
5. I could make pasta. We could order out.
6. Gregory and Hugh both earn good grades. They compete to see who can score higher.
7. The temperature was rising. Clouds covered the sky.
8. I was hired for the job. I have an extensive background in information technology.
9. Mr. Wu grows prize-winning roses. He is thinking about photographing them for a book.
10. I commit my afternoons to studying in the library. Mark spends his time practicing the saxophone.

SPEAKING APPLICATION

Take turns with a partner. Describe your ideal vacation. Be sure to include at least four compound and/or complex sentences that contain coordinating and subordinating conjunctions.

WRITING APPLICATION

Write a paragraph about a fictional character who finds a treasure. Use compound and/or complex sentences that contain coordinating and subordinating conjunctions in your paragraph.

4.3 Varying Sentences

Vary your sentences to develop a rhythm, to achieve an effect, or to emphasize the connections between ideas. There are several ways you can vary your sentences.

Varying Sentence Length

To emphasize a point or surprise a reader, include a short, direct sentence to interrupt the flow of long sentences. Notice the effect of the last sentence in the following paragraph.

EXAMPLE   The Jacobites derived their name from *Jacobus,* the Latin name for King James II of England, who was dethroned in 1688 by William of Orange during the Glorious Revolution. Unpopular because of his Catholicism and autocratic ruling style, James fled to France to seek the aid of King Louis XIV. In 1690, James, along with a small body of French troops, landed in Ireland in an attempt to regain his throne. His hopes ended at the Battle of the Boyne.

Some sentences contain only one idea and can't be broken. It may be possible, however, to state the idea in a shorter sentence. Other sentences contain two or more ideas and might be shortened by breaking up the ideas.

LONGER SENTENCE   Many of James II's predecessors were able to avoid major economic problems, but James had serious economic problems.

MORE DIRECT   Unlike many of his predecessors, James II was unable to avoid major economic problems.

LONGER SENTENCE   James tried to work with Parliament to develop a plan of taxation that would be fair and reasonable, but members of Parliament rejected his efforts, and James dissolved the Parliament.

SHORTER SENTENCES   James tried to work with Parliament to develop a fair and reasonable taxation plan. However, because members of Parliament rejected his efforts, James dissolved the Parliament.

Varying Sentence Beginnings

Another way to create sentence variety is to start sentences with different parts of speech.

WAYS TO VARY SENTENCE BEGINNINGS	
Start With a Noun	Formal gardens are difficult to create.
Start With an Adverb	Naturally, formal gardens are difficult to create.
Start With an Adverbial Phrase	Because of their complexity, formal gardens are difficult to create.
Start With a Participial Phrase	Having tried to create formal gardens, I know how hard it is.
Start With a Prepositional Phrase	For the average person, formal gardens are very difficult to create.
Start With an Infinitive Phrase	To create a beautiful and functional formal garden was my goal.

See Practice 4.3A

Using Inverted Word Order

You can also vary sentence beginnings by reversing the traditional subject–verb order to create verb–subject order. You can reverse order by starting the sentence with a **participial phrase** or a **prepositional phrase.** You can also move a complement to the beginning of the sentence.

SUBJECT–VERB ORDER

The students waited for directions.

The students walked into the test center.

The sound of wind filled the forest.

The wind was blowing.

VERB–SUBJECT ORDER

Waiting for directions were the students.
participial phrase

Into the test center walked the students.
prepositional phrase

Filling the forest was the sound of wind.
participial phrase

Blowing was the wind.
predicate adjective

See Practice 4.3B

PRACTICE 4.3A ▷ **Revising to Vary Sentence Beginnings**

Read each sentence. Rewrite each sentence to begin with the part of speech or phrase indicated in parentheses. You may need to add a word or phrase.

EXAMPLE   Bob left the office; he was finished for the day. (participial phrase)

ANSWER   *Finished for the day, Bob left the office.*

1. Barbara checked the telephone directory to get the number. (infinitive phrase)

2. My CD player is an older model, but it has excellent speakers. (prepositional phrase)

3. The committee approved the plan; the vote was overwhelming. (adverb phrase)

4. Joey accepted the award; he was grinning happily. (participial phrase)

5. The child drank lemonade at the fair. (prepositional phrase)

6. He framed the picture. (infinitive phrase)

7. They rested on the sidelines. (adverb)

8. The dog watched me through the window. (prepositional phrase)

9. Dinner was served at the hotel. (prepositional phrase)

10. The lion attacked the deer with agility. (prepositional phrase)

PRACTICE 4.3B ▷ **Inverting Sentences to Vary Subject-Verb Order**

Read each sentence. Rewrite each sentence by inverting subject-verb order to verb-subject order.

EXAMPLE   The falcon soared in the sky.

ANSWER   *In the sky soared the falcon.*

11. The cruise ship moved toward the shore.

12. The skier raced away from the starting gate.

13. My little sister attends kindergarten at that school.

14. Your painting is hanging in the art gallery.

15. The little baby lamb pranced at the back of the herd.

16. The flea market was packed with hundreds of bargain hunters.

17. The bunny hopped into the meadow.

18. The bride sat inside the long, black car.

19. The treasure was buried beneath the large rock.

20. The leaves fell onto the picnic blanket.

SPEAKING APPLICATION

Take turns with a partner. Choose three sentences from Practice 4.3A. Say each sentence, but change the directive in the parentheses. Your partner should follow the directive to revise how the sentence begins.

WRITING APPLICATION

Write three sentences about any subject of your choice. Then, exchange papers with a partner. Your partner should invert the order of your sentences from subject-verb order to verb-subject order.

Hasty writers sometimes omit crucial words, punctuate awkwardly, or leave their thoughts unfinished, causing two common sentence errors: **fragments** and **run-ons**.

Recognizing Fragments

Although some writers use them for stylistic effect, **fragments** are generally considered errors in standard English.

> **Do not capitalize and punctuate phrases, subordinate clauses, or words in a series as if they were complete sentences.**

4.4.1 RULE

Reading your work aloud to listen for natural pauses and stops should help you avoid fragments. Sometimes, you can repair a fragment by connecting it to words that come before or after it.

> **One way to correct a fragment is to connect it to the words in a nearby sentence.**

4.4.2 RULE

PARTICIPIAL FRAGMENT	inspired by the knowledge of the professor
ADDED TO A NEARBY SENTENCE	**Inspired by the knowledge of the professor**, Peri sat through the lecture again.
PREPOSITIONAL FRAGMENT	before her assistant
ADDED TO A NEARBY SENTENCE	The professor entered the class **before her assistant**.
PRONOUN AND PARTICIPIAL FRAGMENT	the one filled with apples
ADDED TO NEARBY SENTENCE	The basket I want is **the one filled with apples**.

Another way to correct a fragment is to add any sentence part that is needed to make the fragment a complete sentence.

Remember that every complete sentence must have both a subject and a verb and express a complete thought. Check to see that each of your sentences contains all of the parts necessary to be complete.

NOUN FRAGMENT

the van of happy young teenagers

COMPLETED SENTENCES

The van of happy young teenagers
subject

parked at the field.
verb

We quietly listened to
subject   verb

the van of happy young teenagers .
direct object

Notice what missing sentence parts must be added to the following types of phrase fragments to make them complete.

	FRAGMENTS	COMPLETED SENTENCES
Noun Fragment With Participial Phrase	the other team beaten by us	The other team was beaten by us.
Verb Fragment	will be at the game tomorrow	I will be at the game tomorrow.
Prepositional Fragment	in the locker room	I put the helmets in the locker room.
Participial Fragment	found under the bench	The water bottle found under the bench is mine .
Gerund Fragment	teaching children to play hockey	Teaching children to play hockey is rewarding .
Infinitive Fragment	to meet the new coach	I expect to meet the new coach.

You may need to attach a **subordinate clause** to a main clause to correct a fragment.

A **subordinate clause** contains a subject and a verb but does not express a complete thought and cannot stand alone as a sentence. Link it to a main clause to make the sentence complete.

ADJECTIVAL CLAUSE FRAGMENT	which was being held inside
COMPLETED SENTENCE	I enjoyed watching the basketball game, **which was being held inside**.

ADVERBIAL CLAUSE FRAGMENT	after she practiced her graduation speech
COMPLETED SENTENCE	**After she practiced her graduation speech**, she was ready for the commencement.

NOUN CLAUSE FRAGMENT	whatever food is served for breakfast
COMPLETED SENTENCE	We always enjoy **whatever food is served for breakfast**.

Series Fragments A fragment is not always short. A long series of words still needs to have a subject and a verb and express a complete thought. It may be a long fragment masquerading as a sentence.

SERIES FRAGMENT	COMPLETE SENTENCE
after studying modern dance, with its infrequent steps and movements, in the style typical of present-day theater	After studying modern dance, with it's infrequent steps and movements, in the style typical of present-day theater, I was able to prepare for the show thoroughly.

See Practice 4.4A

Avoiding Run-on Sentences

A **run-on** sentence is two or more sentences capitalized and punctuated as if they were a single sentence.

> **Use punctuation and conjunctions to correctly join or separate parts of a run-on sentence.**

There are two kinds of **run-ons: fused sentences**, which are two or more sentences joined with no punctuation, and **comma splices**, which have two or more sentences separated only by commas rather than by commas and conjunctions.

FUSED SENTENCE	The employee worked late every day he was the employee of the month.
COMMA SPLICE	Only one dog was at the show, the others never came.

As with fragments, proofreading or reading your work aloud will help you find run-ons. Once found, they can be corrected by adding punctuation and conjunctions or by rewording the sentences.

FOUR WAYS TO CORRECT RUN-ONS		
	RUN-ON	CORRECTION
With End Marks and Capitals	The snow fell heavily in the living room the family huddled by the fireplace.	The snow fell heavily. In the living room, the family huddled by the fireplace.
With Commas and Conjunctions	The button needed to be sewn we could not locate the thread.	The button needed to be sewn, but we could not locate the thread.
With Semicolons	Our town has many patriotic events, for example, it hosts picnics and fireworks on July 4th.	Our town has many patriotic events; for example, it hosts picnics and fireworks on July 4th.
By Rewriting	The class began late, the professor wasn't there on time.	The class began late because the professor wasn't there on time.

See Practice 4.4B

PRACTICE 4.4A ▷ **Identifying and Correcting Fragments**

Read each sentence. If an item contains a fragment, rewrite it to make a complete sentence. If an item contains a complete sentence, write *correct*.

EXAMPLE   Adjusting the turntable again.

ANSWER   *Adjusting the turntable again, I finally got it right.*

1. The panel discussing a school-wide celebration.

2. Unfortunately, the flowers delivered to the wrong address.

3. Between you and me.

4. The mirror that Mother wanted.

5. After we left the music store went to eat lunch.

6. Please be quiet.

7. Their eyes met.

8. Their faces shining with awe at seeing the famous portrait.

9. Working with children.

10. Classified ads filling the pages of the newspaper.

PRACTICE 4.4B ▷ **Revising to Eliminate Run-on Sentences**

Read each sentence. Correct each run-on by correctly joining or separating the sentence parts.

EXAMPLE   I play first base, Sasha is the catcher.

ANSWER   *I play first base, and Sasha is the catcher.*

11. There are two choices, I don't like either.

12. The new mall will have over one hundred shops enclosed parking will be attached.

13. Eggs can be prepared in many ways, my favorite is scrambled eggs.

14. It rains a lot in the spring, it rained all last week.

15. I want to become a doctor I want to help people.

16. The couple just got married, their guests showered them with rose petals.

17. Some plants have medicinal properties, for example, mint leaves can aid in digestion.

18. Sherlock Holmes is a fictional detective, who also plays the violin.

19. A category 1 hurricane has the lowest wind speeds, a category 5 has the highest.

20. I prefer summer days, I do not enjoy cold weather.

SPEAKING APPLICATION

Take turns with a partner. Say sentence fragments. Your partner should make each fragment a complete sentence.

WRITING APPLICATION

Find and read a newspaper or magazine article. Choose one paragraph and change several correct sentences into run-on sentences. Then, exchange papers with a partner, and have your partner correct the run-ons.

4.5 Misplaced and Dangling Modifiers

Careful writers put modifiers as close as possible to the words they modify. When modifiers are misplaced or left dangling in a sentence, the result may be illogical or confusing.

Recognizing Misplaced Modifiers

A **misplaced modifier** is placed too far from the modified word and appears to modify the wrong word or words.

RULE 4.5.1

> A **misplaced modifier** seems to modify the wrong word in the sentence.

MISPLACED MODIFIER The woman ran over a rock **riding on the bike trail**.

CORRECTION The woman **riding on the bike trail** ran over a rock.

MISPLACED MODIFIER We heard the radio playing **while driving home**.

CORRECTION **While driving home**, we heard the radio playing.

Recognizing Dangling Modifiers

With **dangling modifiers,** the word that should be modified is missing from the sentence. Dangling modifiers usually come at the beginning of a sentence and are followed by a comma. The subject being modified should come right after the comma.

RULE 4.5.2

> A **dangling modifier** seems to modify the wrong word or no word at all because the word it should modify has been omitted from the sentence.

See Practice 4.5A

DANGLING PARTICIPIAL PHRASE	Estimating carefully, the school loan was paid off accurately. (*Who* did the estimating?)
CORRECTED SENTENCE	Estimating carefully, **the student** accurately paid off the school loan.

Dangling participial phrases are corrected by adding missing words and making other needed changes.

Dangling infinitive phrases and elliptical clauses can be corrected in the same way. First, identify the subject of the sentence. Then, make sure each subject is clearly stated. You may also need to change the form of the verb.

DANGLING INFINITIVE PHRASE	To get on the plane, the ticket must be checked. (*Who* is getting on the plane?)
CORRECTED SENTENCE	To get on the plane, **the travelers** must present their tickets.
DANGLING ELLIPTICAL CLAUSE	While floating down the canal, houses, boats, and other buildings were sighted. (*Who* was floating and sighted the other buildings?)
CORRECTED SENTENCE	While floating down the canal, **we** saw houses, boats, and other buildings.

EL8

A dangling adverbial clause may also occur when the antecedent of a pronoun is not clear.

DANGLING ADVERBIAL CLAUSE	When she graduated from high school, Amy's mother planned a picnic in the park. (*Who* graduated from high school, Amy or her mother?)
CORRECTED SENTENCE	**When Amy graduated from high school**, her mother planned a picnic in the park.

See Practice 4.5B

Misplaced and Dangling Modifiers

PRACTICE 4.5A Identifying and Correcting Misplaced Modifiers

Read each sentence. Then, rewrite each sentence, putting the misplaced modifiers closer to the words they should modify. If a sentence is correct, write *correct*.

EXAMPLE   The horse gallops around the paddock with white hooves.

ANSWER   *The horse with white hooves gallops around the paddock.*

1. Oranges are juicy that come from Florida.
2. Olivia gave her bike to her younger sister with a gel seat.
3. The pecan tree was hit by lightning with a forked trunk.
4. The woman crossed the street walking her dog.
5. The coat is in the hall closet that you need.
6. Emilio wants a hamburger and coffee cooked medium well.
7. Stephanie bought new glasses in the city with bifocals.
8. Carolyn called her parents elated by the good news.
9. Gloria purchased a necklace in Austin with a gold clasp.
10. The dog was groomed with a curly tail.

PRACTICE 4.5B Identifying and Correcting Dangling Modifiers

Read each sentence. Then, rewrite the sentences, correcting any dangling modifiers by supplying missing words or ideas.

EXAMPLE   Reading the first page, the book was too difficult.

ANSWER   *Reading the first page, I realized the book was too difficult.*

11. Turning the corner, a beautiful sunset could be seen.
12. While opening the box, a mistake had been made.
13. Closing the car door, her keys were still in the ignition.
14. To play baseball, a glove is needed.
15. Having finished the book, it was very late.
16. While eating breakfast, the phone rang.
17. Reaching the stop sign, an accident blocked the right lane.
18. Working too fast, an error was made.
19. While speaking on the phone, her dog ran out the door.
20. When he turned four, his brother was born.

SPEAKING APPLICATION

Take turns with a partner. Tell about an exciting experience that you have had. Use modifiers in your sentences. Your partner should listen for and identify the modifiers, and tell whether they are correctly placed.

WRITING APPLICATION

Use sentences 12, 14, and 16 as models to write your own sentences with dangling modifiers. Then, rewrite each sentence to correct the dangling modifiers.

112 **Effective Sentences**

4.6 Faulty Parallelism

Good writers try to present a series of ideas in similar grammatical structures so the ideas will read smoothly. If one element in a series is not parallel with the others, the result may be jarring or confusing.

Recognizing the Correct Use of Parallelism

To present a series of ideas of equal importance, you should use parallel grammatical structures.

> **Parallelism** involves presenting equal ideas in words, phrases, clauses, or sentences of similar types.

4.6.1 RULE

PARALLEL WORDS

The doctor looked **calm** , **focused** , and **determined** .

PARALLEL PHRASES

The greatest feeling I know is **to teach a skill to someone** and **then to see that person apply the skill** .

PARALLEL CLAUSES

The sunscreen **that you recommended** and **that my son needs** is on sale.

PARALLEL SENTENCES

It couldn't be , of course. **It could never, never be** . –Dorothy Parker

Correcting Faulty Parallelism

Faulty parallelism occurs when a writer uses unequal grammatical structures to express related ideas.

> Correct a sentence containing faulty parallelism by rewriting it so that each parallel idea is expressed in the same grammatical structure.

4.6.2 RULE

Faulty parallelism can involve words, phrases, and clauses in a series or in comparisons.

Nonparallel Words, Phrases, and Clauses in a Series
Always check for parallelism when your writing contains items in a series.

Correcting Faulty Parallelism in a Series

NONPARALLEL
STRUCTURES

Marking, sewing, and alteration are three
gerund   gerund   noun
steps in the tailoring process.

CORRECTION

Marking, sewing, and altering are three
gerund   gerund   gerund
steps in the tailoring process.

NONPARALLEL
STRUCTURES

I could not wait to try my new skis, to ski
infinitive phrase
down the slope, and visiting the cozy lodge.
infinitive phrase   participial phrase

CORRECTION

I could not wait to try my new skis, to ski
infinitive phrase
down the slope, and to visit the cozy lodge.
infinitive phrase   infinitive phrase

NONPARALLEL
STRUCTURE

Some people feel that badminton is
noun clause
not a sport, but it requires practice and
independent clause
dedication.

CORRECTION

Some people feel that badminton is not
noun clause
a sport, but that it requires practice and
noun clause
dedication.

Another potential problem involves correlative conjunctions, such as *both ... and* or *not only ... but also*. Though these conjunctions connect two related items, writers sometimes misplace or split the first part of the conjunction. The result is faulty parallelism.

NONPARALLEL	Sue **not only** won the "Best Pie" competition **but also** the county title.
PARALLEL	Sue won **not only** the "Best Pie" competition **but also** the county title.

Nonparallel Words, Phrases, and Clauses in Comparisons
As the saying goes, you cannot compare apples with oranges. In writing comparisons, you generally should compare a phrase with the same type of phrase and a clause with the same type of clause.

Correcting Faulty Parallelism in Comparisons

NONPARALLEL
STRUCTURES

Many people prefer **baseball** to **watching**
<small>noun</small>
golf.
<small>gerund phrase</small>

CORRECTION

Many people prefer **baseball** to **golf**.
<small>noun</small>   <small>noun</small>

NONPARALLEL
STRUCTURES

I left my class **at 2:00 P.M.** rather than
<small>prepositional phrase</small>
walking out at 3:00 P.M.
<small>participial phrase</small>

CORRECTION

I left my class **at 2:00 P.M.** rather than
<small>prepositional phrase</small>
at the usual 3:00 P.M.
<small>prepositional phrase</small>

NONPARALLEL
STRUCTURES

Tate delights **in busy days** as much as
<small>subject</small>   <small>prepositional phrase</small>
relaxing days delight other **people**.
<small>subject</small>   <small>direct object</small>

CORRECTION

Tate delights **in busy days** as much as
<small>subject</small>   <small>prepositional phrase</small>
other **people** delight **in relaxing days**.
<small>subject</small>   <small>prepositional phrase</small>

See Practice 4.6A

4.7 Faulty Coordination

When two or more independent clauses of unequal importance are joined by *and*, the result can be faulty **coordination**.

Recognizing Faulty Coordination

To *coordinate* means to "place side by side in equal rank." Two independent clauses that are joined by the coordinating conjunction *and*, therefore, should have equal rank.

RULE **4.7.1**

> Use *and* or other coordinating conjunctions only to connect ideas of equal importance.

CORRECT COORDINATION   Phil designed a house, **and** Morgan built it.

Sometimes, however, writers carelessly use *and* to join main clauses that either should not be joined or should be joined in another way so that the real relationship between the clauses is clear. Faulty coordination puts all the ideas on the same level of importance, even though logically they should not be.

FAULTY COORDINATION   Production of aircraft accelerated in World War II, **and** aircraft became a decisive factor in the war.

I didn't do well, **and** the test was easy.

The speaker looked tired, **and** she was rambling as she spoke.

Occasionally, writers will also string together so many ideas with *and's* that the reader is left breathless.

STRINGY SENTENCE   The fighter jet that flew over the airstrip did a few dips and turns, **and** the people on the ground craned their necks to watch, **and** everyone applauded and cheered.

Correcting Faulty Coordination

Faulty coordination can be corrected in several ways.

> **One way to correct faulty coordination is to put unrelated ideas into separate sentences.**

4.7.2 RULE

When faulty coordination occurs in a sentence in which the main clauses are not closely related, separate the clauses and omit the coordinating conjunction.

FAULTY COORDINATION	Production of aircraft accelerated in World War II, **and** aircraft became a decisive factor in the war.
CORRECTION	Production of aircraft accelerated in World War II. Aircraft became a decisive factor in the war.

> **You can correct faulty coordination by putting less important ideas into subordinate clauses or phrases.**

4.7.3 RULE

If one main clause is less important than, or subordinate to, the other, turn it into a subordinate clause. You can also reduce a less important idea to a phrase.

FAULTY COORDINATION	I didn't do well, **and** the test was easy.
CORRECTION	I didn't do well, **even though** the test was easy.
FAULTY COORDINATION	The speaker looked tired, **and** she was rambling as she spoke.
CORRECTION	Rambling as she spoke, the speaker looked tired.

Stringy sentences should be broken up and revised using any of the three methods just described. Following is one way that the stringy sentence on the previous page can be revised.

REVISION OF A STRINGY SENTENCE	The fighter jet that flew over the airstrip did a few dips and turns. Craning their necks, the people on the ground applauded and cheered.

See Practice 4.6B

PRACTICE 4.6A	**Revising to Eliminate Faulty Parallelism**

Read each sentence. Then, rewrite the sentence to correct any nonparallel structures.

EXAMPLE   She not only plays golf but also soccer.

ANSWER   *She plays not only golf but also soccer.*

1. The new employee was energetic, helpful, and often arrived early.

2. I hate cleaning as much as medicine.

3. Going there is better than to stay home.

4. The picture is old, torn, and looks fragile.

5. Katy not only will go to the parade but also to the science fair.

6. I would choose reading a book over a movie.

7. I see trees swaying, ducks swimming, and flying birds.

8. He both wanted to stay in his house and to move to the country.

9. I think I sang well because I practiced a lot rather than because the nerves weren't there.

10. Laughing, telling jokes, and to play games makes the time go by faster.

PRACTICE 4.6B	**Revising to Eliminate Faulty Coordination**

Read each sentence. Then, rewrite each sentence, to correct the faulty coordination.

EXAMPLE   It was true the Clays needed a babysitter, and they had five kids.

ANSWER   *It was true that the Clays, who had five kids, needed a babysitter.*

11. I have read many biographies, and all of them have been popular for years.

12. I plan to study chemistry in college, and biology is another course I'd like to take.

13. Eduardo bought a bike and it has 15 speeds.

14. Learning to parallel park was difficult for me, and I finally mastered the technique.

15. The car is a minivan, and has room for eight.

16. The truck had a full load, and it slowed going uphill.

17. There are guided tours and we will join them.

18. Oak trees lined the street, and it was called Grand Avenue.

19. Kit is attending an Ivy League university and she graduated from high school with honors.

20. Australia is a country as well as a continent and is located in the Southern Hemisphere.

SPEAKING APPLICATION

Take turns with a partner. Tell several things you plan to do with your family or friends. Your partner should listen for and correct any faulty parallelism in your description.

WRITING APPLICATION

Use sentences 14, 15, and 16 as models to write three sentences that contain faulty coordination. Exchange papers with a partner, and correct each other's work.

VERB USAGE

Use strong verbs to set the stage of the action in your writing.

WRITE GUY *Jeff Anderson, M.Ed.*

WHAT DO YOU NOTICE?

Uncover the verbs as you zoom in on these sentences from the novel *Hard Times* by Charles Dickens.

MENTOR TEXT

"We hope to have, before long, a board of fact, composed of commissioners of fact, who will force the people to be a people of fact, and of nothing but fact."

Now, ask yourself the following questions:

- What tense is the verb in the clause *We hope to have, before long, a board of fact?* What tense is the verb in the clause *who will force the people to be a people of fact?*
- Why did the author use two different verb tenses in the same sentence?

The verb *hope* in the clause *We hope to have, before long, a board of fact* is written in the present tense. The verb *will force* in the clause *who will force the people to be a people of fact* is written in the future tense. Dickens used the present tense of the verb *hope* to indicate that the narrator was expressing his wishes at the time he was speaking. He used *will force,* the future tense of the verb *force,* to explain that the narrator expected the commissioners to act in the future.

Grammar for Writers Although there are subtle differences between verb tenses, the variations are important. Think of tenses as a time travel tool you can use to help guide readers through the sequence of action in your writing.

How can I help my verbs to relax?

Try adjusting their tenses!

5.1 Verb Tenses

Besides expressing actions or conditions, verbs have different **tenses** to indicate when the action or condition occurred.

RULE 5.1.1 A **tense** is the form of a verb that shows the time of an action or a condition.

EL5

The Six Verb Tenses

There are six tenses that indicate when an action or a condition of a verb is, was, or will be in effect. Each of these six tenses has at least two forms.

RULE 5.1.2 Each tense has a **basic** and a **progressive** form.

The chart that follows shows examples of the six tenses.

THE BASIC FORMS OF THE SIX TENSES	
Present	Sandy acts in plays.
Past	She acted in last year's school musical.
Future	She will act in a play this spring.
Present Perfect	She has acted since she was a young child.
Past Perfect	She had acted in the high school's holiday musical.
Future Perfect	She will have acted in many plays by the time she gets to college.
Present	We go to the beach on summer vacation.
Past	We went to the beach last summer.
Future	We will go to the beach next summer.
Present Perfect	We have gone to other places, too.
Past Perfect	We had gone to the lake in July.
Future Perfect	We will have gone to different beaches during summer vacations.

See Practice 5.1A

Basic Verb Forms or Tenses

Verb tenses are identified simply by their tense names. The **progressive tenses,** however, are identified by their tense names plus the word *progressive.* Progressive tenses show that an action is or was happening for a period of time.

The chart below shows examples of the six tenses in their progressive form or tense. Note that all of these progressive tenses end in *-ing.* (See the section on verb conjugation later in this chapter for more about the progressive tense.)

THE PROGRESSIVE TENSES	
Present Progressive	Sandy is acting in a play.
Past Progressive	She was acting in elementary school.
Future Progressive	She will be acting in the spring.
Present Perfect Progressive	She has been acting in many different kinds of plays.
Past Perfect Progressive	She had been acting only in small parts, but she now plays lead roles.
Future Perfect Progressive	Next season, she will have been acting for a decade.

The Emphatic Form

There is also a third form or tense, the **emphatic,** which exists only for the present and past tenses. The **present emphatic** is formed with the helping verbs *do* or *does,* depending on the subject. The **past emphatic** is formed with *did.* The purpose of the emphatic tense is to put more emphasis on, or to stress, the action of the verb.

THE EMPHATIC TENSES OF THE PRESENT AND THE PAST	
Present Emphatic	The president does speak about issues that I think are important. The student council does act on students' complaints.
Past Emphatic	My dad did get a promotion to vice-president of his company. My mom did insist that I finish my homework before I could meet my friends.

See Practice 5.1B

PRACTICE 5.1A > Identifying Verb Tenses

Read each sentence. Then, write the verb used in each sentence, and the tense of the verb.

EXAMPLE   Lucy has crossed the parking lot.

ANSWER   *has crossed* — *present perfect*

1. I often swim in the pool.
2. The plane took off right on time.
3. Abe has toured the Texas State Capitol.
4. By the end of the week, the competition will have hosted over three hundred athletes.
5. Sea scavengers will eat almost any detritous on the ocean floor.
6. By next week, I will have seen that movie three times.
7. Victor had visited his grandparents all summer.
8. My sister will enter all four skateboard competitions.
9. Andie and I wait at the intersection.
10. Bruce spoke to Natalia about the meeting.

PRACTICE 5.1B > Recognizing Tenses or Forms of Verbs

Read each sentence. Then, write the verb, and the tense of the verb.

EXAMPLE   We have been climbing.

ANSWER   *have been climbing* — *present perfect progressive*

11. I did formulate a hypothesis.
12. Gary was sledding all afternoon.
13. Ruth had been studying for days.
14. Chisom will be hiding the presents.
15. We had been driving through three states.
16. They have been preparing for the science fair.
17. Damon does concede graciously.
18. Francine is paddling down the river.
19. I do recommend that restaurant.
20. Pedro will have been rehearsing for weeks.

SPEAKING APPLICATION

Take turns with a partner. Using complete sentences, describe the objects around you. Your partner should repeat each sentence, chang the tense of the verb that you used. Be sure to use all six verb tenses.

WRITING APPLICATION

Using at least three progressive tenses, write a paragraph, describing a fictional action scene. Underline each verb or verb phrase and write the form of each verb.

The Four Principal Parts of Verbs

Every verb in the English language has four **principal parts** from which all of the tenses are formed.

> A verb has four principal parts: the **present,** the **present participle,** the **past,** and the **past participle.**

5.1.3 RULE

The chart below shows the principal parts of the verbs *leave, present,* and *run.*

THE FOUR PRINCIPAL PARTS			
PRESENT	PRESENT PARTICIPLE	PAST	PAST PARTICIPLE
leave	leaving	left	(have) left
present	presenting	presented	(have) presented
run	running	ran	(have) run

The first principal part, the present, is used for the basic forms of the present and future tenses, as well as for the emphatic forms or tenses. The present tense is formed by adding an -*s* or -*es* when the subject is *he, she, it,* or a singular noun. The future tense is formed with the helping verb *will. (I will leave. Mary will present. Carl will run.)* The present emphatic is formed with the helping verb *do* or *does. (I do leave. Mary does present. Carl does run.)* The past emphatic is formed with the helping verb *did. (I did leave. Mary did present. Carl did run.)*

EL6

The second principal part, the present participle, is used with helping verbs for all of the progressive forms. *(I am leaving. Mary is presenting. Carl is running.)*

The third principal part, the past, is used to form the past tense. *(I left. Mary presented. Carl ran.)* As in the example *ran,* the past tense of a verb can change its spelling. (See the next section for more information.)

The fourth principal part, the past participle, is used with helping verbs to create the perfect tenses. *(I have left. Mary had presented. Carl had run.)*

See Practice 5.1C
See Practice 5.1D

PRACTICE 5.1C > **Recognizing the Four Principal Parts of Verbs**

Read each sentence. Then, write the principal part and label as *present, present participle, past,* or *past participle.*

EXAMPLE   The Rangers are winning at halftime.

ANSWER   *winning* — present participle

1. I never eat alone in the cafeteria.
2. Our manager is driving to the other branches today.
3. The bus departed ahead of schedule.
4. Every student grasped the meaning of the story.
5. She is using an ointment to rub on her sore knee.
6. Bobby has completed his workout already.
7. By the end of the month, the proposal gained much support.
8. Some of my classmates find the assignment challenging.
9. Most applicants have submitted a cover letter with their resumes.
10. I am taking extra classes to get additional credits.

PRACTICE 5.1D > **Identifying the Four Principal Parts of Verbs**

Read each sentence. Then, write the verb or verb phrase in each sentence, and the principal part used to form each verb.

EXAMPLE   You have passed the test.

ANSWER   *have passed* — past participle

11. Maria found the lost wallet.
12. The plane had risen above the clouds.
13. Armand is announcing his desire to run for class president.
14. Ray and Benjamin completed their entrance exams.
15. I am joining a gym to work out more often.
16. Roger stored all his belongings in his car.
17. Jack attempts to train his new puppy.
18. We vacationed the entire month of August.
19. I am looking for my camera.
20. Marta buys herself a necklace.

SPEAKING APPLICATION

Take turns with a partner. Tell a fictional short story about a day in the life of a pet dog. Use each of the four principal parts of a verb in your story.

WRITING APPLICATION

Use sentence 18 as the first sentence in a short essay about your dream vacation. Be sure to include the four principal parts of some verbs in your essay.

Regular and Irregular Verbs

The way the past and past participle forms of a verb are formed determines whether the verb is **regular** or **irregular.**

Regular Verbs The majority of verbs are regular. Regular verbs form their past and past participles according to a predictable pattern.

> A **regular verb** is one for which the past and past participle are formed by adding *-ed* or *-d* to the present form.

5.1.4 RULE

In the chart below, notice that a final consonant is sometimes doubled to form the present participle, the past, and the past participle. A final *e* may also be dropped to form the participle.

See Practice 5.1E
See Practice 5.1F

PRINCIPAL PARTS OF REGULAR VERBS			
PRESENT	PRESENT PARTICIPLE	PAST	PAST PARTICIPLE
advance	advancing	advanced	(have) advanced
grip	gripping	gripped	(have) gripped
predict	predicting	predicted	(have) predicted

Irregular Verbs Although most verbs are regular, many of the most common verbs are irregular. Irregular verbs do not use a predictable pattern to form their past and past participles.

> An **irregular verb** is one whose past and past participle are *not* formed by adding *-ed* or *-d* to the present form.

5.1.5 RULE

Usage Problems Remembering the principal parts of irregular verbs can help you avoid usage problems. One common usage problem is using a principal part that is not standard.

INCORRECT   My mom **teached** me how to cook.

CORRECT   My mom **taught** me how to cook.

A second usage problem is confusing the past and past participle when they have different forms.

INCORRECT Mike **done** his chores before he went to school.

CORRECT Mike **did** his chores before he went to school.

Some common irregular verbs are shown in the charts that follow. Use a dictionary if you are not sure how to form the principal parts of an irregular verb.

IRREGULAR VERBS WITH THE SAME PRESENT, PAST, AND PAST PARTICIPLE			
PRESENT	PRESENT PARTICIPLE	PAST	PAST PARTICIPLE
burst	bursting	burst	(have) burst
cost	costing	cost	(have) cost
cut	cutting	cut	(have) cut
hit	hitting	hit	(have) hit
hurt	hurting	hurt	(have) hurt
let	letting	let	(have) let
put	putting	put	(have) put
set	setting	set	(have) set
shut	shutting	shut	(have) shut
split	splitting	split	(have) split
spread	spreading	spread	(have) spread

Note About *Be: Be* is one of the most irregular of all of the verbs. The present participle of *be* is *being.* The past participle is *been.* The present and the past depend on the subject and tense of the verb.

CONJUGATION OF *BE*		
	SINGULAR	PLURAL
Present	I am. You are. He, she, or it is.	We are. You are. They are.
Past	I was. You were. He, she, or it was.	We were. You were. They were.
Future	I will be. You will be. He, she, or it will be.	We will be. You will be. They will be.

IRREGULAR VERBS WITH THE SAME PAST AND PAST PARTICIPLE			
PRESENT	PRESENT PARTICIPLE	PAST	PAST PARTICIPLE
bring	bringing	brought	(have) brought
build	building	built	(have) built
buy	buying	bought	(have) bought
catch	catching	caught	(have) caught
fight	fighting	fought	(have) fought
find	finding	found	(have) found
get	getting	got	(have) got or (have) gotten
hold	holding	held	(have) held
keep	keeping	kept	(have) kept
lay	laying	laid	(have) laid
lead	leading	led	(have) led
leave	leaving	left	(have) left
lose	losing	lost	(have) lost
pay	paying	paid	(have) paid
say	saying	said	(have) said
sell	selling	sold	(have) sold
send	sending	sent	(have) sent
shine	shining	shone or shined	(have) shone or (have) shined
sit	sitting	sat	(have) sat
sleep	sleeping	slept	(have) slept
spend	spending	spent	(have) spent
stand	standing	stood	(have) stood
stick	sticking	stuck	(have) stuck
sting	stinging	stung	(have) stung
strike	striking	struck	(have) struck
swing	swinging	swung	(have) swung
teach	teaching	taught	(have) taught
win	winning	won	(have) won
wind	winding	wound	(have) wound

IRREGULAR VERBS THAT CHANGE IN OTHER WAYS			
PRESENT	PRESENT PARTICIPLE	PAST	PAST PARTICIPLE
arise	arising	arose	(have) arisen
become	becoming	became	(have) become
begin	beginning	began	(have) begun
bite	biting	bit	(have) bitten
break	breaking	broke	(have) broken
choose	choosing	chose	(have) chosen
come	coming	came	(have) come
do	doing	did	(have) done
draw	drawing	drew	(have) drawn
drink	drinking	drank	(have) drunk
drive	driving	drove	(have) driven
eat	eating	ate	(have) eaten
fall	falling	fell	(have) fallen
fly	flying	flew	(have) flown
give	giving	gave	(have) given
go	going	went	(have) gone
grow	growing	grew	(have) grown
know	knowing	knew	(have) known
lie	lying	lay	(have) lain
ride	riding	rode	(have) ridden
ring	ringing	rang	(have) rung
rise	rising	rose	(have) risen
run	running	ran	(have) run
see	seeing	saw	(have) seen
sing	singing	sang	(have) sung
sink	sinking	sank	(have) sunk
speak	speaking	spoke	(have) spoken
swim	swimming	swam	(have) swum
take	taking	took	(have) taken
tear	tearing	tore	(have) torn
throw	throwing	threw	(have) thrown
wear	wearing	wore	(have) worn
write	writing	wrote	(have) written

See Practice 5.1G
See Practice 5.1H

PRACTICE 5.1E > **Recognizing Principal Parts of Regular Verbs**

Read each group of regular verbs. Then, write the missing principal part of the verb.

EXAMPLE   named, naming, named

ANSWER   *name*

1. balance, balanced, (have) balanced
2. permitting, permit, permitted
3. matched, match, matching
4. interrupting, (have) interrupted, interrupt
5. fastened, (have) fastened, fasten
6. promised, promising, (have) promised
7. (have) removed, remove, removing
8. slap, slapped, slapping
9. tugging, tugged, (have) tugged
10. claimed, (have) claimed, claim

PRACTICE 5.1F > **Using the Correct Form of Regular Verbs**

Read each sentence. Then, choose the correct verb form from those given in parentheses to complete each sentence.

EXAMPLE   Harry (damaging, damaged) his car in the accident.

ANSWER   *damaged*

11. Mr. Wayne (stay, stayed) at a five-star hotel.
12. I have (stopped, stop) spending so much money on video games.
13. I am (filled, filling) my tank with gas.
14. Shana and Joe are (smiling, smile) at us from the bus.
15. Sunblock (protect, protected) her skin from harmful rays.
16. Zac is (explained, explaining) what happened during the fire drill.
17. Both my parents (admire, admiring) my independent spirit.
18. Mr. Fitch (demand, demanded) the attention of the entire class.
19. Silvio's food always (smelling, smells) really good.
20. Depak and Tony have (apologize, apologized) for being late.

SPEAKING APPLICATION

Take turns with a partner. Tell about your last summer vacation. Use as many principal parts of verbs as you can in your description.

WRITING APPLICATION

Write a paragraph about an idea for a movie. Use at least three regular verbs and different principal parts of those verbs.

PRACTICE 5.1G **Recognizing Principal Parts of Irregular Verbs**

Read each verb. Then, write the present participle, past, and past participle of each verb.

EXAMPLE   steal

ANSWER   *stealing, stole, (have) stolen*

1. hide
2. get
3. do
4. forget
5. understand
6. write
7. split
8. overdo
9. begin
10. let

PRACTICE 5.1H **Supplying the Correct Form of Irregular Verbs**

Read each sentence. Then, write the correct form of the irregular verb that is italicized. If the sentence is correct, write *correct*.

EXAMPLE   I have *ate* a delicious dinner.

ANSWER   *eaten*

11. The news *spreaded* all over the country.
12. The sun *rising* well before I was out of bed.
13. Peter *drawed* the short straw, so he went first.
14. The truck was *drove* by an experienced driver.
15. My mother *forbidden* me to leave dirty dishes in the sink.
16. I have *forgave* Gino for being late to dinner.
17. Angelina *strove* to be the fastest runner on the field.
18. Beatrice has *shook* the bottle of salad dressing.
19. I have *forgot* his gift in the car.
20. Albert *lended* me his jacket.

SPEAKING APPLICATION

Take turns with a partner. Tell what you did during your free time yesterday and what you plan to do during that time today. Use irregular verbs in your description. Your partner should listen for and identify each irregular verb that you use.

WRITING APPLICATION

Write a paragraph about a happy time in your life. Use four different irregular verbs, using four different principal parts of that verb in your paragraph.

Verb Conjugation

The **conjugation** of a verb displays all of its different forms.

> **A conjugation** is a complete list of the singular and plural forms of a verb in a particular tense.

 5.1.6 RULE

The singular forms of a verb correspond to the singular personal pronouns (*I, you, he, she, it*), and the plural forms correspond to the plural personal pronouns (*we, you, they*).

To conjugate a verb, you need the four principal parts: the present (*choose*), the present participle (*choosing*), the past (*chose*), and the past participle (*chosen*). You also need various helping verbs, such as *has, have,* or *will*.

Notice that only three principal parts—the present, the past, and the past participle—are used to conjugate all six of the basic forms.

CONJUGATION OF THE BASIC FORMS OF *CHOOSE*		SINGULAR	PLURAL
Present	First Person Second Person Third Person	I choose. You choose. He, she, or it chooses.	We choose. You choose. They choose.
Past	First Person Second Person Third Person	I chose. You chose. He, she, or it chose.	We chose. You chose. They chose.
Future	First Person Second Person Third Person	I will choose. You will choose. He, she, or it will choose.	We will choose. You will choose. They will choose.
Present Perfect	First Person Second Person Third Person	I have chosen. You have chosen. He, she, or it has chosen.	We have chosen. You have chosen. They have chosen.
Past Perfect	First Person Second Person Third Person	I had chosen. You had chosen. He, she, or it had chosen.	We had chosen. You had chosen. They had chosen.
Future Perfect	First Person Second Person Third Person	I will have chosen. You will have chosen. He, she, or it will have chosen.	We will have chosen. You will have chosen. They will have chosen.

See Practice 5.1l

Conjugating the Progressive Tense With *Be*

As you learned earlier, the **progressive tense** shows an ongoing action or condition. To form the progressive tense, use the present participle form of the verb (the *-ing* form) with a form of the verb *be*.

CONJUGATION OF THE PROGRESSIVE FORMS OF *CHOOSE*		SINGULAR	PLURAL
Present Progressive	First Person Second Person Third Person	I am choosing. You are choosing. He, she, or it is choosing.	We are choosing. You are choosing. They are choosing.
Past Progressive	First Person Second Person Third Person	I was choosing. You were choosing. He, she, or it was choosing.	We were choosing. You were choosing. They were choosing.
Future Progressive	First Person Second Person Third Person	I will be choosing. You will be choosing. He, she, or it will be choosing.	We will be choosing. You will be choosing. They will be choosing.
Present Perfect Progressive	First Person Second Person Third Person	I have been choosing. You have been choosing. He, she, or it has been choosing.	We have been choosing. You have been choosing. They have been choosing.
Past Perfect Progressive	First Person Second Person Third Person	I had been choosing. You had been choosing. He, she, or it had been choosing.	We had been choosing. You had been choosing. They had been choosing.
Future Perfect Progressive	First Person Second Person Third Person	I will have been choosing. You will have been choosing. He, she, or it will have been choosing.	We will have been choosing. You will have been choosing. They will have been choosing.

See Practice 5.1J

PRACTICE 5.1I	**Conjugating the Basic Forms of Verbs**

Read each word. Then, conjugate each verb using the subject indicated in parentheses. Write the verbs in the past, future, present perfect, past perfect, and future perfect forms.

EXAMPLE   grabs (he)

ANSWER   *he grabbed, he will grab, he has grabbed, he had grabbed, he will have grabbed*

1. informs (she)
2. hide (I)
3. shake (they)
4. deliver (we)
5. chases (it)
6. grow (you)
7. pretends (he)
8. give (I)
9. get (you)
10. fit (we)

PRACTICE 5.1J	**Conjugating the Progressive Forms of Verbs**

Read each sentence. Then, conjugate the progressive form of each verb indicated in parentheses.

EXAMPLE   I manage. (past progressive, future perfect progressive)

ANSWER   *I was managing. I will have been managing.*

11. He holds. (past progressive, future progressive)
12. We keep. (present perfect progressive, future perfect progressive)
13. They sink. (past perfect progressive, past progressive)
14. I fall. (future progressive, present perfect progressive)
15. She bites. (past perfect progressive, past progressive)
16. You prepare. (past progressive, future progressive)
17. I offer. (present perfect progressive, past perfect progressive)
18. They remove. (future perfect progressive, past progressive)
19. We scream. (past perfect progressive, future progressive)
20. He unites. (past progressive, future perfect progressive)

SPEAKING APPLICATION

Take turns with a partner. Say five verbs. Your partner should conjugate each verb for all six basic forms.

WRITING APPLICATION

Choose three verbs not used in Practice 5.1J and conjugate each verb for all six progressive forms.

5.2 The Correct Use of Tenses

The basic, progressive, and emphatic forms of the six tenses show time within one of three general categories: **present, past,** and **future.** This section will explain how each verb form has a specific use that distinguishes it from the other forms.

Present, Past, and Future Tense

Good usage depends on an understanding of how each form works within its general category of time to express meaning.

Uses of Tense in Present Time
Three different forms can be used to express present time.

RULE 5.2.1

> The three forms of the **present tense** show present actions or conditions as well as various continuing actions or conditions.

EXPRESSING PRESENT TENSE	
Present	I explore .
Present Progressive	I am exploring .
Present Emphatic	I do explore .

The main uses of the basic form of the present tense are shown in the chart below.

EXPRESSING PRESENT TENSE	
Present Action	Two dogs play in the park.
Present Condition	They are both excited.
Regularly Occurring Action	They go to the dog run on weekends.
Regularly Occurring Condition	The dog run is open all day.
Constant Action	Dogs pant when they run.
Constant Condition	Dogs are good pets.

See Practice 5.2A

Historical Present The present tense may also be used to express historical events. This use of the present, called the **historical present tense,** is occasionally used in narration to make past actions or conditions sound more lively.

THE HISTORICAL PRESENT TENSE	
Past Actions Expressed in Historical Present Tense	Michelangelo sits quietly and thinks about the block of marble in front of him.
Past Condition Expressed in Historical Present Tense	The people of Renaissance Italy are aware of Michelangelo's artistic genius and love his work.

The **critical present tense** is most often used to discuss deceased authors and their literary achievements.

THE CRITICAL PRESENT TENSE	
Action Expressed in Critical Present	Shakespeare writes plays about historical figures and about fictional ones.
Condition Expressed in Critical Present	Shakespeare is also a writer of sonnets.

The **present progressive tense** is used to show a continuing action or condition of a long or short duration.

USES OF THE PRESENT PROGRESSIVE TENSE	
Long Continuing Action	We are working on a group project.
Short Continuing Action	We are researching the ecology of our area.
Continuing Condition	We are enjoying working together.

USES OF THE PRESENT EMPHATIC TENSE	
Emphasizing a Statement	Marco does enjoy sculpting figures.
Denying a Contrary Assertion	No, he does not enjoy painting.
Asking a Question	Does he sculpt with clay?
Making a Sentence Negative	He does not want people to watch him work.

See Practice 5.2B

PRACTICE 5.2A > **Identifying Tense in Present Time**

Read each sentence. Then, label the verb form *present*, *present progressive*, or *present emphatic*.

EXAMPLE   I give Lisa my attention.

ANSWER   *present*

1. Rachel is training for a marathon.
2. Carlos is wrapping the presents for the celebration.
3. High tide occurs twice a day.
4. We do run the risk of losing our turn.
5. Nathan is cooking steaks on the grill.
6. Despite his tight schedule, Ralph finds time to exercise.
7. Jonathan does study very hard for exams.
8. Sagan grows stronger every year.
9. Catie is hoping for another chance to complete.
10. I do e-mail her whenever I get the chance.

PRACTICE 5.2B > **Supplying Verbs in Present Time**

Read each sentence. Then, rewrite each sentence, using the tense indicated in parentheses.

EXAMPLE   Becky puts the chair in the basement. (present progressive)

ANSWER   *Becky is putting the chair in the basement.*

11. Hassan is thinking about attending college after high school. (present)
12. Constance felt elated after winning the close game. (present emphatic)
13. Clarence reaches for the top of the cupboard. (present progressive)
14. Kelly keeps up with current events. (present emphatic)
15. Upon reflection, Warren does remember the event. (present)
16. Anya is keeping a close watch on her younger brother. (present)
17. Jackie loves babysitting. (present emphatic)
18. We do recommend learning about different cultures. (present)
19. Walter is helping those in need. (present emphatic)
20. Jose dives off the dock into the cold water. (present progressive)

SPEAKING APPLICATION

Take turns with a partner. Describe what is happening in your classroom right now, using present, present progressive, and present emphatic forms of verbs.

WRITING APPLICATION

Write a humorous short story, describing, in present tense, a fictional character's encounter with an alien from outerspace. Use the different forms of present-tense verbs in your short story.

Uses of the Past Tense

There are seven verb forms that express past actions or conditions.

> The seven forms that express **past tense** show actions and conditions that began at some time in the past.

FORMS EXPRESSING PAST TENSE	
Past	I teach.
Present Perfect	I have taught.
Past Perfect	I had taught.
Past Progressive	I was teaching.
Present Perfect Progressive	I have been teaching.
Past Perfect Progressive	I had been teaching.
Past Emphatic	I did teach.

The uses of the most common form, the past, are shown below.

USES OF THE PAST TENSE	
Completed Action	Barbara checked Lynn's grammar.
Completed Condition	Barbara was thorough in her review.

See Practice 5.2C

Notice in the chart above that the time of the action or the condition could be changed from indefinite to definite if such words as *last week* or *yesterday* were added to the sentences.

Present Perfect The **present perfect tense** always expresses indefinite time. Use it to show actions or conditions continuing from the past to the present.

USES OF THE PRESENT PERFECT TENSE	
Completed Action (Indefinite Time)	I have taken ballet lessons.
Completed Condition (Indefinite Time)	I have been in the ballet studio.
Action Continuing to Present	I have practiced for many hours.
Condition Continuing to Present	I have wanted to perform for others.

Past Perfect The **past perfect tense** expresses an action that took place before another action.

USES OF THE PAST PERFECT TENSE	
Action Completed Before Another Action	I had found a job with a veterinarian before the school year ended.
Condition Completed Before Another Condition	The job has been a great experience, and it was a good way to learn about animals.

These charts show the **past progressive** and **emphatic tenses.**

USES OF THE PROGRESSIVE TENSE TO EXPRESS PAST TIME	
Past Progressive	LONG CONTINUING ACTION Bob was going to run for office. SHORT CONTINUING ACTION He was planning to talk to the current president. CONTINUOUS CONDITION He wanted to be sure he had enough time to do the work.
Present Perfect Progressive	CONTINUING ACTION Bob has been working on his campaign for several weeks.
Past Perfect Progressive	CONTINUING ACTION INTERRUPTED He had been attending meetings, but he wanted to do more for the school.

USES OF THE PAST EMPHATIC TENSE	
Emphasizing a Statement	The test did seem easy when I first read it over.
Denying a Contrary Assertion	I didn't do as well as I'd hoped.
Asking a Question	Why did I feel so overconfident?
Making a Sentence Negative	He will not go out the night before the next test.

See Practice 5.2D

PRACTICE 5.2C ▷ **Identifying Tense in Past Time**

Read each sentence. Then, write the verb in each sentence that shows past time and identify the form of the tense.

EXAMPLE   After sleeping for hours,
          I had awoken to the sound
          of wind chimes.

ANSWER   *had awoken* — past perfect

1. All morning, the actor had been attempting to learn his lines.

2. I had finished the adventure novel in only fourteen hours!

3. The hesitant girl did ride the roller coaster.

4. We had been searching for the perfect pet.

5. Despite my attempts to stay organized, my homework vanished under a pile of papers.

6. The disappointed cheerleader has decided to try out for the gymnastics team.

7. We did not comprehend the importance of the occasion.

8. Todd had been surfing at the same beach since the age of sixteen.

9. The student was hoping for good grades and lots of college acceptance letters.

10. I stopped being concerned about what other people thought of my artwork.

PRACTICE 5.2D ▷ **Supplying Verbs in Past Time**

Read each sentence. Then, rewrite each sentence and change the verb to the tense indicated in parentheses.

EXAMPLE   Before the storm, everyone *bought* canned goods. (past perfect)

ANSWER   *Before the storm, everyone had bought canned goods.*

11. Getting ready for college requires careful planning and preparation. (past emphatic)

12. The high school athletes receive the trophy, grinning all the while. (past progressive)

13. The dog climbed into the back seat of my car. (past perfect progressive)

14. By eight o'clock, everyone goes home. (past emphatic)

15. The students listen carefully to the two-hour lecture. (past perfect progressive)

16. After a long, difficult week, Karan groaned whenever she sat down. (past progressive)

17. The students work cooperatively. (past perfect progressive)

18. Joe lifts heavy weights every day. (past emphatic)

19. All day long, Pax gnaws on a bone. (past)

20. The corn pops loudly, attracting puzzled looks from the cat. (past perfect progressive)

SPEAKING APPLICATION

Take turns with a partner. Tell about a time you helped another person. Use verbs in at least four of the past tense forms. Your partner should listen for and identify the past-tense verbs.

WRITING APPLICATION

Write a paragraph about your most memorable birthday. Include at least four verbs in different forms of the past tense, and underline each past-tense verb.

Uses of the Future Tense

The **future tense** shows actions or conditions that will happen at a later date.

RULE 5.2.3

> The future tense expresses actions or conditions that have not yet occurred.

FORMS EXPRESSING FUTURE TENSE	
Future	I will work.
Future Perfect	I will have worked.
Future Progressive	I will be working.
Future Perfect Progressive	I will have been working.

USES OF THE FUTURE AND THE FUTURE PERFECT TENSE	
Future	I will paint with watercolors. I will be painting this afternoon.
Future Perfect	I will have painted every day this week. By the time of the art exhibition, I will have painted for two years.

Notice in the next chart that the **future progressive** and the **future perfect progressive tenses** express only future actions.

USES OF THE PROGRESSIVE TENSE TO EXPRESS FUTURE TIME	
Future Progressive	Ling will be gardening all weekend.
Future Perfect Progressive	By Monday, she will have been gardening for three days, and her knees will be sore.

The basic forms of the present and the present progressive tense are often used with other words to express future time.

EXAMPLES   My favorite band **plays** in town next month.

I **am going** to be in line for tickets.

See Practice 5.2E
See Practice 5.2F

PRACTICE 5.2E > **Identifying Tense in Future Time**

Read each sentence. Then, write the future-tense verbs in each sentence and identify the form of the tense.

EXAMPLE   Everyone will be hungry tonight.

ANSWER   *will be* — *future*

1. The concert will be starting in a few minutes.
2. The clerk will have mailed your tickets by tomorrow.
3. In January, we will have been living in this house for seven years.
4. The committee will have made its decision by next week.
5. This time next month, we will have been collecting shells on a beach in Mexico.
6. A heavy rain will soak the area tonight.
7. The travel agent will make the reservations.
8. Thomas will be photographing the wedding.
9. The sun will rise in the east.
10. Caryn will be putting the baby to bed.

PRACTICE 5.2F > **Supplying Verbs in Future Time**

Read each sentence. Then, rewrite each sentence, filling in the blank with the future tense of the verb indicated in parentheses.

EXAMPLE   Those tight shoes _____ your feet later. (hurt, future)

ANSWER   *Those tight shoes will hurt your feet later.*

11. I _____ all the seeds. (plant, future perfect)
12. I _____ disappointed if all my friends are away this summer. (be, future)
13. Ginger _____ college next year. (graduate, future perfect)
14. I _____ to London for the weekend. (fly, future perfect progressive)
15. By the time we stop, we _____ over thirteen hours. (travel, future perfect)
16. The coach told us that we _____ this weekend. (practice, future progressive)
17. By tomorrow, I _____ all of the details. (memorize, future perfect)
18. My instructor _____ his lectures to be recorded. (allow, future progressive)
19. The new teacher _____ able to meet her students. (be, future perfect)
20. Someone _____ the package on the table. (leave, future)

SPEAKING APPLICATION

Take turns with a partner. Tell about your plans for the upcoming weekend. Use future-tense verbs in your sentences. Your partner should listen for and name the future-tense verbs that you use.

WRITING APPLICATION

Rewrite your corrections for sentences 13, 16, and 17, changing the verbs to include other future-tense verbs. Make sure your sentences still make sense.

Sequence of Tenses

A sentence with more than one verb must be consistent in its time sequence.

> When showing a sequence of events, do not shift tenses unnecessarily.

EXAMPLES   Jose **will run** track, then he **will take** a shower.

Kima **has studied** for her test, and she **has finished** her research paper.

I **swam** and **surfed** in the ocean.

Sometimes, however, it is necessary to shift tenses, especially when a sentence is complex or compound-complex. The tense of the main verb often determines the tense of the verb in the subordinate clause. Moreover, the form of the participle or infinitive often depends on the tense of the verb in the main clause.

Verbs in Subordinate Clauses It is frequently necessary to look at the tense of the main verb in a sentence before choosing the tense of the verb in the subordinate clause.

> The tense of a verb in a subordinate clause should follow logically from the tense of the main verb.

INCORRECT   I **will know** that Dad **fixed** the car.

CORRECT   I **know** that Dad **fixed** the car.

As you study the combinations of tenses in the charts on the next pages, notice that the choice of tenses affects the logical relationship between the events being expressed. Some combinations indicate that the events are **simultaneous**—meaning that they occur at the same time. Other combinations indicate that the events are **sequential**—meaning that one event occurs before or after the other.

SEQUENCE OF EVENTS		
MAIN VERB	**SUBORDINATE VERB**	**MEANING**
MAIN VERB IN PRESENT TENSE		
I understand...	**PRESENT** that he drives a car. **PRESENT PROGRESSIVE** that he is driving a car. **PRESENT EMPHATIC** that he does drive a car.	Simultaneous events: All events occur in present time.
I understand...	**PAST** that he drove a car. **PRESENT PERFECT** that he has driven a car. **PAST PERFECT** that he had driven a car. **PAST PROGRESSIVE** that he was driving a car. **PRESENT PERFECT PROGRESSIVE** that he has been driving a car. **PAST PERFECT PROGRESSIVE** that he had been driving a car. **PAST EMPHATIC** that he did drive a car.	Sequential events: The driving comes before the understanding.
I understand...	**FUTURE** that he will drive a car. **FUTURE PERFECT** that he will have driven a car. **FUTURE PROGRESSIVE** that he will be driving a car. **FUTURE PERFECT PROGRESSIVE** that he will have been driving a car.	Sequential events: The understanding comes before the driving.

SEQUENCE OF EVENTS		
MAIN VERB	SUBORDINATE VERB	MEANING
MAIN VERB IN PAST TENSE		
I understood…	**PAST** that he drove a car. **PAST PROGRESSIVE** that he was driving a car. **PAST EMPHATIC** that he did drive a car.	Simultaneous events: All events take place in the past.
I understood…	**PAST PERFECT** that he had driven a car. **PAST PERFECT PROGRESSIVE** that he had been driving a car.	Sequential events: The driving came before the understanding.
MAIN VERB IN FUTURE TENSE		
I will understand…	**PRESENT** if he drives a car. **PRESENT PROGRESSIVE** if he is driving a car. **PRESENT EMPHATIC** if he does drive a car.	Simultaneous events: All events take place in future time.
I will understand…	**PAST** if he drove a car. **PRESENT PERFECT** if he has driven a car. **PRESENT PERFECT PROGRESSIVE** if he has been driving a car. **PAST EMPHATIC** if he did drive a car.	Sequential events: The driving comes before the understanding.

Time Sequence With Participles and Infinitives Frequently, the form of a participle or infinitive determines whether the events are simultaneous or sequential. Participles can be present (*winning*), past (*won*), or perfect (*having won*). Infinitives can be present (*to win*) or perfect (*to have won*).

> **The form of a participle or an infinitive should logically relate to the verb in the same clause or sentence.**

5.2.6 RULE

To show simultaneous events, you will generally need to use the present participle or the present infinitive, whether the main verb is present, past, or future.

Simultaneous Events

| IN PRESENT TIME | **Winning** the game, the team **celebrates**. |
| | present ⸱ present |

| IN PAST TIME | **Winning** the game, the team **celebrated**. |
| | present ⸱ past |

| IN FUTURE TIME | **Winning** the game, the team **will celebrate**. |
| | present ⸱ future |

To show sequential events, use the perfect form of the participle and infinitive, regardless of the tense of the main verb.

Sequential Events

IN PRESENT TIME	**Having won** the game, the team **is celebrating**.
	perfect ⸱ present progressive
	(They won *before* they celebrated.)

IN PAST TIME	**Having won** the game, the team **celebrated**.
	perfect ⸱ past
	(They won *before* they celebrated.)

SPANNING PAST AND FUTURE TIME	**Having won** the game, the team **will celebrate**.
	perfect ⸱ future
	(They will celebrate *after* winning.)

See Practice 5.2G
See Practice 5.2H

PRACTICE 5.2G ▷ Identifying the Time Sequence in Sentences With More Than One Verb

Read each sentence. Write the verb of the event that happens second in each sentence.

EXAMPLE   We will go to school after we have eaten breakfast.

ANSWER   *will go*

1. John feels that he did his job correctly.

2. The group wished that they had completed the project ahead of time.

3. I wrote a letter after I finished my homework.

4. Troy sat down and thought about his writing assignment.

5. After seeing John play basketball, the coach added him to the team.

6. When she heard what the plan was, she became excited.

7. When I woke up, I realized the solution.

8. Because we played with the friendly dog, he came back every afternoon.

9. You will see that you have chosen well.

10. I admired the mural that she had painted on the wall.

PRACTICE 5.2H ▷ Recognizing and Correcting Errors in Tense Sequence

Read each sentence. Then, if a sentence has an error in tense sequence, rewrite it to correct the error. If a sentence is correct, write *correct*.

EXAMPLE   The squirrel stuffed the acorn into its mouth and scampers up the tree.

ANSWER   *The squirrel stuffed the acorn into its mouth and scampered up the tree.*

11. All of the students studied hard and learn the material.

12. Have you read the book and discuss it with the teacher?

13. The violinist listens carefully and imitated her instructor.

14. Last night, the wind blew hard and knocks down the fence.

15. Fernando wore his favorite jacket to the dance and enjoyed himself.

16. I took the rotten apple and throw it away.

17. Has she written and edit her paper yet?

18. Ice burst the pipes and floods the basement.

19. Have you seen and driven the model car?

20. I went to the mall to buy a shirt and ate Chinese food.

SPEAKING APPLICATION

Take turns with a partner. Tell about something fun that you like to do. Use two verbs in your sentences. Your partner should listen to and identify the sequence of events in your sentences.

WRITING APPLICATION

Use sentences 11, 14, and 20 as models to write your own sentences with incorrect tense sequence. Then, exchange papers with a partner. Your partner should rewrite your sentences, using the correct sequence in tense.

Modifiers That Help Clarify Tense

The time expressed by a verb can often be clarified by adverbs such as *often*, *sometimes*, *always*, or *frequently* and phrases such as *once in a while*, *within a week*, *last week*, or *now and then*.

> **Use modifiers when they can help clarify tense.**

5.2.7 RULE

In the examples below, the modifiers that help clarify the tense of the verb are highlighted in orange. Think about how the sentences would read without the modifiers. Modifiers help to make your writing more precise and interesting.

EXAMPLES   Julia **works** **every afternoon** at the store.

She **rearranges** the sale racks **once a day**.

She **rearranges** the sale racks **now and then**.
(These two sentences have very different meanings.)

Occasionally, she **buys** something at the store.

She **always** **uses** her employee discount.

By next month, Julia **will have worked** at the store for two years.

Julia also **talks** to her friends **every night**.

Talking on the phone **is** **now** one of her favorite pastimes.

Sometimes, two friends **attempt** to call her at once.

She **always** **tries** not to keep them waiting too long.

See Practice 5.2I
See Practice 5.2J

| PRACTICE 5.2I | **Identifying Modifiers That Help Clarify Tense** |

Read each sentence. Then, write the modifier in each sentence that helps clarify the verb tense.

EXAMPLE   My parents are going to Europe next week.

ANSWER   *next week*

1. Pamela has asked me to help her with her math homework tonight.

2. The Bearcats won the game yesterday.

3. My English class is always very interesting.

4. Occasionally, we receive a heavy downpour.

5. Sometimes, my father wakes up at 5:00 A.M.

6. Suddenly, the showers stopped and a rainbow appeared.

7. Last Thursday, we watched a film about Earth Day.

8. Each weekday, he works at the store after school.

9. Last summer, we did not receive much rain.

10. Mom seldom returns from her office before 6:00 P.M.

| PRACTICE 5.2J | **Supplying Modifiers to Clarify Meaning** |

Read each sentence. Then, fill in the blank with a modifier that will clarify the meaning of each sentence.

EXAMPLE   Whitney _____ sings at parties.

ANSWER   *always*

11. _____, I will work at the garden supply store.

12. _____, we listened to my father tell a story.

13. _____, Tory walks five miles to the park.

14. The barred owl is _____ seen in the woods.

15. We will _____ meet the new principal.

16. I take piano lessons _____.

17. The tone of the drama class is _____ uplifting.

18. Mr. Roberts _____ lets everyone give his or her opinion.

19. We _____ eat healthy meals.

20. My mom _____ likes to invite our relatives to the house.

SPEAKING APPLICATION

Take turns with a partner. Tell each other about trips that you have taken. Use modifiers that help clarify tense in your sentences. Your partner should listen for and identify the modifiers in your sentences.

WRITING APPLICATION

Use your corrections for sentences 11, 17, and 20 as models to write your own sentences. Rewrite the sentences to include different modifiers that clarify meaning.

5.3 The Subjunctive Mood

There are three **moods,** or ways in which a verb can express an action or condition: **indicative, imperative,** and **subjunctive.** The **indicative** mood, which is the most common, is used to make factual statements (*Karl is helpful.*) and to ask questions (*Is Karl helpful?*). The **imperative** mood is used to give orders or directions (*Be helpful.*).

Using the Subjunctive Mood

There are two important differences between verbs in the **subjunctive** mood and those in the indicative mood. First, in the present tense, third-person singular verbs in the subjunctive mood do not have the usual *-s* or *-es* ending. Second, the subjunctive mood of *be* in the present tense is *be;* in the past tense, it is *were,* regardless of the subject.

INDICATIVE MOOD	SUBJUNCTIVE MOOD
I want to be sure that she drives slowly.	I suggest that she drive slowly.
She is not punctual.	I insist that she be punctual.
I was angry that she was late.	If she were late, I'd be angry.

> Use the subjunctive mood (1) in clauses beginning with *if* or *that* to express an idea that is contrary to fact or (2) in clauses beginning with *that* to express a request, a demand, or a proposal.

5.3.1 RULE

Expressing Ideas Contrary to Fact Ideas that are contrary to fact are commonly expressed as wishes or conditions. Using the subjunctive mood in these situations shows that the idea expressed is not true now and may never be true.

EXAMPLES   Tracy wishes that she **were** better at piano.

She wishes that her fingers **were** more agile.

She could have performed in the recital if she **were** a better pianist.

RULE 5.3.2 Some *if* clauses do not take a subjunctive verb. If the idea expressed may be true, an indicative form is used.

EXAMPLES   I told my mom that **if** I **was** finished with my homework, I'd go shopping with her.

If we **want** to avoid the crowds, we should go now.

Expressing Requests, Demands, and Proposals Verbs that request, demand, or propose are often followed by a *that* clause containing a verb in the subjunctive mood.

REQUEST   We request that people **be** silent during the show.

DEMAND   It is required that people **be** silent during the show.

PROPOSAL   He proposed that people **be** silent during the show. See Practice 5.3A

Auxiliary Verbs That Express the Subjunctive Mood

Because certain helping verbs suggest conditions contrary to fact, they can often be used in place of the subjunctive mood.

RULE 5.3.3 *Could, would,* or *should* can be used with a verb to express the subjunctive mood.

The sentences on the left in the chart below have the usual subjunctive form of the verb *be: were.* The sentences on the right have been reworded with *could, would,* and *should.*

THE SUBJUNCTIVE MOOD WITH AUXILIARY VERBS	
WITH FORMS OF *BE*	WITH *COULD, WOULD,* OR *SHOULD*
If the car **were** working, I'd drive.	If the car **would** work, I'd drive.
If I **were** to learn to drive, I'd go anywhere.	If I **would** learn to drive, I'd go anywhere.
If you **were** to learn to drive, could I ride with you?	If you **should** learn to drive, could I ride with you?

See Practice 5.3B

PRACTICE 5.3A Identifying Mood (Indicative, Imperative, Subjunctive)

Read each sentence. Then, identify whether each sentence expresses the *indicative, imperative,* or *subjunctive* mood.

EXAMPLE   I wish that today were Friday.

ANSWER   *subjunctive*

1. If I were an actor, I'd like to work on Broadway.
2. Walk the dog right now.
3. They requested that the flowers be delivered.
4. I demand that the package be ready by noon.
5. The caterers arrived just in time.
6. Turn over the pancakes so they don't burn.
7. If you were to help me, I would finish sooner.
8. Did Carol volunteer at the rummage sale all day?
9. If you were to open the windows, the paint would dry faster.
10. I wish that I were going with you.

PRACTICE 5.3B Supplying Auxiliary Verbs to Express the Subjunctive Mood

Read each sentence. Then, rewrite each sentence and complete it by supplying an auxiliary verb to express the subjunctive mood.

EXAMPLE   If I were in your place, I ____ be so happy.

ANSWER   *If I were in your place, I would be so happy.*

11. If I were stronger, I ____ lift heavier objects.
12. If you ____ leave, I ____ be sad.
13. If I were an inch taller, I ____ be the same height as my father.
14. The house ____ be cooler if you were to turn off the oven.
15. If you were to go to San Antonio, what ____ you see?
16. I ____ make a roast for dinner tonight.
17. We ____ not be so rushed if the deadline was extended.
18. He decided that the mortgage ____ be paid early.
19. This meeting ____ run more smoothly if they weren't so many interruptions.
20. If I ____ get home earlier, I ____ exercise more often.

SPEAKING APPLICATION

Take turns with a partner. Say sentences that express the indicative, imperative, and subjunctive moods. Your partner should listen for and identify which mood each of your sentences express.

WRITING APPLICATION

Use the auxiliary verbs that you used to rewrite sentences 15, 16, and 17 to write sentences of your own. Be sure that your sentences still express the subjunctive mood.

5.4 Voice

This section discusses a characteristic of verbs called **voice**.

RULE 5.4.1

Voice or tense is the form of a verb that shows whether the subject is performing the action or is being acted upon.

In English, there are two voices: **active** and **passive.** Only action verbs can indicate the active voice; linking verbs cannot.

Active and Passive Voice or Tense

If the subject of a verb performs the action, the verb is active; if the subject receives the action, the verb is passive.

Active Voice Any action verb can be used in the active voice. The action verb may be transitive (that is, it may have a direct object) or intransitive (without a direct object).

RULE 5.4.2

A verb is active if its subject performs the action.

In the examples below, the subject performs the action. In the first example, the verb *telephoned* is transitive; *team* is the direct object, which receives the action. In the second example, the verb *developed* is transitive; *pictures* is the direct object. In the third example, the verb *gathered* is intransitive; it has no direct object. In the last example, the verb *worked* is intransitive and has no direct object.

ACTIVE
VOICE

The captain **telephoned** the **team**.
    transitive verb   direct object

Bill **developed** twenty-five **pictures** of the ocean.
    transitive verb   direct object

Telephone messages **gathered** on the desk while
                    intransitive verb
she was away.

Bill **worked** quickly.
    intransitive verb

See Practice 5.4A
See Practice 5.4B

Passive Voice Most action verbs can also be used in the passive voice.

> **A verb is passive if its action is performed upon the subject.**

In the following examples, the subjects are the receivers of the action. The first example names the performer, the captain, as the object of the preposition *by* instead of the subject. In the second example, no performer of the action is mentioned.

PASSIVE VOICE   The **team** **was telephoned** by the captain.
receiver of action   verb

The **messages** **were gathered** into neat piles.
receiver of action   verb

> **A passive verb is always a verb phrase made from a form of *be* plus the past participle of a verb. The tense of the helping verb *be* determines the tense of the passive verb.**

The chart below provides a conjugation in the passive voice of the verb *affect* in the three moods. Notice that there are only two progressive forms and no emphatic form.

THE VERB *AFFECT* IN THE PASSIVE VOICE	
Present Indicative	He is affected.
Past Indicative	He was affected.
Future Indicative	He will be affected.
Present Perfect Indicative	He has been affected.
Past Perfect Indicative	He had been affected.
Future Perfect Indicative	He will have been affected.
Present Progressive Indicative	He is being affected.
Past Progressive Indicative	He was being affected.
Present Imperative	(You) be affected.
Present Subjunctive	(if) he be affected
Past Subjunctive	(if) he were affected

See Practice 5.2C

Using Active and Passive Voice

Writing that uses the active voice tends to be much more lively than writing that uses the passive voice. The active voice is usually more direct and economical. That is because active voice shows someone doing something.

Use the active voice whenever possible.

ACTIVE
VOICE
Melissa **created** a clay sculpture.

PASSIVE
VOICE
A clay sculpture **was created** by Melissa.

The passive voice has two uses in English.

Use the passive voice when you want to emphasize the receiver of an action rather than the performer of an action.

EXAMPLE
Andrew **was given** the highest grades.

Use the passive voice to point out the receiver of an action whenever the performer is not important or not easily identified.

EXAMPLE
The T-shirts in the store **were marked** down, so we bought three.

The active voice lends more excitement to writing, making it more interesting to readers. In the example below, notice how the sentence you just read has been revised to show someone doing something, rather than something just happening.

EXAMPLE
The store manager **marked** down the T-shirts, so we bought three.
(*Who* marked down the shirts so we could buy three?)

See Practice 5.4D

PRACTICE 5.4A > **Recognizing Active Voice (Active Tense)**

Read each sentence. Write the active verb(s) in each sentence and identify them as *transitive* or *intransitive*.

EXAMPLE   The early frost damaged and ruined the crops.

ANSWER   *damaged* — transitive
           ruined — transitive

1. The new law protects consumers.
2. Shelly agreed to edit and rewrite the last part of the play.
3. The heavy wind blew down several trees.
4. Everyone enjoyed the festival.
5. The delivery truck comes once a week.
6. Fry the eggs on both sides.
7. Maddie tilled the soil and planted the seeds in the ground.
8. The soldiers are prepared for any kind of situation.
9. They ate dinner and discussed their mutual interests.
10. We called Alana and asked her to be a part of our group.

PRACTICE 5.4B > **Using Active Verbs**

Read each item. Then, write different sentences, using each item as active verbs.

EXAMPLE   created, gave

ANSWER   *Bill created a fictional character and gave it a funny name.*

11. delivered, signed
12. writes, erases
13. slept, woke
14. answered, wept
15. opened, flew
16. laugh, cry
17. bought, sold
18. winks, waves
19. toured, sang
20. adores, spoils

SPEAKING APPLICATION

Take turns with a partner. Say sentences in the active voice. Your partner will listen to and identify the active verbs in each of your sentences.

WRITING APPLICATION

Write a short paragraph about your dream vacation. Use active verbs in your description.

PRACTICE 5.4C ▷ Forming the Tenses of Passive Verbs

Read each verb. Then, using the subject indicated in parentheses, conjugate each verb in the passive voice for the present indicative, past indicative, future indicative, present perfect indicative, past perfect indicative, and future perfect indicative.

EXAMPLE   reword (it)

ANSWER   *it is reworded, it was reworded, it will be reworded, it has been reworded, it had been reworded, it will have been reworded*

1. borrow (it)

2. promise (I)

3. ask (she)

4. earn (it)

5. maintain (we)

6. lift (he)

7. follow (she)

8. buy (it)

9. tell (she)

10. carry (it)

PRACTICE 5.4D ▷ Supplying Verbs in the Active Voice

Read each sentence. Then, complete each sentence by suppling a verb in the active voice.

EXAMPLE   Politics _____ the conversation all evening.

ANSWER   *dominated*

11. Guests from several nations _____ freely at the reception.

12. Charlotte _____ the numerous compliments.

13. They _____ the winning essay today.

14. These pants _____ two sizes in the dryer.

15. The wind _____ waves across the water.

16. Preston _____ new flowers in his garden.

17. Olivia _____ her bike for the first time today.

18. I _____ the towels and swimsuits to take to the beach.

19. The dog _____ his tail back and forth.

20. The committee _____ to adjourn for the evening.

SPEAKING APPLICATION

Take turns with a partner. Say six verbs. Your partner should say the basic forms of each verb in the passive voice.

WRITING APPLICATION

Choose three of your corrected sentences for Practice 5.4D and rewrite each of them to show the passive voice.

CHAPTER 6

PRONOUN USAGE

Use each case of pronoun correctly to help create a smooth flow and rhythm in your writing.

WRITE GUY *Jeff Anderson, M.Ed.*

WHAT DO YOU NOTICE?

Discover pronouns as you zoom in on lines from the poem "Lines Composed a Few Miles Above Tintern Abbey" by William Wordsworth.

MENTOR TEXT

> . . . And I have felt
> A presence that disturbs me with the joy
> Of elevated thoughts; a sense sublime
> Of something far more deeply interfused,
> Whose dwelling is the light of setting suns . . .

Now, ask yourself the following questions:

- Which two forms of the first-person pronoun *I* are used in this verse?
- Why does the poet use the word *whose* in the final line?

The poet uses the nominative form *I* in the opening words *I have felt* because it performs the action of the verb. He uses the objective case *me* in the next line because *me* is the object of the verb *disturbs*. The poet uses *whose*—the possessive form of the pronoun *who*—to show ownership of the noun *dwelling*.

Grammar for Writers Look for commonly misspelled pronouns when you edit your writing. For example, the possessive pronoun *whose* is sometimes confused with the contraction *who's*, which is the shortened form of the words *who is* or *who has*.

Is that your nominative or possessive case?

My mom is on my case again.

6.1 Case

Nouns and pronouns are the only parts of speech that have **case**.

RULE 6.1.1

Case is the form of a noun or a pronoun that shows how it is used in a sentence.

The Three Cases

Nouns and pronouns have three cases, each of which has its own distinctive uses.

RULE 6.1.2

The three cases of nouns and pronouns are the **nominative,** the **objective,** and the **possessive.**

CASE	USE IN SENTENCE
Nominative	As the Subject of a Verb, Predicate Nominative, or Nominative Absolute
Objective	As the Direct Object, Indirect Object, Object of a Preposition, Object of a Verbal, or Subject of an Infinitive
Possessive	To Show Ownership

Case in Nouns
The case, or form, of a noun changes only to show possession.

NOMINATIVE   The **key** had been hidden for weeks.

(*Key* is the subject of the verb *had been hidden.*)

OBJECTIVE   We tried to find the **key**.

(*Key* is the object of the infinitive *to find.*)

POSSESSIVE   The **key's** location could not be determined.

(The form changes when *'s* is added to show possession.)

Case in Pronouns

Personal pronouns often have different forms for all three cases. The pronoun that you use depends on its function in a sentence.

NOMINATIVE	OBJECTIVE	POSSESSIVE
I	*me*	*my, mine*
you	*you*	*your, yours*
he, she, it	*him, her, it*	*his, her, hers, its*
we, they	*us, them*	*our, ours*
		their, theirs

EXAMPLES   **I** read the magazines about cars.

Martha sent the tickets to **me**.

See Practice 6.1A   The magazine about cars is **mine**.

The Nominative Case in Pronouns

The **nominative case** is used when a personal pronoun acts in one of three ways.

> Use the **nominative case** when a pronoun is the subject of a verb, the subject of a predicate nominative, or the subject of a pronoun in a nominative absolute.

6.1.3 RULE

A **nominative absolute** consists of a noun or nominative pronoun followed by a participial phrase. It functions independently from the rest of the sentence.

EXAMPLE   **We having opened our history books,** our

teacher assigned us to read about the Civil War

and its outcome.

NOMINATIVE PRONOUNS	
As the Subject of a Verb	I will consult the book while she looks up the author.
As a Predicate Nominative	The owners were she and he.
In a Nominative Absolute	We having finished the soup, the server cleared and washed the dishes.

Nominative Pronouns in Compounds

When you use a pronoun in a compound subject or predicate nominative, check the case either by mentally crossing out the other part of the compound or by inverting the sentence.

COMPOUND SUBJECT

The pilot and **I** inspected the flight plan.

(**I** inspected the flight plan.)

She and her sister swam in the pool.

(**She** swam in the pool.)

COMPOUND PREDICATE NOMINATIVE

The fastest swimmers were Dan and **he**.

(Dan and **he** were the fastest swimmers.)

The supervisors were Rae and **I**.

(Rae and **I** were the supervisors.)

Nominative Pronouns With Appositives

When an appositive follows a pronoun that is being used as a subject or predicate nominative, the pronoun should stay in the nominative case. To check that you have used the correct case, either mentally cross out the appositive or isolate the subject and verb.

SUBJECT

We coaches use clipboards.

(**We** use clipboards.)

PREDICATE NOMINATIVE

The supervisors were **we** seniors.

(**We** were the supervisors.)

APPOSITIVE AFTER NOUN

The team racers, who were **he** and **I**, won the trophy cup.

(**He** and **I** won the trophy cup.)

See Practice 6.1B

PRACTICE 6.1A > Identifying Case

Read each sentence. Then, label the underlined pronoun *nominative*, *objective*, or *possessive*.

EXAMPLE   The dappled horse is <u>ours</u>.

ANSWER   *possessive*

1. Did she buy this sweater or did she knit <u>it</u>?
2. The train let <u>its</u> passengers off at Union Station.
3. <u>She</u> followed the directions on the back of the box.
4. Can <u>you</u> tell me which helmet is for sale?
5. Carlos bought <u>her</u> a necklace for graduation.
6. <u>We</u> promise not to let you down!
7. The investment made <u>them</u> a lot of money.
8. Are <u>you</u> the winner of the contest?
9. According to the law, the house should be <u>hers</u>.
10. The woman in the photograph is <u>she</u>.

PRACTICE 6.1B > Supplying Pronouns in the Nominative Case

Read each sentence. Then, supply the correct pronoun from the choices in parentheses to complete each sentence.

EXAMPLE   When Lena left the store, (she, her) forgot her keys.

ANSWER   *she*

11. It was (he, him) whom the director chose.
12. Both my brother and (me, I) plan to go to the graduation ceremony.
13. My aunt and (she, her) used the same recipe.
14. (Them, They) are panning for gold in California.
15. The man sitting on the bench is (he, him).
16. (She, her) was eager to get the voyage underway.
17. Keisha and (her, she) finished before anyone else.
18. (Us, We) began to wonder if the scent was coming from the garden.
19. As Jason sat waiting in the lobby, (him, he) became more calm.
20. The losers of the tournament were (they, them).

SPEAKING APPLICATION

Take turns with a partner. Tell about a television show you saw recently. Your partner should listen for pronouns in your sentences and tell whether each one is possessive, nominative, or objective.

WRITING APPLICATION

Write a paragraph about a trip that you have taken. Underline all pronouns in the nominative case in your paragraph.

The Objective Case

Objective pronouns are used for any kind of object in a sentence as well as for the subject of an infinitive.

> Use the **objective case** for the object of any verb, preposition, or verbal or for the subject of an infinitive.

OBJECTIVE PRONOUNS	
Direct Object	The hockey puck hit him in the jaw.
Indirect Object	My sister sent me many beautiful pictures from Israel.
Object of Preposition	The coach stood in front of us on the new soccer field.
Object of Participle	The basketball coach awaiting them seemed aggravated.
Object of Gerund	Confronting them at the party will make a big scene.
Object of Infinitive	I am required to pick her up at the airport.
Subject of Infinitive	The teacher wanted her to stay after class.

Objective Pronouns in Compounds

As with the nominative case, errors with objective pronouns most often occur in compounds. To find the correct case, mentally cross out the other part of the compound.

EXAMPLES

The loud sirens alarmed Bill and **her**.
(The loud sirens alarmed **her**.)

Laura painted Alex and **me** a picture of my house.
(Laura painted **me** a picture of my house.)

Note About *Between:* Be sure to use the objective case after the preposition *between.*

INCORRECT   This password is between you and **I**.

CORRECT   This password is between you and **me**.

Objective Pronouns With Appositives

Use the objective case when a pronoun that is used as an object or as the subject of an infinitive is followed by an appositive.

EXAMPLES The contest recipe intimidated **us** bakers.

My uncle brought **us** nieces rabbits.

See Practice 6.1C The captain asked **us** troops to march forward.

The Possessive Case

One use for the **possessive case** is before gerunds. A **gerund** is a verbal form ending in *-ing* that is used as a noun.

Use the **possessive case** before gerunds.

EXAMPLES **Your** storytelling was very exciting.

We considered **his** storytelling to be exciting and fun.

Ryan consents to **our** attending the meeting.

Common Errors in the Possessive Case

Be sure not to use an apostrophe with a possessive pronoun because possessives already show ownership. Spellings such as *her's, our's, their's,* and *your's* are incorrect.

In addition, be sure not to confuse possessive pronouns and contractions that sound alike. *It's* (with an apostrophe) is the contraction for *it is* or *it has. Its* (without the apostrophe) is a possessive pronoun that means "belonging to it." *You're* is a contraction of *you are;* the possessive form of *you* is *your.*

POSSESSIVE PRONOUNS The garden has served **its** purpose.

Don't forget **your** flowers.

CONTRACTIONS **It's** likely we will see you again.

You're the only senior in your group this

See Practice 6.1D afternoon.

PRACTICE 6.1C › **Supplying Pronouns in the Objective Case**

Read each sentence. Then, write the correct pronoun from the choices in parentheses to complete each sentence.

EXAMPLE   Please ask (him, he) to join us for dinner.

ANSWER   *him*

1. We bought Rhiannon and (she, her) some potted flowers.
2. The soldier ordered (he, him) to stand at attention.
3. The incident was between Neil and (her, she).
4. Please tell (us, we) another joke.
5. We ordered (he, him) a new pair of boots.
6. I have to choose between (they, them).
7. The teacher asked Julie and (she, her) to comment on the essay.
8. Will you allow George and (he, him) to revise their essays?
9. My father gave (I, me) a ring that belonged to my grandmother.
10. Have you asked (her, she) to show you how to use the computer program?

PRACTICE 6.1D › **Recognizing Pronouns in the Possessive Case**

Read each sentence. Then, write the correct pronoun from the choices in parentheses to complete each sentence.

EXAMPLE   Everyone agreed with (us, our) inviting them to the dance.

ANSWER   *our*

11. Mom agreed to (their, they) painting the fence.
12. The deed proved that the house was (his, him).
13. (They, Their) treehouse is six feet off the ground.
14. My sister was happy about (my, me) learning to swim.
15. We thought (she, her) story was the best.
16. (His, Him) being so happy was due to the puppy in the yard.
17. (Us, Our) whistling caused several birds to respond.
18. The colorful garden with the orange lilies is (my, mine).
19. (Their, they) request has been fulfilled.
20. I appreciate you for always bringing (you, your) camera to the games.

SPEAKING APPLICATION

Take turns with a partner. Tell about an upcoming school event. Use three or more objective pronouns in your description. Your partner should listen for and identify each objective pronoun that you use.

WRITING APPLICATION

Write four sentences using the following possessive pronouns: *your, our, my,* and *her*.

6.2 Special Problems With Pronouns

Choosing the correct case is not always a matter of choosing the form that "sounds correct," because writing is usually more formal than speech. For example, it would be incorrect to say, "John is smarter than *me*." because the verb is understood in the sentence: "John is smarter than *I [am]*."

Using *Who* and *Whom* Correctly

In order to decide when to use *who* or *whom* and the related forms *whoever* and *whomever*, you need to know how the pronoun is used in a sentence and what case is appropriate.

> **Who** is used for the nominative case. **Whom** is used for the objective case.

6.2.1 RULE

CASE	PRONOUNS	USE IN SENTENCES
Nominative	*who* *whoever*	As the Subject of a Verb or Predicate Nominative
Objective	*whom* *whomever*	As the Direct Object, Object of a Verbal, Object of a Preposition, or Subject of an Infinitive
Possessive	*whose* *whoever*	To Show Ownership

EXAMPLES
I know **who** cooked that lasagna.

Kate took **whoever** was off for vacation to the beach.

Ken did not know **whom** the teacher chose.

Whose car is sitting in the driveway?

The nominative and objective cases are the source of certain problems. Pronoun problems can appear in two kinds of sentences: direct questions and complex sentences.

In Direct Questions

Who is the correct form when the pronoun is the subject of a simple question. *Whom* is the correct form when the pronoun is the direct object, object of a verbal, or object of a preposition.

Questions in subject–verb word order always begin with *who*. However, questions in inverted order never correctly begin with *who*. To see if you should use *who* or *whom*, reword the question as a statement in subject–verb word order.

EXAMPLES   **Who** wants to go to the skateboard park?

Whom did you go with yesterday?

(You went with whom yesterday.)

In Complex Sentences

Follow these steps to see if the case of a pronoun in a subordinate clause is correct. First, find the subordinate clause. If the complex sentence is a question, rearrange it in subject–verb order. Second, if the subordinate clause is inverted, rearrange the words in subject–verb word order. Finally, determine how the pronoun is used in the subordinate clause.

EXAMPLE   **Who** , may I ask, has read the play?

REARRANGED   I may ask **who** has read the play.

USE OF PRONOUN   (subject of the verb *has read*)

EXAMPLE   Is Alicia the one **whom** they chose to speak?

REARRANGED   They chose **whom** could speak.

USE OF PRONOUN   (object of the verb *chose*)

Note About Whose: The word *whose* is a possessive pronoun; the contraction *who's* means "who is" or "who has."

POSSESSIVE PRONOUN   **Whose** book is this?

CONTRACTION   **Who's** [who has] taken my book?   See Practice 6.2A

Pronouns in Elliptical Clauses

An **elliptical clause** is one in which some words are omitted but still understood. Errors in pronoun usage can easily be made when an elliptical clause that begins with *than* or *as* is used to make a comparison.

6.2.2 RULE

> In **elliptical clauses** beginning with *than* or *as*, use the form of the pronoun that you would use if the clause were fully stated.

The case of the pronoun is determined by whether the omitted words fall before or after the pronoun. The omitted words in the examples below are shown in brackets.

WORDS OMITTED BEFORE PRONOUN

You made more for Brent than **me**.

(You made more for Brent than [you made] me.)

WORDS OMITTED AFTER PRONOUN

Blake is as determined as **he**.

(Blake is as determined as he [is].)

Mentally add the missing words. If they come *before* the pronoun, choose the objective case. If they come *after* the pronoun, choose the nominative case.

CHOOSING A PRONOUN IN ELLIPTICAL CLAUSES
1. Consider the choices of pronouns: nominative or objective.
2. Mentally complete the elliptical clause.
3. Base your choice on what you find.

The case of the pronoun can sometimes change the entire meaning of the sentence.

NOMINATIVE PRONOUN

He liked jogging more than **I**.

He liked jogging more than **I** [did].

OBJECTIVE PRONOUN

He liked jogging more than **me**.

He liked jogging more than [he liked] **me**.

See Practice 6.2B

PRACTICE 6.2A > **Choosing *Who* or *Whom* Correctly**

Read each sentence. Then, write *who* or *whom* to complete each sentence.

EXAMPLE   (Who, Whom) did she think would be here?

ANSWER   *Who*

1. (Who, Whom) did the teacher chose to be the school representative?

2. Meghan chose the person (who, whom) she believed was best qualified for the job.

3. From (who, whom) were you expecting a call?

4. Marshall was the person (who, whom) called early this morning.

5. (Who, Whom) was the last person chosen?

6. To (who, whom) should I address my letter?

7. (Who, Whom) did they trust with their important documents?

8. That man is the one (who, whom) received the award.

9. With (who, whom) did you travel to Venice?

10. Jorge is the student (whom, who) can best play the part of Romeo.

PRACTICE 6.2B > **Identifying the Correct Pronoun in Elliptical Clauses**

Read each sentence. Then, complete each elliptical clause by choosing the correct pronoun in parentheses and adding the missing words in brackets.

EXAMPLE   Kendra tried as hard as (she, her) could.

ANSWER   *Kendra tried as hard as she could [try].*

11. Due to her insightful remarks, Carly impressed Rosa as much as (we, us).

12. This year, Henry sank more foul shots than (he, him).

13. More praise was given to my sister than (I, me).

14. Petra has a newer car than (he, him).

15. She was as close to the exit as (I, me).

16. I have trained as hard as (they, them).

17. My brother is a better drummer than (I, me).

18. More work was given to me than (her, she).

19. You are better prepared than (she, her).

20. During the tryouts, more catches were made by Wai than (he, him).

SPEAKING APPLICATION

Take turns with a partner. Tell the name of a favorite book. Then, have your partner ask questions, using the pronouns *who* and *whom*, to obtain information about the book's characters.

WRITING APPLICATION

Write six comparisons using correct pronouns in elliptical phrases, and add the missing words in brackets.

CHAPTER 7

AGREEMENT

Recognizing the importance of subject-verb and pronoun-antecedent agreement will help you craft clear sentences.

WRITE GUY *Jeff Anderson, M.Ed.*

WHAT DO YOU NOTICE?

Find evidence of agreement as you zoom in on this sentence from the introduction to *Frankenstein* by Mary Wollstonecraft Shelley.

MENTOR TEXT

> At first we spent our pleasant hours on the lake or wandering on its shores; and Lord Byron, who was writing the third canto of *Childe Harold*, was the only one among us who put his thoughts upon paper.

Now, ask yourself the following questions:

- Why does the author use the singular verb *was*?
- What is the antecedent of the pronoun *his*?

The verb *was* in the second clause is singular because the subject is one person—Lord Byron. The author uses *was* a second time to keep agreement in number and consistency in tense. The singular, masculine noun *Lord Byron* is the antecedent of the singular, masculine pronoun *his*, so they agree in number and gender.

Grammar for Writers Writers often use multiple clauses or phrases to craft complex sentences. When you write complex sentences, determine the subject and make sure the predicate and any pronouns that follow agree in number and gender.

Do your subjects and predicates always agree?

I don't know. I'll have to ask them.

7.1 Subject–Verb Agreement

For a subject and a verb to agree, both must be singular, or both must be plural. In this section, you will learn how to make sure singular and plural subjects and verbs agree.

Number in Nouns, Pronouns, and Verbs

In grammar, **number** indicates whether a word is singular or plural. Only three parts of speech have different forms that indicate number: nouns, pronouns, and verbs.

RULE 7.1.1

> **Number** shows whether a noun, pronoun, or verb is singular or plural.

Recognizing the number of most nouns is seldom a problem because most form their plurals by adding -s or -es. Some, such as *mouse* or *ox,* form their plurals irregularly: *mice, oxen.*

Pronouns, however, have different forms to indicate their number. The chart below shows the different forms of personal pronouns in the nominative case, the case that is used for subjects.

PERSONAL PRONOUNS		
SINGULAR	PLURAL	SINGULAR OR PLURAL
I	*we*	*you*
he, she, it	*they*	

The grammatical number of verbs is sometimes difficult to determine. That is because the form of many verbs can be either singular or plural, and they may form plurals in different ways.

SINGULAR   He **helps** .

He **has helped** .

PLURAL   We **help** .

We **have helped** .

Some verb forms can be only singular. The personal pronouns *he*, *she*, and *it* and all singular nouns call for singular verbs in the present and the present perfect tense.

ALWAYS SINGULAR

She **speaks**.

She **has spoken**.

Allie **speaks**.

Kurt **has spoken**.

She **sees**.

She **has seen**.

The verb *be* in the present tense has special forms to agree with singular subjects. The pronoun *I* has its own singular form of *be*; so do *he*, *she*, *it*, and singular nouns.

ALWAYS SINGULAR

I **am** seventeen.

She **is** beautiful.

Ricky **is** home.

She **is** healthy.

All singular subjects except *you* share the same past tense verb form of *be*.

ALWAYS SINGULAR

I **was** going on vacation.

He **was** company chairman.

Laura **was** early to class.

He **was** getting into the cab.

See Practice 7.1A

A verb form will always be singular if it has had an *-s* or *-es* added to it or if it includes the words *has*, *am*, *is*, or *was*. The number of any other verb depends on its subject.

The chart on the next page shows verb forms that are always singular and those that can be singular or plural.

VERBS THAT ARE ALWAYS SINGULAR	VERBS THAT CAN BE SINGULAR OR PLURAL
(he, she, Jane) sees	(I, you, we, they) see
(he, she, Jane) has seen	(I, you, we, they) have seen
(I) am	(you, we, they) are
(he, she, Jane) is	(you, we, they) were
(I, he, she, Jane) was	

Singular and Plural Subjects

When making a verb agree with its subject, be sure to identify the subject and determine its number.

RULE 7.1.2

A singular subject must have a singular verb. A plural subject must have a plural verb.

SINGULAR SUBJECT AND VERB	PLURAL SUBJECT AND VERB
The police officer works in New York City.	These police officers work in New York City.
He was being cryptic about their vacation destination.	They were being cryptic about their vacation destination.
Brent looks through a dictionary for the correct spelling.	Brent and Emmett look through a dictionary for the correct spelling.
Texas is a large state in the United States.	Texas and California are large states in the United States.
Ricky takes first aid and health.	Ricky and Nick take first aid and health.
Thomas is planning a vacation to go see the Alamo in Texas.	Thomas and Gene are planning a vacation to go see the Alamo in Texas.
Christy plays piano for the church choir.	Christy and Amy play piano for the church choir.
She looks through the microscope.	They look through the microscope.
Terrance has been studying how to prevent diseases.	They have been studying how to prevent diseases.

See Practice 7.1B

PRACTICE 7.1A **Identifying Number in Nouns, Pronouns, and Verbs**

Read each word or group of words. Then, write whether the word or words are *singular, plural,* or *both.*

EXAMPLE   he

ANSWER   *singular*

1. table
2. knows
3. mice
4. us
5. are
6. you see
7. boxes
8. exposes
9. children
10. it

PRACTICE 7.1B **Identifying Singular and Plural Subjects and Verbs**

Read each sentence. Then, write the subject and verb in each sentence and label them *plural* or *singular.*

EXAMPLE   The note was left on the coffee table.

ANSWER   *subject: note; verb: was — singular*

11. Recent weather reports indicate record-breaking snow this year.
12. Her strong legs come from her daily hour of running.
13. A cared for flowerbed provides a great deal of beauty to a home.
14. This sport coat is very versatile.
15. My cats provide me with great companionship.
16. Our teacher grades our midterms on a curve.
17. The stained-glass windows have adorned the old building.
18. From a distance, the oil painting looks exactly like the tranquil lake.
19. Tommy has run the mile faster than anyone else on the team.
20. Is Arnie next up at bat?

SPEAKING APPLICATION

Take turns with a partner. Tell about a time when you overcame a fear that you had. Your partner should listen for and name the plural and singular nouns and verbs that you use.

WRITING APPLICATION

For each sentence in Practice 7.1B, change the subject from singular to plural or plural to singular. Make sure that the verb in each sentence agrees with your new subject.

Intervening Phrases and Clauses

When you check for agreement, mentally cross out any words that separate the subject and verb.

> **A phrase or clause that interrupts a subject and its verb does not affect subject–verb agreement.**

In the first example below, the singular subject *discovery* agrees with the singular verb *interests* despite the intervening prepositional phrase *of hidden jewels,* which contains a plural noun.

EXAMPLES The **discovery** of hidden jewels **interests** many people.

The **fundraisers**, whose goal is nearly reached, **require** more donations.

Intervening parenthetical expressions—such as those beginning with *as well as, in addition to, in spite of,* or *including*—also have no effect on the agreement of the subject and verb.

EXAMPLES Your **presentation**, in addition to the data gathered by others, **is helping** to generate new ideas.

Francisco's **trip**, including visits to England, France, and Italy, **is lasting** three months.

See Practice 7.1C

Relative Pronouns as Subjects

When *who, which,* or *that* acts as a subject of a subordinate clause, its verb will be singular or plural depending on the number of the antecedent.

> **The antecedent of a relative pronoun determines its agreement with a verb.**

EXAMPLES He is the only **one** of the tourists **who has** the ability to speak Spanish.

(The antecedent of *who* is *one*.)

He is the only one of several **tourists who have** the ability to speak Spanish.

(The antecedent of *who* is *tourists*.)

Compound Subjects

A **compound subject** has two or more simple subjects, which are usually joined by *or* or *and*. Use the following rules when making compound subjects agree with verbs.

Subjects Joined by *And*

Only one rule applies to compound subjects connected by *and:* The verb is usually plural, whether the parts of the compound subject are all singular, all plural, or mixed.

> **A compound subject joined by *and* is generally plural and must have a plural verb.**

7.1.5 RULE

TWO SINGULAR SUBJECTS   A **snowstorm** and a **rainstorm hit** the state.

TWO PLURAL SUBJECTS   **Puppies** and **kittens chase** the ball across the yard.

A SINGULAR SUBJECT AND A PLURAL SUBJECT   The brown **puppy** and the gray **kittens chase** the ball across the yard.

There are two exceptions to this rule. The verb is singular if the parts of a compound subject are thought of as one item or if the word *every* or *each* precedes the compound subject.

Bacon and eggs was all she could cook for breakfast.

Every weather center and emergency network in the United States issues warnings for severe weather.

Singular Subjects Joined by *Or* or *Nor*
When both parts of a compound subject connected by *or* or *nor* are singular, a singular verb is required.

> **RULE 7.1.6** Two or more singular subjects joined by *or* or *nor* must have a singular verb.

EXAMPLE An **ice storm** or **rainstorm makes** driving difficult.

Plural Subjects Joined by *Or* or *Nor*
When both parts of a compound subject connected by *or* or *nor* are plural, a plural verb is required.

> **RULE 7.1.7** Two or more plural subjects joined by *or* or *nor* must have a plural verb.

EXAMPLE Neither **rainstorms** nor **windstorms cause** as much mess as sandstorms.

Subjects of Mixed Number Joined by *Or* or *Nor*
If one part of a compound subject is singular and the other is plural, the verb agrees with the subject that is closer to it.

> **RULE 7.1.8** If one or more singular subjects are joined to one or more plural subjects by *or* or *nor*, the subject closest to the verb determines agreement.

EXAMPLES Neither **Katherine** nor my **sisters have packed**.

Neither my **sisters** nor **Katherine has packed**. See Practice 7.1D

PRACTICE 7.1C > **Identifying Intervening Phrases and Clauses**

Read each sentence. Then, write the intervening phrase or clause between the subject and verb in each sentence.

EXAMPLE The students in my class work hard on the project.

ANSWER *in my class*

1. The neighborhood where I live has many new homes.

2. Sap, which comes from trees, is used to make deliciously sweet syrup.

3. Her favorite book, a classic piece of literature, sits on her nightstand.

4. These dribbling drills, along with the sprints, are really exhausting.

5. The collection of films, which was critically acclaimed, won several awards.

6. The cake, with its three layers, served 100 people at the party.

7. The rock band, popular with everyone, will play at the pavilion tonight.

8. Jasmine, who is the smartest student in our class, always answers the questions.

9. The discovery of gold in Alaska in the 1800s, led to a gold rush.

10. The smoke alarm in the kitchen was just replaced.

PRACTICE 7.1D > **Making Verbs Agree With Singular and Compound Subjects**

Read each sentence. Then, fill in the blank with the form of a verb that agrees with the singular or compound subject.

EXAMPLE Either tomato sauce or tomato paste _____ used in this recipe.

ANSWER *is*

11. The hikers _____ from their long excursion.

12. Neither Yen nor I _____ horror movies.

13. Either roses or a tree _____ planted in front of the house.

14. Neither she nor he _____ Spanish.

15. The cost of replacing the windows _____ covered by my insurance.

16. Neither Kathy nor the children _____ anywhere near the window.

17. A nice card _____ a person's day.

18. Shovels and plows _____ the streets after a blizzard.

19. Studying or reading _____ a productive way to spend a rainy afternoon.

20. Every Saturday, Chico and I _____ chess.

SPEAKING APPLICATION

Take turns with a partner. Use sentences with intervening clauses to tell about a trip you would love to take someday. Your partner should listen for and identify the intervening clauses in your sentences.

WRITING APPLICATION

Use sentence 13 as a model to write three similar sentences. Replace the subject in sentence 13 with three different subjects.

Confusing Subjects

Some kinds of subjects have special agreement problems.

Hard-to-Find Subjects and Inverted Sentences
Subjects that appear after verbs are said to be **inverted.**
Subject–verb order is usually inverted in questions. To find out
whether to use a singular or plural verb, mentally rearrange the
sentence into subject–verb order.

RULE
7.1.9

> A verb must still agree in number with a subject that comes
> after it.

EXAMPLE On the board **are** two dinner **specials**.

REARRANGED IN
SUBJECT–VERB ORDER
Two dinner **specials are** on the board.

The words *there* and *here* often signal an inverted sentence.
These words never function as the subject of a sentence.

EXAMPLES There **are** the news **photographs**.

Here **is** the current **information**.

Note About *There's* and *Here's*: Both of these contractions
contain the singular verb *is: there is* and *here is*. They should be
used only with singular subjects.

CORRECT **There's** only one **class** scheduled.

Here's a name **tag** to pin on your shirt. See Practice 7.1E

Subjects With Linking Verbs
Subjects with linking verbs may also cause agreement problems.

RULE
7.1.10

> A linking verb must agree with its subject, regardless of the
> number of its predicate nominative.

EXAMPLES   The **branches are** full of leaves.

The big **flood was** the motivation for building the new dam.

In the first example, the plural verb *are* agrees with the plural subject *branches*. In the next example, the singular subject *reason* takes the singular verb *is*.

Collective Nouns

Collective nouns name groups of people or things. Examples include *audience*, *class*, *club*, and *committee*.

> A collective noun takes a singular verb when the group it names acts as a single unit. A collective noun takes a plural verb when the group acts as individuals.

SINGULAR   The plane **crew leaves** in December.

(The members act as a unit.)

PLURAL   The plane **crew were going** on separate routes.

(The members act individually.)

Nouns That Look Like Plurals

Some nouns that end in -*s* are actually singular. For example, nouns that name branches of knowledge, such as *civics*, and those that name single units, such as *mumps*, take singular verbs.

> Use singular verbs to agree with nouns that are plural in form but singular in meaning.

SINGULAR   **Mathematics is** my easiest subject.

When words such as *ethics* and *politics* do not name branches of knowledge but indicate characteristics, their meanings are plural. Similarly, such words as *eyeglasses*, *pants*, and *scissors* generally take plural verbs.

PLURAL   The **acoustics** in the theater **are** excellent.

Indefinite Pronouns

Some indefinite pronouns are always singular, some are always plural, and some may be either singular or plural. Prepositional phrases do not affect subject–verb agreement.

Singular indefinite pronouns take singular verbs. Plural indefinite pronouns take plural verbs.

SINGULAR   *anybody, anyone, anything, each, either, everybody, everyone, everything, neither, nobody, no one, nothing, somebody, someone, something*

PLURAL   *both, few, many, others, several*

SINGULAR   **Everyone** on the rescue mission **has arrived**.

PLURAL   **Many** of the windows **were replaced**.

The pronouns *all, any, more, most, none,* and *some* usually take a singular verb if the antecedent is singular, and a plural verb if it is plural.

SINGULAR   **Some** of the building **was ruined** by the wind.

PLURAL   **Some** of the alliances **are** stronger than in the past.

Titles of Creative Works and Names of Organizations

Plural words in the title of a creative work or in the name of an organization do not affect subject–verb agreement.

A title of a creative work or name of an organization is singular and must have a singular verb.

EXAMPLES **Doctors without Borders is** a helpful group

in the event of a disaster.

(organization)

The ***Mona Lisa*** by Leonardo da Vinci **is** a

famous painting.

(creative work)

Amounts and Measurements

Although they appear to be plural, most amounts and measurements actually express single units or ideas.

> A noun expressing an amount or measurement is usually singular and requires a singular verb.

7.1.16 | RULE

EXAMPLES **Five hundred million dollars is** the cost to build

new highways in the state.

(*Five hundred million dollars is one sum of money.*)

Five blocks was our distance from the nearest

coffee shop.

(*Five blocks is a single distance.*)

Three quarters of the town **votes**

in the school board election.

(*Three quarters is one part of a town.*)

Half of the flowers **were uprooted**.

(*Half* refers to a number of individual flowers, and not part of an individual flower, so it is plural.)

See Practice 7.1F

PRACTICE 7.1E > **Identifying Subjects and Verbs in Inverted Sentences**

Read each sentence. Then, identify the subject and verb in each sentence.

EXAMPLE   These are the best players on the team.

ANSWER   subject: *players*; verb: *are*

1. Here are all the possible paint colors.

2. There is only one viable option to choose.

3. Can she be trusted?

4. There is no one here at the moment.

5. At the bottom of the laundry basket is your favorite pair of running shorts.

6. Along the route were various gas stations and visitor centers.

7. Where did you put my keys?

8. Among the contestants is a girl from Burundi.

9. Here is my favorite story from my childhood.

10. Are two cups of flour enough for this recipe?

PRACTICE 7.1F > **Making Verbs Agree With Confusing Subjects**

Read each sentence. Then, write the correct verb from the choices in parentheses to complete each sentence.

EXAMPLE   The film series (begins, begin) next week.

ANSWER   *begins*

11. The distance of the race (is, are) 5 kilometers.

12. Two thirds of the meal (was, were) consumed by the guests.

13. The senior class (was, were) visiting separate sites.

14. His pants (were, was) torn when he leapt over the fence.

15. *Sense and Sensibility* (is, are) a great work of literature.

16. American studies (was, were) her minor in college.

17. Several of the animals (was, were) released from captivity.

18. Everyone (agrees, agree) that the fundraiser was a huge success.

19. The least of your concerns (is, are) how to get the house ready in time.

20. Neither Charles nor Yvette (have, has) the folder.

SPEAKING APPLICATION

Take turns with a partner. Say five inverted sentences. Your partner should identify the subject and verb in each of your sentences.

WRITING APPLICATION

Write three sentences that include confusing subjects. Underline the subject in each sentence, and make sure that the verb agrees with the subject.

7.2 Pronoun–Antecedent Agreement

Like a subject and its verb, a pronoun and its antecedent must agree. An **antecedent** is the word or group of words for which the pronoun stands.

Agreement Between Personal Pronouns and Antecedents

While a subject and verb must agree only in number, a personal pronoun and its antecedent must agree in three ways.

> A personal pronoun must agree with its antecedent in number, person, and gender.

7.2.1 RULE

The **number** of a pronoun indicates whether it is singular or plural. **Person** refers to a pronoun's ability to indicate either the person speaking (first person), the person spoken to (second person), or the person, place, or thing spoken about (third person). **Gender** is the characteristic of nouns and pronouns that indicates whether the word is *masculine* (referring to males), *feminine* (referring to females), or *neuter* (referring to neither males nor females).

The only pronouns that indicate gender are third-person singular personal pronouns.

GENDER OF THIRD-PERSON SINGULAR PRONOUNS	
Masculine	*he, him, his*
Feminine	*she, her, hers*
Neuter	*it, its*

In the example below, the pronoun *her* agrees with the antecedent *First Lady* in number (both are singular), in person (both are third person), and in gender (both are feminine).

EXAMPLE   The First Lady shared **her** dreams with the
reporter.

Agreement in Number

There are three rules to keep in mind to determine the number of compound antecedents.

Use a singular personal pronoun when two or more singular antecedents are joined by *or* or *nor*.

EXAMPLES   Either Kate **or** Brianna will bring **her** sample of a casserole to the sale.

Neither Bianca **nor** Belinda will wear **her** new dress tonight.

Use a plural personal pronoun when two or more antecedents are joined by *and*.

EXAMPLE   Bobby **and** I are training for **our** marathon.

An exception occurs when a distinction must be made between individual and joint ownership. If individual ownership is intended, use a singular pronoun to refer to a compound antecedent. If joint ownership is intended, use a plural pronoun.

SINGULAR   **Ben and Adie** read **her** favorite book.

PLURAL   **Bea and Adie** bought **their** favorite books.

SINGULAR   Neither **Alice nor Rosalie** let me use **her** cellphone.

PLURAL   Neither **Alice nor Rosalie** let me use **their** cellphone.

The third rule applies to compound antecedents whose parts are mixed in number.

Use a plural personal pronoun if any part of a compound antecedent joined by *or* or *nor* is plural.

See Practice 7.2A

EXAMPLE   If either the **agent** or the **actresses**
arrive, take **them** to the VIP lounge.

Agreement in Person and Gender Avoid shifts in person or gender
of pronouns.

> As part of pronoun–antecedent agreement, take care not to shift
> either person or gender.

RULE 7.2.5

SHIFT IN
PERSON
Vincent is planning to visit Italy because **you**
can taste authentic Italian food.

CORRECT
Vincent is planning to visit Italy because **he**
wants to taste authentic Italian food.

SHIFT IN
GENDER
The **lion** threw **its** head back, roared, and stood
on **his** hind legs.

CORRECT
The **lion** threw **its** head back, roared, and stood
on **its** hind legs.

Generic Masculine Pronouns Traditionally, a masculine pronoun
has been used to refer to a singular antecedent whose gender is
unknown. Such use is called *generic* because it applies to both
masculine and feminine genders. Many writers now prefer to use
his or her, he or she, him or her, or to rephrase a sentence to
eliminate the situation.

> When gender is not specified, either use *his or her* or rewrite
> the sentence.

RULE 7.2.6

EXAMPLES   Each **player** found a useful playbook in which
to record **his or her plays** during the game.

Players found useful playbooks in which
See Practice 7.2B
to record **their plays** during the game.

PRACTICE 7.2A Making Personal Pronouns Agree With Their Antecedents

Read each sentence. Then, rewrite each sentence to include the correct personal pronoun. If the sentence is correct, write *correct.*

EXAMPLE   My brothers and I are planning a surprise for their parents.

ANSWER   *My brothers and I are planning a surprise for our parents.*

1. Neither of the birds ate their seeds.

2. Joe and Laura's sister can't find their toothbrush.

3. Neither Sean nor John had any trouble choosing their topic.

4. The doctor and his assistant published her discoveries.

5. The boy used his hands to make shadow animals.

6. Danielle and her brother are coaching her sister's soccer team.

7. When my parents and my brother ski, he always wear a helmet.

8. Either Julio or Pete will shave their beard.

9. The Brady twins rode their bikes home.

10. Boris and Leo improved his performance by practicing more often.

PRACTICE 7.2B Revising for Agreement in Person and Gender

Read each sentence. Then, revise each sentence so that the personal pronoun agrees with the antecedent.

EXAMPLE   With a gleam in his eyes, the baby shook its rattle.

ANSWER   *With a gleam in his eyes, the baby shook his rattle.*

11. Each girl must submit their report.

12. Those hikers will soon realize that you cannot walk for miles in unsturdy shoes.

13. Either Jerome or Ralph can use their ticket for the ride.

14. We learned in chemistry that you should record all of your observations.

15. All of the team members washed his or her uniform.

16. Meghan's doll looks as if she is real.

17. Their mother accompanied each athlete.

18. The welders wear goggles so that your eyes will be protected.

19. As the car pulled away, it left a trail of smoke in his wake.

20. A bee's sting is her defense.

SPEAKING APPLICATION

Take turns with a partner. Tell each other about a family pet or a favorite relative. Use several different pronouns in your sentences. Your partner should name the personal pronouns you use and tell if they agree with their antecedents.

WRITING APPLICATION

Use sentences 14, 15, and 19 as models to write similar sentences. Then, exchange papers with a partner. Your partner should revise each sentence to make the personal pronoun agree with the antecedent.

Agreement With Indefinite Pronouns

When an indefinite pronoun, such as *each, all,* or *most,* is used with a personal pronoun, the pronouns must agree.

> **Use a plural personal pronoun when the antecedent is a plural indefinite pronoun.**

7.2.7 RULE

EXAMPLES **Many** of the graduates were excited about **their** college choices.

All the graduates remembered to bring **their** caps.

When both pronouns are singular, a similar rule applies.

> **Use a singular personal pronoun when the antecedent is a singular indefinite pronoun.**

7.2.8 RULE

In the first example, the personal pronoun *his* agrees in number with the singular indefinite pronoun *one.* The gender (masculine) is determined by the word *boys.*

EXAMPLES Only **one** of the boys studied **his** class notes.

One of the boys remembered to bring **his** notes.

If other words in the sentence do not indicate a gender, you may use *him or her, he or she, his or her* or rephrase the sentence.

EXAMPLES **Each** of the politicians practiced **his or her** stump speech.

The **politicians** practiced **their** stump speeches.

For indefinite pronouns that can be either singular or plural, such as *all, any, more, most, none,* and *some,* agreement depends on the antecedent of the indefinite pronoun.

EXAMPLES   **Most** of the trip had lost **its** excitement.
(The antecedent of *most* is *trip,* which is singular.)

Most of the customers wanted **their** accounts credited.
(The antecedent of *most* is *customers,* which is plural.)

Some of the book **was** too torn to read.
(The antecedent of *some* is *book,* which is singular.)

All of the rackets **were** on the shelf in the garage.
(The antecedent of *all* is *rackets,* which is plural.)

In some situations, strict grammatical agreement may be illogical. In these situations, either let the meaning of the sentence determine the number of the personal pronoun, or reword the sentence.

ILLOGICAL   When **each of the pagers** buzzed, I answered **it** as quickly as possible.

MORE LOGICAL   When **each of the pagers** buzzed, I answered **them** as quickly as possible.

MORE LOGICAL   When **all of the pagers** buzzed, I answered **them** as quickly as possible.   See Practice 7.2C

Agreement With Reflexive Pronouns

Reflexive pronouns, which end in *-self* or *-selves,* should only refer to a word earlier in the same sentence.

RULE 7.2.9

A reflexive pronoun must agree with an antecedent that is clearly stated.

EXAMPLES   **Benjamin** threw a party for **himself**.

You should consider **yourself** special.

Efficient **workers** would rather handle things **themselves**.   See Practice 7.2D

PRACTICE 7.2C	**Making Personal and Indefinite Pronouns Agree**

Read each sentence. Then, fill in the blanks with an appropriate personal pronoun that agrees with the indefinite pronoun to complete each sentence.

EXAMPLE   Each of the girls has sold _____ quota of cookies.

ANSWER   *her*

1. Most of the fans brought blankets with _____.
2. No one on the girls' team wears _____ cap at a meet.
3. Much of the glass has smudges on _____.
4. Few of the voters changed _____ minds after the debate.
5. I think some of the tourists brought cameras with _____.
6. None of the students handed in _____ assignments late.
7. Most of the furniture has scratches on _____.
8. Everyone in the club brings _____ own opinions to the meetings.
9. Has any boy decided on _____ project yet?
10. All of the musicians are tuning _____ instruments.

PRACTICE 7.2D	**Supplying Reflexive Pronouns**

Read each sentence. Then, fill in the blanks by writing the correct reflexive pronoun that agrees with the antecedent in each sentence.

EXAMPLE   Carlos wrote _____ a message.

ANSWER   *himself*

11. Christina and he left by _____.
12. Myra bought _____ a new jacket.
13. Pablo and I can handle the nominations committee's work by _____.
14. Steve made _____ a costume.
15. Grandma's stories about how she got _____ into sticky situations are very amusing.
16. Mom knitted _____ a sweater.
17. The babies look at _____ in the mirror.
18. Please make _____ comfortable in the living room.
19. Gina helped _____ to some mashed potatoes.
20. The lady fanned _____ to cool down.

SPEAKING APPLICATION

Take turns with a partner. Choose three indefinite pronouns. Your partner should say sentences, using a personal pronoun that agrees with each indefinite pronoun.

WRITING APPLICATION

Use sentences 11, 12, and 18 as models to write three similar sentences. Then, exchange papers with a partner. Your partner should rewrite each sentence, using the correct reflexive pronoun that agrees with the antecedent.

7.3 Special Problems With Pronoun Agreement

This section will show you how to avoid some common errors that can obscure the meaning of your sentences.

Vague Pronoun References

One basic rule governs all of the rules for pronoun reference.

> **To avoid confusion, a pronoun requires an antecedent that is either stated or clearly understood.**

The pronouns *which, this, that,* and *these* should not be used to refer to a vague or overly general idea.

In the following example, it is impossible to determine exactly what the pronoun *these* stands for because it may refer to three different groups of words.

VAGUE REFERENCE	Kay was singing, the guests were happy, and the catered food was delicious. **These** made our birthday party a joyful occasion.

This vague reference can be corrected in two ways. One way is to change the pronoun to an adjective that modifies a specific noun. The second way is to revise the sentence so that the pronoun *these* is eliminated.

CORRECT	Kay was singing, the guests were happy, and the catered food was delicious. **These pleasures** made our birthday party a joyful occasion.
CORRECT	Kay's singing, the guests' happiness, and the delicious catered food made our birthday party a joyful occasion.

The personal pronouns *it, they,* and *you* should always have a clear antecedent.

7.3.2   RULE

In the next example, the pronoun *it* has no clearly stated antecedent.

VAGUE REFERENCE   Winnie is studying medical advancements next month. **It** should be very educational.

Again, there are two methods of correction. The first method is to replace the personal pronoun with a specific noun. The second method is to revise the sentence entirely in order to make the whole idea clear.

CORRECT   Winnie is studying medical advancements next month. **The experience** should be very educational.

CORRECT   **Winnie's study** of medical advancements should be very educational.

In the next example, the pronoun *they* is used without an accurate antecedent.

VAGUE REFERENCE   I enjoyed reading Shakespeare in class, but **he** never explained his symbolism in tragedy.

CORRECT   I enjoyed reading Shakespeare in class, but **the professor** never explained Shakespeare's symbolism in tragedy.

VAGUE REFERENCE   When we arrived at the game, **they** told us which player was about to throw the opening pitch.

CORRECT   When we arrived at the game, **the announcer** told us which player was about to throw the opening pitch.

Use *you* only when the reference is truly to the reader or listener.

VAGUE
REFERENCE
You couldn't understand a word the musician sang.

CORRECT
We couldn't understand a word the musician sang.

VAGUE
REFERENCE
In the school my grandfather went to, **you** were expected to be polite to everyone.

CORRECT
In the school my grandfather went to, **students** were expected to be polite to everyone.

Note About *It*: In many idiomatic expressions, the personal pronoun *it* has no specific antecedent. In statements such as "It is late," *it* is an idiom that is accepted as standard English.

See Practice 7.3A

Ambiguous Pronoun References

A pronoun is **ambiguous** if it can refer to more than one antecedent.

A pronoun should never refer to more than one antecedent.

In the following sentence, *he* is confusing because it can refer to either *Wilson* or *Jason*. Revise such a sentence by changing the pronoun to a noun or rephrasing the sentence entirely.

AMBIGUOUS
REFERENCE
Wilson told Jason about the dolphins **he** spotted.

CORRECT
Wilson told Jason about the dolphins **Wilson** spotted.

(Wilson knew about the dolphins.)

Do not repeat a personal pronoun in a sentence if it can refer to a different antecedent each time.

AMBIGUOUS REPETITION	When Tina asked her mother if **she** could borrow the earrings, **she** said that **she** needed them.
CLEAR	When Tina asked her mother if **she** could borrow the earrings, **Tina** said that **she** needed them.
CLEAR	When Tina asked her mother if **she** could borrow the earrings, her **mother** said that **she** needed them **herself**.

Notice that in the first sentence above, it is unclear whether *her* is referring to Tina or to her mother. To eliminate the confusion, Tina's name was used in the second sentence. In the third sentence, the reflexive pronoun *herself* helps to clarify the meaning.

Avoiding Distant Pronoun References

A pronoun should be placed close to its antecedent.

> **A personal pronoun should always be close enough to its antecedent to prevent confusion.**

7.3.6 RULE

A distant pronoun reference can be corrected by moving the pronoun closer to its antecedent or by changing the pronoun to a noun. In the example below, *it* is too far from the antecedent *knee*.

| DISTANT REFERENCE | Betty shifted her weight from her injured knee. Three days ago, she had slipped and fallen down the stairs. Now **it** was in a brace. |
| CORRECT | Betty shifted her weight from her injured knee. Three days ago, she had slipped and fallen down the stairs. Now her **knee** was in a brace. (*Knee* replace the pronoun *it*.) |

See Practice 7.3B

PRACTICE 7.3A > **Correcting Vague Pronouns**

Read each sentence. Then, rewrite each sentence to avoid the use of vague pronouns.

EXAMPLE At the annual picnic, they always feature fried chicken.

ANSWER *The annual picnic always features fried chicken.*

1. It was past midnight when the snow stopped.
2. In that game, you can only reach "home" with an exact roll of the dice.
3. In Boston, they often drop their *r*'s.
4. It isn't fun going to a party alone.
5. It suggests in the article that Andrews is running for office.
6. The boys promptly wrote thank-you notes, which shocked their mother.
7. During the fire drill, they spoke about safety.
8. They can't do anything to prevent the crops from freezing.
9. She heard that they had discovered a new type of fuel.
10. To make a claim on the frontier, you had to live there.

PRACTICE 7.3B > **Recognizing Ambiguous Pronouns**

Read each sentence. Then, rewrite each sentence to avoid the use of ambiguous pronouns.

EXAMPLE Phillippe told Jack that he would wait until after his football practice.

ANSWER *Phillippe told Jack that he would wait until after Jack's football practice.*

11. Siobhan and Barbara shared her lunch.
12. After Nancy had spoken to Rebecca, she felt much calmer.
13. Mr. Patel asked Tate to repeat the experiment he had just completed.
14. The approaches to the bridges were clogged, as they often were at rush hour.
15. The window looked out over the garden, but it was overgrown with weeds.
16. While Bert wheeled his small son around the park, he was very content.
17. Kumar informed Hank that he would have to leave soon.
18. The coach told James that he would not renew his contract.
19. Alice told Bella that she was getting a promotion.
20. Plant the bulbs by the new bushes and water them.

SPEAKING APPLICATION

Take turns with a partner. Use sentences from Practice 7.3A as models to say similar sentences that contain vague pronoun references. Your partner should reword each sentence to make it clearer.

WRITING APPLICATION

Use sentences 11, 13, and 15 as models to write similar sentences. Then, exchange papers with a partner. Your partner should rewrite each sentence, correcting the ambiguous pronoun references.

USING MODIFIERS

Knowing how to use modifiers to make comparisons will help you write vivid descriptions.

CHAPTER 8

WRITE GUY *Jeff Anderson, M.Ed.*

WHAT DO YOU NOTICE?

Focus on comparisons as you zoom in on these lines from the poem "Song" by John Donne.

MENTOR TEXT

> Sweetest love, I do not go,
>   For weariness of thee,
> Nor in hope the world can show
>   A fitter love for me . . .

Now, ask yourself the following questions:

- Which degrees of comparison does the poet use?
- What comparisons are made?

The adjective *sweetest* is in the superlative degree, as shown by the ending *-est,* and the *-er* ending on the adjective *fitter* shows the comparative degree. The speaker of the poem compares the person he loves to all others when he says *sweetest.* By using the adjective *fitter,* the poet compares his love to the love the world could show him.

Grammar for Writers Writers can use different degrees of comparison to create more interesting and dynamic descriptions. Check how many items you are comparing to figure out which degree to use.

How can I compare thee to a summer's day?

You could say I was cooler.

8.1 Degrees of Comparison

In the English language, there are three degrees, or forms, of most adjectives and adverbs that are used in comparisons.

Recognizing Degrees of Comparison

In order to write effective comparisons, you first need to know the three degrees.

The three degrees of comparison are the positive, the comparative, and the superlative.

The following chart shows adjectives and adverbs in each of the three degrees. Notice the three different ways that modifiers are changed to show degree: (1) by adding -*er* or -*est*, (2) by adding *more* or *most*, and (3) by using entirely different words.

DEGREES OF ADJECTIVES		
POSITIVE	COMPARATIVE	SUPERLATIVE
funny	funnier	funniest
pleasant	more pleasant	most pleasant
bad	worse	worst
DEGREES OF ADVERBS		
slowly	more slowly	most slowly
pleasantly	more pleasantly	most pleasantly
badly	worse	worst

See Practice 8.1A

Regular Forms

Adjectives and adverbs can be either **regular** or **irregular,** depending on how their comparative and superlative degrees are formed. The degrees of most adjectives and adverbs are formed regularly. The number of syllables in regular modifiers determines how their degrees are formed.

Use -*er* or *more* to form the comparative degree and -*est* or *most* to form the superlative degree of most one- and two-syllable modifiers.

EXAMPLES	silly	sillier	silliest
	careful	more careful	most careful

> **All adverbs that end in -*ly* form their comparative and superlative degrees with *more* and *most*.**

EXAMPLES	cleverly	more cleverly	most cleverly
	cowardly	more cowardly	most cowardly

> **Use *more* and *most* to form the comparative and superlative degrees of all modifiers with three or more syllables.**

EXAMPLES	delicate	more delicate	most delicate
	dependable	more dependable	most dependable

Note About Comparisons With *Less* and *Least*: *Less* and *least* can be used to form another version of the comparative and superlative degrees of most modifiers.

See Practice 8.1B

EXAMPLES	delicate	less delicate	least delicate
	dependable	less dependable	least dependable

Irregular Forms

The comparative and superlative degrees of a few commonly used adjectives and adverbs are formed in unpredictable ways.

> **The irregular comparative and superlative forms of certain adjectives and adverbs must be memorized.**

In the chart on the following page, the form of some irregular modifiers differs only in the positive degree. The modifiers *bad*, *badly*, and *ill*, for example, all have the same comparative and superlative degrees *(worse, worst)*.

IRREGULAR MODIFIERS		
POSITIVE	COMPARATIVE	SUPERLATIVE
bad, badly, ill	worse	worst
far (distance)	farther	farthest
far (extent)	further	furthest
good, well	better	best
late	later	last or latest
little (amount)	less	least
many, much	more	most

RULE
 8.1.6

Bad is an adjective. Do not use it to modify an action verb. *Badly* is an adverb. Use it after an action verb but not after a linking verb.

INCORRECT   The chorus sang its program **bad**.

CORRECT   The chorus sang its program **badly**.

INCORRECT   Our team feels **badly** about losing the game.

CORRECT   Our team feels **bad** about losing the game.

Note About *Good* and *Well*: *Good* is always an adjective and cannot be used as an adverb after an action verb. It can, however, be used as a predicate adjective after a linking verb.

INCORRECT   My band played **good** at last night's concert.

CORRECT   My band sounded **good** at last night's concert.

Well is generally an adverb. However, when *well* means "healthy," it is an adjective and can be used after a linking verb.

CORRECT   Marnie plays chess **well**.

CORRECT   Marnie should be **well** soon.

See Practice 8.1C
See Practice 8.1D

PRACTICE 8.1A > **Recognizing Positive, Comparative, and Superlative Degrees of Comparison**

Read each sentence. Then, identify the degree of comparison of the underlined word or words as *positive*, *comparative*, or *superlative*.

EXAMPLE   They have been waiting <u>longer</u> than we have.

ANSWER   *comparative*

1. The room will look <u>brighter</u> with a fresh coat of paint.
2. We congratulated the <u>proud</u> parents.
3. That was the <u>heaviest</u> rainfall to date.
4. Greta was voted <u>most likely</u> to succeed.
5. If I had been <u>more careful</u>, I wouldn't have made that mistake.
6. Luviano's serves the <u>spiciest</u> food in town.
7. The cat moved <u>stealthily</u> along the side of the house.
8. Surely the koala bear is one of the <u>laziest</u> animals.
9. An ice pack may make you feel <u>more comfortable</u>.
10. The stubborn child shook his head <u>vigorously</u>.

PRACTICE 8.1B > **Forming Regular Comparative and Superlative Degrees of Comparison**

Read each sentence. Then, rewrite each sentence with the correct comparative or superlative degree of the modifier indicated in parentheses.

EXAMPLE   My uncle was _____ than I expected. (generous)

ANSWER   *My uncle was more generous than I expected.*

11. This chair is _____ than that one. (comfortable)
12. Anthony made the mistake of wearing the _____ of his shirts. (itchy)
13. That shirt is the _____ of all the shirts on display. (bright)
14. I am _____ than I was yesterday. (sleepy)
15. Carly is _____ now than ever before. (happy)
16. These apples will ripen _____ if they are put in a paper bag. (quickly)
17. Please let me try on the _____ size. (small)
18. I was _____ by her attitude than by her lateness. (disappointed)
19. I am never _____ than when I relax on the swing. (tranquil)
20. That picture is the _____ of them all. (stunning)

SPEAKING APPLICATION

Take turns with a partner. Compare the size of objects found in your classroom. Use comparative, superlative, and positive degrees of comparison. Your partner should listen for and identify which degree of comparison you are using.

WRITING APPLICATION

Rewrite sentences 13, 15, and 17, changing the modifiers in parentheses. Then, exchange papers with a partner. Your partner should write the correct degree of the modifiers you provided.

PRACTICE 8.1C Supplying Irregular Comparative and Superlative Forms

Read each modifier. Then, write its irregular comparative and superlative forms.

EXAMPLE   good

ANSWER   *better, best*

1. much
2. ill
3. badly
4. many
5. well
6. late
7. bad
8. little (amount)
9. far (extent)
10. far (distance)

PRACTICE 8.1D Supplying Irregular Modifiers

Read each sentence. Then, fill in the blank with the form of the modifier in parentheses that best completes each sentence.

EXAMPLE   I delivered my monologue in the play _____ than I ever had before. (good)

ANSWER   *better*

11. Cheryl was clearly the _____ player in the game tonight. (good)
12. Denora was the _____ student in the class to hand in her paper. (late)
13. Six miles is the _____ I have ever run. (far)
14. I felt terrible yesterday, but I'm feeling _____ today. (well)
15. According to the poll, _____ people favor the independent candidate. (many)
16. My dad said that buying a new television was the _____ thing from his mind at the time. (far)
17. The doctor was treating the _____ case of hiccups that she had ever encountered. (bad)
18. Hudson plays the clarinet really _____ . (good)
19. Scottie feels lightheaded, but Ilene seems even _____ . (bad)
20. The lid will probably fit better if you apply _____ pressure. (little)

SPEAKING APPLICATION

Take turns with a partner. Say sentences with irregular comparative and superlative forms. Your partner should listen for and identify the irregular comparative and superlative forms.

WRITING APPLICATION

Write pairs of sentences using the following modifiers correctly: *more* and *most, better* and *best, less* and *least, farthest* and *furthest*.

8.2 Making Clear Comparisons

The comparative and superlative degrees help you make comparisons that are clear and logical.

Using Comparative and Superlative Degrees

One basic rule that has two parts covers the correct use of comparative and superlative forms.

8.2.1 | RULE

> Use the **comparative degree** to compare two persons, places, or things. Use the **superlative degree** to compare three or more persons, places, or things.

The context of a sentence should indicate whether two items or more than two items are being compared.

COMPARATIVE Driving a car is **harder** than it looks.

I'm **less confident** than I thought I'd be.

Gas **costs more** than I thought it would.

SUPERLATIVE Driving a car is the **hardest** thing I've done.

I'm the **least confident** driver in the class.

Gas is **most expensive** at the station on Broadway.

In informal writing, the superlative degree is sometimes used just for emphasis, without any specific comparison.

EXAMPLE Ella was **most treacherously** betrayed.

Note About Double Comparisons: A double comparison is caused by using both -er and more or both -est and most to form a regular modifier or by adding an extra comparison form to an irregular modifier.

See Practice 8.2A
See Practice 8.2B

INCORRECT Jane is **more younger** than my sister Meg.

CORRECT Jane is **younger** than my sister Meg.

PRACTICE 8.2A Supplying the Comparative and Superlative Degrees of Modifiers

Read each sentence. Then, fill in the blank with the correct form of the underlined modifier.

EXAMPLE   The film is <u>good</u>, but the book is
_____.

ANSWER   *better*

1. The old line of cars is selling <u>well</u>, but we hope the new line will sell even _____.

2. We drove <u>far</u> to reach the store and even _____ to reach a restaurant.

3. Marilyn looks <u>better</u> in green than in blue, but she looks _____ in red.

4. Jonas has <u>little</u> patience for board games and even _____ for word games.

5. Camilla has <u>much</u> interest in chemistry and even _____ in physics.

6. I ran quite <u>far</u> yesterday, but I intend to run even _____ today.

7. There were <u>many</u> guests at Hakim's party, but there were _____ at Marshall's.

8. I still feel <u>ill</u> this morning, but I felt _____ last night after I ate.

9. He arrived <u>late</u>, but I arrived even _____.

10. She is <u>shy</u>, but Yen is the _____ in the class.

PRACTICE 8.2B Revising Sentences to Correct Errors in Modifier Usage

Read each sentence. Then, rewrite each sentence, correcting any errors in the usage of modifiers to make comparisons. If a sentence contains no errors, write *correct*.

EXAMPLE   Adam is tallest than his friend Harry.

ANSWER   *Adam is taller than his friend Harry.*

11. Which of your parents is most likely to drive us to school?

12. The movie was worst than we expected.

13. Which of the two campsites is farthest?

14. Sean arrived at the library more later than Tommy.

15. Jeremy's plan is most viable than Katie's plan.

16. Edgar is the better player on the football team.

17. Kairi is the more talented of her three sisters.

18. Winston is the funnier student in our class.

19. This road will be the muddiest in town after the snow melts.

20. Wear a warmest coat and leave the other in the closet.

SPEAKING APPLICATION

Take turns with a partner. Compare two movies. Your partner should listen for and identify the comparisons in your sentences.

WRITING APPLICATION

Write three sentences with errors in modifier usage. Then, exchange papers with a partner. Your partner should correct your sentences.

Using Logical Comparisons

Two common usage problems are the comparison of unrelated items and the comparison of something with itself.

Balanced Comparisons
Be certain that things being compared in a sentence are similar.

> **Your sentences should only compare items of a similar kind.**

8.2.2 RULE

The following unbalanced sentences illogically compare dissimilar things.

UNBALANCED   I prefer **Monet's paintings** to **Renoir**.

CORRECT   I prefer **Monet's paintings** to **Renoir's**.

UNBALANCED   The **length of the sofa** is longer than the **wall**.

CORRECT   The **length of the sofa** is longer than the **length of the wall**.

Note About *Other* **and** *Else* **in Comparisons**
Another illogical comparison results when something is inadvertently compared with itself.

> **When comparing one of a group with the rest of the group, make sure that your sentence contains the word** *other* **or the word** *else*.

8.2.3 RULE

Adding *other* or *else* when comparing one person or thing with a group will make the comparison clear and logical.

ILLOGICAL   Dad's meals are tastier than anybody's.
(Dad's meals cannot be tastier than themselves.)

See Practice 8.2C
See Practice 8.2D

LOGICAL   Dad's meals are tastier than anybody **else's**.

PRACTICE 8.2C ▶ Revising to Make Comparisons Balanced and Logical

Read each sentence. Then, rewrite each sentence, correcting the unbalanced or illogical comparison.

EXAMPLE   Andre's car is newer than his mother.

ANSWER   *Andre's car is newer than his mother's.*

1. My grandmother is older than anyone in the family.

2. The damage from yesterday's snowstorm is greater than last month.

3. Katya's dress is prettier than Jennifer.

4. Teddy's bowl of noodles was bigger than his father.

5. The test Freddie took is harder than Sonny.

6. Mr. Cassar lived longer than anyone in his family.

7. The boy who sits next to me speaks Spanish more fluently than anyone.

8. Your bonsai plant looks healthier than my sister.

9. At that store, shoes are less expensive than this store.

10. The Bulldogs are better than any football team.

PRACTICE 8.2D ▶ Writing Clear Comparisons

Read each sentence. Then, rewrite each sentence, filling in the blanks to make a comparison that is clear and logical.

EXAMPLE   John's voice is deeper than _____.

ANSWER   *John's voice is deeper than Pete's.*

11. Dionne's work is more legible than _____.

12. The storm we had on Saturday night was worse than _____.

13. Feeding the whales is more fun than _____.

14. Contact with poison ivy can hurt as much as _____.

15. Listening to music is more relaxing than _____.

16. A moose's antlers are bigger than _____.

17. His report on the history of Japan was more fascinating than _____ report.

18. Ask Margie to check the records because she is more thorough than _____.

19. The colors in that painting are similar to _____.

20. Wing's paper is longer than _____ in the class.

SPEAKING APPLICATION

Take turns with a partner. Say sentences that have unbalanced or illogical comparisons. Your partner should restate your sentences, using balanced and logical comparisons.

WRITING APPLICATION

Use sentences 11, 13, and 17 as models to write similar sentences. Then, exchange papers with a partner. Your partner should fill in the blanks to make the comparison in each sentence clear and logical.

Avoiding Comparisons With Absolute Modifiers

Some modifiers cannot be used logically to make comparisons because their meanings are *absolute*—that is, their meanings are entirely contained in the positive degree. For example, if a line is *vertical*, another line cannot be *more* vertical. Some other common absolute modifiers are *dead, entirely, fatal, final, identical, infinite, opposite, perfect, right, straight,* and *unique.*

> **Avoid using absolute modifiers illogically in comparisons.**

8.2.4 RULE

INCORRECT	The leaves on the trees look **more dead** in winter.
CORRECT	The leaves on the trees look **dead** in winter.

Often, it is not only the word *more* or *most* that makes an absolute modifier illogical; sometimes it is best to replace the absolute modifier with one that expresses the intended meaning more precisely.

ILLOGICAL	Some people believe that the stock exchange is the **most perfect** way to set prices.
CORRECT	Some people believe that the stock exchange is the **best** way to set prices.

Sometimes an absolute modifier may overstate the meaning that you want.

ILLOGICAL	The soccer loss to the rival team was the **most fatal** to our record this year.
CORRECT	The soccer loss to the rival team was the **most severe** to our record this year.

See Practice 8.2E
See Practice 8.2F

In the preceding example, *most fatal* is illogical because something is either fatal or it is not. However, even *fatal* is an overstatement. *Most severe* better conveys the intended meaning.

PRACTICE 8.2E > **Revising Sentences to Correct Comparisons Using Absolute Modifiers**

Read each sentence. Then, correct each illogical comparison by using more precise words.

EXAMPLE   The universe may be very infinite.

ANSWER   *The universe may be infinite.*

1. Jason's opinions are the most opposite of mine.

2. This model comes in a more infinite number of colors than that one.

3. Be sure the two poles are most perpendicular.

4. The judge's decision is extremely absolute.

5. The two lines in the figure on this page are more parallel.

6. Mom should treat us more equally.

7. His report was more complete than mine.

8. This step is more irrevocable than the last one.

9. A scorpion's sting is more fatal than the bite of a brown recluse spider.

10. The flowers I picked yesterday are less dead than the ones you picked.

PRACTICE 8.2F > **Revising Overstated Absolute Modifiers**

Read each sentence. Then, rewrite each sentence, revising the overstated absolute modifier.

EXAMPLE   He has a very unique personality.

ANSWER   *He has a unique personality.*

11. Those two movies are the most identical films I have ever seen.

12. Luis executed the jump shot with a very perfect throw.

13. Turtles can live a long time, but they are not extremely immortal.

14. Juan was determined to do his very absolute best on the test.

15. That pile of papers is more unequal to this one.

16. The results of the election are extremely final.

17. The need for food and shelter is a very universal requirement of all living things.

18. After the storm, the electricity in our house went completely dead.

19. Love can be more eternal than beauty.

20. Roger's new portrait is the most perfect.

SPEAKING APPLICATION

Take turns with a partner. Say sentences that incorrectly use absolute modifiers. Your partner should restate your sentences correctly.

WRITING APPLICATION

Write three sentences with overstated absolute modifiers. Then, exchange papers with a partner. Your partner should revise the overstated absolute modifiers in your sentences.

CHAPTER 9

MISCELLANEOUS PROBLEMS *in* USAGE

To make your writing clearer and more precise, learn the rules for avoiding common problems in usage.

WRITE GUY *Jeff Anderson, M.Ed.*

WHAT DO YOU NOTICE?

Look for pronouns as you zoom in on lines from the poem "The Prelude" by William Wordsworth.

MENTOR TEXT

> And the errors into which I fell, betrayed
> By present objects, and by reasonings false
> From their beginnings, inasmuch as drawn
> Out of a heart that had been turned aside . . .

Now, ask yourself the following questions:

- To what do the pronouns *which* and *that* refer?
- To what does the pronoun *their* refer?

The relative pronouns *which* and *that* are used to refer to things. In the lines above, *which* refers to the noun *errors* and *that* refers to the noun *heart*. The possessive pronoun *their* shows ownership and refers to the noun *reasonings*.

Grammar for Writers Writers can choose from a variety of pronouns to make their writing less repetitive and more interesting. You can avoid some common usage problems by carefully selecting the pronouns that you use in your writing.

Who is a relative pronoun.

To whose relatives are you referring?

9.1 Negative Sentences

In English, only one *no* is needed in a sentence to deny or refuse something. You can express a negative idea with words such as *not* or *never* or with contractions such as *can't, couldn't,* and *wasn't.* (The ending *-n't* in a contraction is an abbreviation of *not.*)

Recognizing Double Negatives

Using two negative words in a sentence when one is sufficient is called a **double negative.** While double negatives may sometimes be used in informal speech, they should be avoided in formal English speech and writing.

RULE 9.1.1

Do not use **double negatives** in formal writing.

The following chart provides examples of double negatives and two ways each can be corrected.

DOUBLE NEGATIVE	CORRECTIONS
I haven't seen no new movies.	I haven't seen any new movies. I have seen no new movies.
I don't have no money for tickets.	I don't have any money for tickets. I have no money for tickets.
I never see nothing when I'm saving money.	I never see anything when I'm saving money. I see nothing when I'm saving money.

Sentences that contain more than one clause can correctly contain more than one negative word. Each clause, however, should contain only one negative word.

EXAMPLES   Because the ball **didn't** go through the goalposts, it **wasn't** a field goal.

When a ball **isn't** properly centered, the kicker **can't** kick it accurately.

Forming Negative Sentences Correctly

There are three common ways to form negative sentences.

Using One Negative Word The most common ways to make a statement negative are to use one **negative word,** such as *never, no,* or *none,* or to add the contraction *-n't* to a helping verb.

> **Use only one negative word in each clause.**

9.1.2 RULE

DOUBLE NEGATIVE	Michael **isn't never** going to beat that time.
PREFERRED	Michael **isn't ever** going to beat that time.
	Michael **is never** going to beat that time.

Using *But* in a Negative Sense When *but* means "only," it usually acts as a negative. Do not use it with another negative word.

DOUBLE NEGATIVE	My paper **didn't** need **but** one more source.
PREFERRED	My paper needed **but** one more source.
	My paper needed **only** one more source.

Using *Barely, Hardly,* and *Scarcely* Each of these words is negative. If you use one of these words with another negative word, you create a double negative.

> **Do not use *barely, hardly,* or *scarcely* with another negative word.**

9.1.3 RULE

DOUBLE NEGATIVE	Our class **hasn't hardly** begun to study space.
PREFERRED	Our class **has hardly** begun to study space.
DOUBLE NEGATIVE	It was cloudy, so the stars **weren't barely** visible.
PREFERRED	It was cloudy, so the stars **were barely** visible.
DOUBLE NEGATIVE	I **couldn't scarcely** even see the moon.
PREFERRED	I **could scarcely** even see the moon.

See Practice 9.1A

Using Negatives to Create Understatement

Sometimes a writer wants to express an idea indirectly, either to minimize the importance of the idea or to draw attention to it. One such technique is called **understatement.**

> Understatement can be achieved by using a negative word and a word with a negative prefix, such as *un-, in-, im-, dis-,* and *under-.*

EXAMPLES   That new movie is **hardly uninteresting** .

I **wasn't uninvolved** with the characters, particularly the leads.

I did **not underestimate** my interest in the plot.

These examples show that the writer is praising the people or things he or she is discussing. In the first example, the writer states that the movie is interesting. In the second example, the writer states that he or she was involved with the characters, especially the leads. In the third example, the writer states that he or she was intersted in the plot.

If you choose to use understatement, be sure to use it carefully so that you do not sound critical when you wish to praise.

EXAMPLES   Although the plot sounded familiar, her short story **wasn't uninvolving** .

She had published the story, so I guess I **shouldn't underestimate** her talent.

In both examples above, the writer is actually making a negative statement. In the first example, the writer thinks the plot is familiar, but still involving. In the second example, the writer seems to think that, because the story was published, the writer must have some talent.

See Practice 9.1B

Revising Sentences to Avoid Double Negatives

Read each sentence. Then, rewrite each sentence to correct the double negative.

EXAMPLE   I won't never tell.

ANSWER   *I won't ever tell.*

1. Miss Conklin had not heard nothing about a special program.

2. We don't have no tickets for tonight's concert.

3. Carlos won't never make that mistake again.

4. Don't hide the keys nowhere obvious.

5. The witness hadn't seen no one suspicious.

6. The professor wouldn't accept no late papers.

7. Paul never did nothing to antagonize the crew members.

8. You should not drive that car nowhere without snow tires.

9. Hardly no one knew the answers on the exam.

10. I can't find my address book nowhere.

Using Negatives to Create Understatement

Read each item. Then, use each item to create understatement.

EXAMPLE   impervious

ANSWER   *Adam isn't impervious to delicious desserts.*

11. incorrect

12. unaffected

13. immature

14. underfed

15. improbable

16. disowned

17. uninterested

18. uninsured

19. indescribable

20. immaterial

SPEAKING APPLICATION

Take turns with a partner. Say sentences that contain double negatives. Your partner should listen to and correct your sentences to avoid the double negatives.

WRITING APPLICATION

Use items 13, 16, and 18 to write other sentences that contain double negatives. Then, exchange papers with a partner. Your partner should correct your sentences.

9.2 Common Usage Problems

(1) a, an The use of the article *a* or *an* is determined by the sound of the word that follows it. *A* is used before consonant sounds, while *an* is used before vowel sounds. Words beginning with *hon-, o-,* or *u-* may have either a consonant or a vowel sound.

EXAMPLES

a high mountain (*h* sound)

a one-time offer (*w* sound)

an honorable person (no *h* sound)

an opening (*o* sound)

an understanding smile (*u* sound)

(2) accept, except *Accept,* a verb, means "to receive." *Except,* a preposition, means "to leave out" or "other than."

VERB   The settlers **accepted** the harsh climate.

PREPOSITION They had everything they needed **except** wool.

(3) adapt, adopt *Adapt* means "to change." *Adopt* means "to take as one's own."

EXAMPLES

Immigrants **adapt** to life in their new land.

They often **adopt** new customs, too.

(4) affect, effect *Affect* is almost always a verb meaning "to influence." *Effect,* usually a noun, means "a result." Sometimes, *effect* is a verb meaning "to bring about" or "to cause."

VERB The president's speech **affected** me deeply.

NOUN Its **effect** was to get me to volunteer to help others.

VERB The speech **effected** a change in my behavior.

(5) aggravate *Aggravate* means "to make worse." Avoid using this word to mean "annoy."

INCORRECT The thieves **aggravated** the police.

PREFERRED Their crimes **are aggravating** the town's peace.

(6) ain't *Ain't,* which was originally a contraction for *am not,* is no longer considered acceptable in standard English. Always use *am not,* and never use *ain't.* The exception is in certain instances of dialogue.

(7) all ready, already *All ready,* which consists of two separate words used as an adjective, means "ready." *Already,* which is an adverb, means "by or before this time" or "even now."

ADJECTIVE	Michael is **all ready** to learn to drive.
ADVERB	He has started studying the manual **already**.

(8) all right, alright *Alright* is a nonstandard spelling. Make sure you use the two-word form.

INCORRECT	With some help from conservationists, the rain forest may be **alright**.
PREFERRED	With some help from conservationists, the rain forest may be **all right**.

(9) all together, altogether *All together* means "together as a single group." *Altogether* means "completely" or "in all."

EXAMPLES	The crew worked **all together** to get the job done.
	They were **altogether** happy to have such good sailors.

(10) among, between Both of these words are prepositions. *Among* shows a connection between three or more items. *Between* generally shows a connection between two items.

EXAMPLES	Orchids may be found **among** the many varieties of plants in the rain forest.
	Small plants grow in the few rays of sunshine that filter **between** the larger plants and the trees.

See Practice 9.2A

(11) anxious This adjective implies uneasiness, worry, or fear. Do not use it as a substitute for *eager.*

INCORRECT	I was **anxious** for the exam period to be over.
PREFERRED	I was **anxious** about how well I'd perform.

(12) anyone, any one, everyone, every one   *Anyone* and *everyone* mean "any person" or "every person." *Any one* means "any single person (or thing)"; *every one* means "every single person (or thing)."

EXAMPLES   **Anyone** can appreciate art.

You can choose **any one** of the art media to explore and learn about.

Everyone might not be able to paint or sculpt.

However, **every one** of us can enjoy some form of art.

(13) anyway, anywhere, everywhere, nowhere, somewhere   These adverbs should never end in *-s*.

INCORRECT   We looked up in the sky; the stars seemed to be **everywheres** we looked.

PREFERRED   We looked up in the sky; the stars seemed to be **everywhere** we looked.

(14) as   Do not use the conjunction *as* to mean "because" or "since."

INCORRECT   I think we should stay indoors today **as** the weather is going to be terrible.

PREFERRED   I think we should stay indoors today **because** the weather is going to be terrible.

(15) as to   *As to* is awkward. Replace it with *about*.

INCORRECT   I'm worried **as to** whether I'll be able to learn to drive my dad's car.

PREFERRED   I'm worried **about** whether I'll be able to learn to drive my dad's car.

(16) at   Do not use *at* after *where*. Simply eliminate *at*.

INCORRECT   I don't know **where** my dog is **at**.

PREFERRED   I don't know **where** my dog is.

(17) at, about Avoid using *at* with *about*. Simply eliminate *at* or *about*.

| INCORRECT | On weekends, I have to be home **at about** 11:00. |
| PREFERRED | On weekends, I have to be home **at** 11:00. |

(18) awful, awfully *Awful* is used informally to mean that something is "extremely bad." *Awfully* is used informally to mean "very." Both words are overused and should be replaced with more descriptive words. In standard English speech and writing, *awful* should only be used to mean "inspiring fear or awe in someone."

OVERUSED	The heat in the desert was **awful**.
PREFERRED	The heat in the desert was **extreme**.
OVERUSED	Dad was **awfully** angry that I'd stayed out late.
PREFERRED	Dad was **very** angry that I'd stayed out late.
OVERUSED	The thunderclouds looked **awful**.
PREFERRED	The thunderclouds looked **threatening**.

(19) awhile, a while *Awhile* is an adverb that means "for a short time." *A while,* which is a noun, means "a period of time." It is usually used after the preposition *for* or *after.*

ADVERB	I waited **awhile** for Sarah to call back.
	Marty practiced his foul shot **awhile**, and finally he could make it easily.
NOUN	After **a while**, we discussed our problem.
	It did take **a while**, but Marty's form improved.

(20) beat, win When you *win*, you "achieve a victory in something." When you *beat* someone or something, you "overcome an opponent."

INCORRECT	My dad was surprised when I **won** him in tennis.
PREFERRED	My dad was surprised when I **beat** him in tennis.
	I was surprised I could **win** against my dad.

See Practice 9.2B

> **PRACTICE 9.2A** **Recognizing Usage
> Problems 1–10**

Read each sentence. Then, choose the correct
item to complete each sentence.

EXAMPLE   Getting enough sleep should have a
good (affect, effect) on your health.

ANSWER   *effect*

1. Some animals (adapt, adopt) quickly to
changes in their environment.

2. The president (accepted, excepted) the
challenge to debate with his opponent.

3. My cousin received (a, an) honorable
discharge from the navy.

4. They should have (all ready, already) left
by now.

5. I (ain't, am not) taking my little brother to the
park today.

6. We should shout the cheer (all together,
altogether).

7. One black orchid grew (among, between)
many white ones.

8. My parents said it was (alright, all right) to
hold the meeting at our house.

9. Perfumes (annoy, aggravate) my sinus
problems.

10. We were (all ready, already) to play
the game.

> **PRACTICE 9.2B** **Recognizing Usage
> Problems 11–20**

Read each sentence. Then, choose the correct
item to complete each sentence.

EXAMPLE   (Anyone, Any one) with a driver's
license is eligible for the contest.

ANSWER   *Anyone*

11. It had been quite (a while, awhile) since we
had seen the ocean.

12. Several horses escaped (as, because) the gate
was left open.

13. We had some questions (as to, about) the
validity of the experiment.

14. We discovered where the best pizza
restaurant (was, was at) in our new town.

15. What could be causing that (awful, terrible)
smell?

16. I've been practicing, so I know I can (beat,
win) you in a game of chess.

17. The students were (anxious, eager) about
taking three tests in one day.

18. I have seen (everyone, every one) of the
movies showing at the movie theater.

19. I hope you are going (somewhere,
somewheres) nice for your birthday.

20. The guests arrived (at, at about) noon.

SPEAKING APPLICATION

Take turns with a partner. Choose any pair of
words from Practice 9.2A (except from #8), and
tell your partner your choices. Your partner
should say two sentences, using both words
correctly.

WRITING APPLICATION

Write two sentences that include usage
problems. Then, exchange papers with a
partner. Your partner should correct your
sentences.

(21) because   Do not use *because* after the phrase *the reason*. Say "The reason is that" or reword the sentence.

INCORRECT   One **reason** to learn another language **is because** it's good to understand how others think.

PREFERRED   One **reason** to learn another language **is that** it's good to understand how others think.

(22) being as, being that   Avoid using either of these expressions. Use *because* instead.

INCORRECT   **Being as** I was leaving work late, I went right home.

PREFERRED   **Because** I was leaving work late, I went right home.

(23) beside, besides   *Beside* means "at the side of" or "close to." *Besides* means "in addition to."

EXAMPLES   In many books, photographs appear **beside** the text.

              Besides being pretty, they complement the text.

(24) bring, take   *Bring* means "to carry from a distant place to a nearer one." *Take* means "to carry from a near place to a far one."

EXAMPLES   Jake will **bring** his uniform home today.

              He can **take** it back after he's washed it.

(25) can, may   Use *can* to mean "have the ability to." Use *may* to mean "have permission to" or "to be likely to."

ABILITY   My dad **can** fix almost any mechanical thing.

PERMISSION   He said I **may** work with him on the car.

POSSIBILITY   He **may** even show me how to change the oil.

(26) clipped words   Avoid using clipped or shortened words, such as *gym* and *photo* in formal writing.

INFORMAL   I'm going to buy the **photo** taken at the prom.

FORMAL   I'm going to buy the **photograph** taken at the prom.

(27) different from, different than   *Different from* is preferred in standard English.

INCORRECT   That college in Iowa is **different than** the one in Ohio.

PREFERRED   That college in Iowa is **different from** the one in Ohio.

(28) doesn't, don't   Do not use *don't* with third-person singular subjects. Instead, use *doesn't.*

INCORRECT   Margaret **don't** have to babysit this evening.

PREFERRED   Margaret **doesn't** have to babysit this evening.

(29) done   *Done* is the past participle of the verb *do.* It should always take a helping verb.

INCORRECT   I **done** the rest of the semester's work.

PREFERRED   I **did** the rest of the semester's work.

(30) due to   *Due to* means "caused by" and should be used only when the words *caused by* can be logically substituted.

INCORRECT   **Due to** a lack of studying, I failed my history test.

PREFERRED   My failing grade on my history test was **due to** a lack of studying.

See Practice 9.2C

(31) each other, one another   These expressions usually are interchangeable. At times, however, *each other* is more logically used in reference to only two and *one another* in reference to more than two.

EXAMPLES   Sandra, Jane, and Patti appreciated **one another's** artistic skill.

The partners relied on **each other** for honest appraisals of their work.

(32) farther, further   *Farther* refers to distance. *Further* means "additional" or "to a greater degree or extent."

EXAMPLES   Africa is **farther** away than South America.

I'd like to do some **further** study on African customs.

(33) fewer, less   Use *fewer* with things that can be counted. Use *less* with qualities and quantities that cannot be counted.

EXAMPLES   **fewer** resources, **less** experience

(34) get, got, gotten   These forms of the verb *get* are acceptable in standard English, but a more specific word is preferable.

INCORRECT   **get** a license, **got** a car, **have gotten** car repairs
PREFERRED   **earn** a license, **bought** a car, **repaired** the car

(35) gone, went   *Gone* is the past participle of the verb *go* and is used only with a helping verb. *Went* is the past tense of *go* and is never used with a helping verb.

INCORRECT   My mom and dad **gone** to work already.

              They could **have went** later this morning.

PREFERRED   My mom and dad **went** to work already.

              They could **have gone** later this morning.

(36) good, lovely, nice   Replace these overused words with a more specific adjective.

WEAK   **good** music, **lovely** decorations, **nice** dance
BETTER   **rhythmic** music, **colorful** decorations, **exciting** dance

(37) in, into   *In* refers to position. *Into* suggests motion.

EXAMPLES   The tourists are **in** the history museum.

              They walked **into** the documents room.

(38) irregardless   Avoid this word in formal speech and writing. Instead, use *regardless*.

(39) just   When you use *just* as an adverb to mean "no more than," place it immediately before the word it modifies.

INCORRECT   My paper **just** needed one more draft.
PREFERRED   My paper needed **just** one more draft.

(40) kind of, sort of   Do not use these phrases in formal speech. Instead, use *rather* or *somewhat*.

See Practice 9.2D

PRACTICE 9.2C ▷ Recognizing Usage Problems 21–30

Read each sentence. Then, choose the correct item to complete each sentence.

EXAMPLE   Who (beside, besides) you is planning to attend?

ANSWER   *besides*

1. The game's cancellation was (due to, because of) rain.

2. How is an alligator different (from, than) a crocodile?

3. Please remember to (bring, take) your jacket home from school today.

4. The reason that the cat ran is (because, that) a dog came into our yard.

5. My new computer (can, may) do more than my old one.

6. The principal announced that we could pick up our (photos, photographs) after school.

7. I sat (besides, beside) the stream and began baiting my fishing line.

8. (Being as, Because) it is after five, the store is closed and will not reopen until tomorrow.

9. I know the right answers, but Thomas (don't, doesn't).

10. We (done, have done) most of the cleaning and should be finished soon.

PRACTICE 9.2D ▷ Revising Sentences to Correct Usage Problems 31–40

Read each sentence. Then, rewrite each sentence, correcting the errors in usage.

EXAMPLE   They canceled the contest because less than 100 people entered.

ANSWER   *They canceled the contest because fewer than 100 people entered.*

11. I consider Victoria to be a nice person.

12. Nathan is kind of excited about taking acting lessons.

13. There was fewer excitement about the party after we found out that it was taking place in the gymnasium.

14. We need to get supplies for the picnic.

15. After he had went only five miles, Brad was ready to quit the race.

16. The rescue team was determined to go irregardless of the risks.

17. She stepped in the room quietly.

18. Many of the football players helped each other learn the new plays.

19. I am confident of just the answers to questions 7 and 8.

20. If you travel just a little further, you will come to Willow Springs.

SPEAKING APPLICATION

Take turns with a partner. Say sentences with usage problems. Your partner should correct each of your sentences.

WRITING APPLICATION

Write a paragraph about a topic of your choice. Include sentences that contain usage problems. Then, exchange papers with a partner. Your partner should correct the usage problems in your paragraph.

(41) lay, lie The verb *lay* means "to put or set (something) down." Its principal parts—*lay, laying, laid, laid*—are followed by a direct object. The verb *lie* means "to recline." Its principal parts—*lie, lying, lay, lain*—are not followed by a direct object.

LAY   **Lay** your tools on the table.

The crew **is laying** down its tools for the evening.

Sally **laid** the hammer and the saw in the toolbox.

She **had laid** them in a dry place so they wouldn't rust.

LIE   After a long day, the mountain climbers **lie** down to rest.

Their climbing tools **are lying** on the ground.

The lead climber **lay** down after planning the next climb.

The trail map **has lain** in his backpack all day.

(42) learn, teach *Learn* means "to receive knowledge." *Teach* means "to give knowledge."

EXAMPLES   It is difficult to **learn** to scuba dive.

An experienced diver can **teach** you the skills.

(43) leave, let *Leave* means "to allow to remain." *Let* means "to permit."

INCORRECT   **Leave** me come along with you to the store.

PREFERRED   **Let** me come along with you to the store.

(44) like, as *Like* is a preposition meaning "similar to" or "such as." It should not be used in place of the conjunction *as*.

INCORRECT   A smart worker is valued **like** a prized possession is valued.

PREFERRED   A smart worker is valued **as** a prized possession is valued.

A smart worker is valued **like** a prized possession.

(45) loose, lose *Loose* is usually an adjective or part of such idioms as *cut loose, turn loose,* or *break loose. Lose* is always a verb and usually means "to miss from one's possession."

EXAMPLES   The torn pocket in your jeans looks **loose**.

If you're not careful, you could **lose** your wallet.

(46) maybe, may be   *Maybe* is an adverb meaning "perhaps." *May be* is a helping verb connected to a main verb.

ADVERB   **Maybe** we can schedule the dance for next month.

VERB   It **may be** too late to schedule it for this month.

(47) of   Do not use *of* after a helping verb such as *should, would, could,* or *must.* Use *have* instead. Do not use *of* after *outside, inside, off,* and *atop.* Simply eliminate *of.*

INCORRECT   We **should of** tried to work together more closely.

PREFERRED   We **should have** tried to work together more closely.

(48) OK, O.K., okay   In informal writing, *OK, O.K.,* and *okay* are acceptably used to mean "all right." Do not use them in standard English speech or writing, however.

INFORMAL   We thought the new eligibility rules were **okay**.

PREFERRED   We thought the new eligibility rules were **fair**.

(49) only   *Only* should be placed immediately before the word it modifies. Placing it elsewhere can lead to confusion.

EXAMPLES   **Only** the settlers used wagons to travel west.
             (No one else used wagons.)

             The settlers used **only** wagons to travel west.
             (They didn't travel in any other way.)

(50) ought   Do not use *ought* with *have* or *had.*

INCORRECT   Dave **hadn't ought** to have raised the membership fee.

PREFERRED   Dave **ought not** to have raised the membership fee.

(51) outside of   Do not use this expression to mean "besides" or "except."

INCORRECT   There are no more classes today **outside of** physics.

PREFERRED   There are no more classes today **except** physics.

(52) plurals that do not end in -s The English plurals of certain nouns from Greek and Latin are formed as they were in their original language. Words such as *criteria*, *media*, and *phenomena* are plural. Their singular forms are *criterion*, *medium*, and *phenomenon*.

INCORRECT	The **media** is an important tool for raising environmental awareness.
PREFERRED	The **media** provide important tools for raising environmental awareness.
	Important tools for raising environmental awareness are available from the **media**.

See Practice 9.2E

(53) precede, proceed *Precede* means "to go before." *Proceed* means "to move or go forward."

EXAMPLES	Final exams will **precede** graduation.
	After graduation, we will **proceed** to celebrate with our families.

(54) principal, principle As an adjective, *principal* means "most important" or "chief." As a noun, it means "a person who has controlling authority," as in a school. *Principle* is always a noun that means "a fundamental law."

ADJECTIVE	My **principal** goal is to graduate with a good average.
NOUN	The student council reports to the **principal**.
NOUN	The **principles** of Project Graduation are to help students safely celebrate their graduation.

(55) real *Real* means "authentic." In formal writing, avoid using *real* to mean "very" or "really."

INCORRECT	In Miami, it is **real** hot during August.
PREFERRED	In Miami, it is **very** hot during August.

(56) says *Says* should not be used as a substitute for *said*.

INCORRECT	Last week, May **says** for me to wait on the corner.
PREFERRED	Last week, May **said** for me to wait on the corner.

(57) seen *Seen* is a past participle and must be used with a helping verb.

INCORRECT   They **seen** the documentary on life in China.

PREFERRED   They **had seen** the documentary on life in China.

(58) set, sit *Set* means "to put (something) in a certain place." Its principal parts—*set, setting, set, set*—are usually followed by a direct object. *Sit* means "to be seated." Its principal parts—*sit, sitting, sat, sat*—are never followed by a direct object.

SET   Please **set** the DVR to record my favorite show.

I **have set** it many times.

Do you need help **setting** it?

Dad **will set** the recorder for his show later.

SIT   Sometimes, it's nice to just **sit** and watch the ocean.

I **am sitting** on a blanket on the sand.

I **can sit** for hours watching the waves.

In fact, I **would sit** here all summer if I could.

(59) so When *so* is used as a coordinating conjunction, it means *and* or *but*. Avoid using *so* when you mean "so that."

INCORRECT   Some animals keep watch **so** others can eat safely.

PREFERRED   Some animals keep watch **so that** others can eat safely.

(60) than, then Use *than* in comparisons. Use *then* as an adverb to refer to time.

EXAMPLES   Tropical climates are hotter **than** temperate climates.

Mornings are cool; **then**, the temperature rises quickly.

(61) that, which, who Use these relative pronouns in the following ways: *that* and *which* refer to things; *who* refers only to people.

EXAMPLES   Weeds **that** have long roots are hard to pull up.

The roots, **which** can extend far underground, often break before I can pull the whole root.

My mom, **who** is a gardener, tells me to dig them out.

(62) their, there, they're   *Their,* a possessive pronoun, always modifies a noun. *There* can be used either as an expletive at the beginning of a sentence or as an adverb showing place or direction. *They're* is a contraction of *they are.*

PRONOUN	The spectators in the stadium will cheer for **their** favorite players.
EXPLETIVE	**There** will be a great deal of noise when the home team takes the field.
ADVERB	The bleachers arc over **there**, to the left and right of the scoreboard.
CONTRACTION	**They're** big enough to fit several hundred fans each.

(63) them   Do not use *them* as a substitute for *those.*

INCORRECT	**Them** boats look close, but they're miles away.
PREFERRED	**Those** boats look close, but they're miles away.

(64) to, too, two   *To,* a preposition, begins a phrase or an infinitive. *Too,* an adverb, modifies adjectives and other adverbs and means "very" or "also." *Two* is a number.

PREPOSITION	**to** the boat, **to** the ocean
INFINITIVE	**to** see dolphins, **to** look for whales
ADVERB	**too** many to count, **too** big to be believed
NUMBER	**two** sea birds, **two** whales jumping

(65) when, where   Do not use *when* or *where* immediately after a linking verb. Do not use *where* in place of *that.*

INCORRECT	Winter is **when** skiers are happiest. They go to **where** there are steep slopes.
PREFERRED	Winter is **the time** skiers are happiest. They go to **places with** steep slopes.

See Practice 9.2F

PRACTICE 9.2E **Recognizing Usage Problems 41–52**

Read each sentence. Then, choose the correct item to complete each sentence.

EXAMPLE   Boris's grandfather (learned, taught) him to play chess.

ANSWER   *taught*

1. (Leave, Let) that poor cat alone!
2. My boss (okayed, approved) my new work schedule.
3. Do you have any idea where I may (have, of) left my keys?
4. I (laid, lay) on the sofa for almost four hours.
5. There (had ought, ought) to be a rule against so much noise across from the library.
6. (Only admit, Admit only) those students who have a ticket.
7. If you don't stop making that sound, I'm going to (lose, loose) my patience!
8. I don't have any plans after school (outside of, except for) doing homework.
9. I waited for (maybe, may be) five seconds, and then I burst out laughing.
10. I began acting (like, as if) I didn't care about the dance, even though I really did care.

PRACTICE 9.2F **Revising Sentences to Correct Usage Problems 53–65**

Read each sentence. Then, rewrite each sentence, correcting the errors in usage.

EXAMPLE   Kareem is the only person which has been friendly to me.

ANSWER   *Kareem is the only person who has been friendly to me.*

11. Marian, please sit the book on the table.
12. Do you want to set downstairs or outside?
13. Daily, at four o'clock, is when I visit my aunt.
14. The principle also teaches history.
15. I have two leave now.
16. Did you pick up them socks that were on the floor in your room?
17. I brought an extra sweater so I wouldn't get cold.
18. I don't know why their not going too the zoo.
19. Keiko seen her sister playing soccer.
20. Marco is more athletic then his brother.

SPEAKING APPLICATION

Reread each sentence in Practice 9.2E. Discuss with a partner which usage errors you've made in past writing assignments.

WRITING APPLICATION

Write four sentences that include usage problems. Then, exchange papers with a partner. Your partner should correct your sentences.

Combining and Varying Sentences

Read the sentences. Then, rewrite each sentence according to the instructions in parentheses.

1. Peace was ushered in at the end of World War II. Prosperity was also ushered in. (Create a compound subject and end with a phrase.)

2. The clothes that I would need for my long journey were in my suitcase. (Invert the subject-verb order.)

3. Steven's group discussed politics to prepare their report. They also discussed the economy. (Create a compound direct object and start with an infinitive.)

4. Susan glanced over her shoulder. She heard a strange sound and wanted to see what had caused it. (Combine the sentences using the conjunction *because*.)

5. We took the shortcut to school even though I much preferred the longer, more scenic way. (Start with an adverb clause.)

6. Jason and Lisa run together every day after school. They are training for the marathon next month. (Combine the sentences using the conjunction *since*.)

7. Karen responded to the suggestion from the group to be flexible. She moved the meeting to another day. (Create a compound verb and start with an infinitive.)

8. The chairman spoke at length during the board meeting last Tuesday. (Start with a prepositional phrase.)

9. A pile of dust and deteriorating pipes were underneath the house. (Invert the subject-verb order.)

10. Styles of dress changed dramatically in the 1960s. Social norms also changed. (Create a compound subject and start with a prepositional phrase.)

PRACTICE 2 **Revising Pronoun and Verb Usage**

Read the sentences. Then, revise each sentence to fix problems in pronoun and verb usage. You may need to reorder, add, or eliminate words.

1. Someone left their jacket in the theater.

2. Whom is in charge of cleaning up the mess?

3. Both Jessica and me am going to the movies.

4. He losed his algebra book for the third time.

5. The person in charge is me.

6. She chasing that dog around the park, but she can't catch him.

7. Them is the first two picked for the team.

8. The novel was really well written, and his plot was very compelling.

9. Him and her sat next to each other.

10. To who should I submit this application?

PRACTICE 3 **Revising for Correct Use of Active and Passive Voice**

Read the sentences. Then, rewrite each sentence in the active voice. You may need to reorder, add, or delete words.

1. Poetry from this collection was beloved by people throughout the world.

2. This winter is being ranked by meteorologists as the coldest winter in decades.

3. Eating fruits and vegetables is believed by many to reduce the risk of heart disease.

4. Its fur is being licked by the cat.

5. Lunch is being served by cafeteria workers from 11:30 until 1:30.

Continued on next page ▶

Cumulative Review Chapters 4–9

PRACTICE 4 ▷ **Correcting Errors in Pronoun and Verb Usage**

Read the sentences. Then, revise each sentence to correct agreement, verb usage, and pronoun usage. If a sentence is already correct, write *correct*.

1. The conductor requested that Sandra and me played the last few bars again.
2. The constant movement of the car caused him to get motion sickness.
3. Us is going to the basketball game on Wednesday night.
4. Henry had went all the way to the soccer game before realizing him had forgets his cleats.
5. Neither Ida nor Jesse had sings the song before.

PRACTICE 5 ▷ **Using Comparative and Superlative Forms Correctly**

Read the sentences. Then, write the appropriate comparative or superlative degree of the modifier in parentheses.

1. The rock concert we went to last night was the (loud) event I have ever attended.
2. Carson completed the exam (fast) than anyone else in the class.
3. Each math problem is (complex) than the next.
4. Shellie is the (strict) of the three of us when it comes to following the rules.
5. This is the (lengthy) book I have ever read.

PRACTICE 6 ▷ **Avoiding Double Negatives**

Read the sentences. Then, choose the word in parentheses that makes each sentence negative without forming a double negative.

1. The farmer wouldn't want (no, any) locusts damaging his crop this year.

2. Velma was extremely stubborn; she didn't want (no one, anyone) telling her what to do.
3. She had done (nothing, anything) like that before.
4. They weren't (nowhere, anywhere) that they had ever been before.
5. Ella would (never, ever) go near the abandoned house.

PRACTICE 7 ▷ **Avoiding Usage Problems**

Read the sentences. Then, choose the correct expression to complete each sentence.

1. Expecting to (loose, lose) the game, Ingrid just went out there and had fun playing.
2. Scott was (accepted, excepted) into his first-choice college.
3. The teacher said we (can, may) try out this plan of ours for a week.
4. Staying up all night can have a bad (effect, affect) on you the next day.
5. There are (less, fewer) people at this track meet (than, then) there were at the previous one.
6. (Since, As) it was not polite to linger, we left immediately after the show.
7. He announced that he was (already, all ready) to go, so we followed him out the door.
8. (Among, Between) the two of us, we can figure out the answer.
9. I (accept, except) your help gratefully; you (can, may) feed the baby.
10. How is today's weather any different (from, than) last week's?

CAPITALIZATION

Use correct conventions of capitalization to shape how you present ideas for your readers.

CHAPTER 10

WRITE GUY *Jeff Anderson, M.Ed.*

WHAT DO YOU NOTICE?

Keep track of capitalization as you zoom in on these lines from the poem "London, 1802" by William Wordsworth.

MENTOR TEXT

> Milton! thou should'st be living at this hour:
> England hath need of thee: she is a fen
> Of stagnant waters: altar, sword, and pen,
> Fireside, the heroic wealth of hall and bower,
> Have forfeited their ancient English dower . . .

Now, ask yourself the following questions:

- Why is the first word in each line capitalized?
- Which words are proper nouns? Which word is a proper adjective? Why are they capitalized?

The first word in each line of a traditional poem is capitalized even if the line starts in the middle of a complete thought. The words *Milton* and *England* are proper nouns naming a specific person and place, so they would be capitalized regardless of their position. Proper adjectives are capitalized because they are derived from proper nouns. The proper adjective *English* in the last line is formed from *England*.

Grammar for Writers Writers use capitalization to help their readers navigate and understand text. Therefore, checking for correct capitalization is an essential step in the writing process.

There are no capitals in your short story.

Maybe I just write small.

10.1 Capitalization in Sentences

Just as road signs help to guide people through a town, capital letters help to guide readers through sentences and paragraphs. Capitalization signals the start of a new sentence or points out certain words within a sentence to give readers visual clues that aid in their understanding.

Using Capitals for First Words

Always capitalize the first word in a sentence.

> Capitalize the first word in **declarative, interrogative, imperative,** and **exclamatory** sentences.

DECLARATIVE **J**ack told me all about it.

INTERROGATIVE **H**ow old are you?

IMPERATIVE **B**e careful on the steps.

EXCLAMATORY **H**eads up!

> Capitalize the first word in **interjections** and **incomplete questions.**

INTERJECTIONS **F**antastic!

INCOMPLETE QUESTIONS **W**ho said? **W**hen?

The word *I* is always capitalized, whether it is the first word in a sentence or not.

> Always capitalize the pronoun *I*.

EXAMPLE Bob, Fred, and **I** went fishing.

> Capitalize the first word after a colon only if the word begins a complete sentence. Do not capitalize the word if it begins a list of words or phrases.

10.1.4 RULE

SENTENCE
FOLLOWING
A COLON

He asked for a ride: **H**e could not take another step.

LIST
FOLLOWING
A COLON

I will leave the following items for you: **m**y toolbox, the saw, and some tape.

> Capitalize the first word in each line of traditional poetry, even if the line does not start a new sentence.

10.1.5 RULE

EXAMPLE

See Practice 10.1A

I think that I shall never see

A poem lovely as a tree. – Joyce Kilmer

Using Capitals With Quotations

There are special rules for using capitalization with **quotations**.

> Capitalize the first word of a **quotation.** However, do not capitalize the first word of a continuing sentence when a quotation is interrupted by identifying words or when the first word of a quotation is the continuation of a speaker's sentence.

10.1.6 RULE

EXAMPLES

Margaret shouted, "**S**top the bus!"

"**A**s I was counting them," she said, "**h**e started to wrap them."

She said that he is "**t**he strongest person

See Practice 10.1B

she knows."

PRACTICE 10.1A Capitalizing Words

Read each sentence. Then, rewrite each sentence, using correct capitalization.

EXAMPLE   oh no! this can't be happening!

ANSWER   *Oh no! This can't be happening!*

1. should we go somewhere this weekend?

2. i have everything that we need for the party: food, decorations, music, and games.

3. stop hovering by the door and come inside.

4. do not go gentle into that good night, old age should burn and rave at close of day. —Dylan Thomas

5. have you ever seen such an entertaining school musical?

6. what? when did you say we need to leave?

7. great news! the debate team finished first in their competition!

8. the mayor announced the outcome: all groups reached an agreement on the site of the new recreation center.

9. this novel has given me some great insights into life during the early twentieth century.

10. i wondered if i had packed enough clothes for my trip.

PRACTICE 10.1B Using Capitals With Quotations

Read each sentence. Then, write the word or words in each sentence that should be capitalized.

EXAMPLE   the actor exclaimed, "wow! the theater is full tonight!"

ANSWER   *The, Wow, The*

11. "my understanding," Juliet said, "was that you would make the presentation."

12. Miranda asked, "does anyone know which is the most direct route to the mall?"

13. "i agree," James replied. "the characters in the story are complex and well-developed."

14. "i am not sure," Roger said, "but i think there is a great place to camp in that wooded area."

15. my mother always said that "time heals all wounds."

16. Michelle wondered, "will you be looking for a new job in April?"

17. "i really feel," Finula said, "that spending time with family should be a priority."

18. cindy remarked that she had "never seen such a crowd of people before."

19. "how do you know that?" he asked. "the announcement was never made."

20. "it wasn't entirely clear to me whether Karla was attending the party," Vinnie said.

SPEAKING APPLICATION

Take turns with a partner. Tell funny stories, using a variety of sentences. Your partner should identify the letters that should be capitalized in your sentences.

WRITING APPLICATION

Write a brief dialogue between you and a friend in which you discuss your interests. Be sure to use capitalization correctly in your quotations.

10.2 Proper Nouns

Capitalization make important words stand out in your writing, such as the names of people, places, countries, book titles, and other proper names. Sometimes proper names are used as nouns and sometimes as adjectives modifying nouns or pronouns.

Using Capitals for Proper Nouns

Nouns, as you may remember, are either **common** or **proper.**

Common nouns, such as *sailor, brother, city,* and *ocean,* identify classes of people, places, or things and are not capitalized.

Proper nouns name specific examples of people, places, or things and should be capitalized.

> Capitalize all **proper** nouns.

RULE 10.2.1

EXAMPLES	**W**endy	**R**everend **B**rown	**G**overnor **J**ohnson
	Atlanta	**T**hird **S**treet	**B**lair **H**ouse
	*E*lizabeth	*M*oby *D*ick	**R.** **M.** **S.** **Q**ueen

Names

Each part of a person's name—the given name, the middle name or initial standing for that name, and the surname—should be capitalized. If a surname begins with *Mc* or *O',* the letter following it is capitalized (McAdams, O'Reilly).

> Capitalize each part of a person's name even when the full name is not used.

RULE 10.2.2

EXAMPLES	**H**al **C**urry	**V.** **R.** **S**mall	**T**homas **H.** **P**erry

Capitalize the proper names that are given to animals.

EXAMPLES	**T**ippy	**L**assie	**P**epper

Geographical and Place Names
If a place can be found on a map, it should generally be
capitalized.

Capitalize geographical and place names.

Examples of different kinds of geographical and place names are
listed in the following chart.

GEOGRAPHICAL AND PLACE NAMES	
Streets	Madison Avenue, First Street, Green Valley Road
Towns and Cities	Dallas, Oakdale, New York City
Counties, States, and Provinces	Champlain County, Texas, Quebec
Nations and Continents	Austria, Kenya, the United States of America, Asia, Mexico, Europe
Mountains	the Adirondack Mountains, Mount Washington
Valleys and Deserts	the San Fernando Valley, the Mojave Desert, the Gobi
Islands and Peninsulas	Aruba, the Faroe Islands, Cape York Peninsula
Sections of a Country	the Northeast, Siberia, the Great Plains
Scenic Spots	Gateway National Park, Carlsbad Caverns
Rivers and Falls	the Missouri River, Victoria Falls
Lakes and Bays	Lake Cayuga, Gulf of Mexico, the Bay of Biscayne
Seas and Oceans	the Sargasso Sea, the Indian Ocean
Celestial Bodies and Constellations	Mars, the Big Dipper, moon, Venus
Monuments and Memorials	the Tomb of the Unknown Soldier, Kennedy Memorial Library, the Washington Monument
Buildings	Madison Square Garden, Fort Hood, the Astrodome, the White House
School and Meeting Rooms	Room 6, Laboratory 3B, the Red Room, Conference Room C

Capitalizing Directions
Words indicating direction are capitalized only when they refer to a section of a country.

EXAMPLES   Cotton was a major crop of the **S**outh.

Columbus sailed **w**est to find the New World.

Capitalizing Names of Celestial Bodies
Capitalize the names of celestial bodies except *moon* and *sun*.

EXAMPLE   **S**aturn is the sixth planet from the **s**un, and it has at least 31 **m**oons.

Capitalizing Buildings and Places
Do not capitalize words such as *theater, hotel, university,* and *park*, unless the word is part of a proper name.

EXAMPLES   She went to Yellowstone **P**ark last summer.

I love to walk in the **p**ark.

Events and Times
Capitalize references to historic events, periods, and documents as well as dates and holidays. Use a dictionary to check capitalization.

Capitalize the names of specific events and periods in history.

SPECIAL EVENTS AND TIMES	
Historic Events	the Battle of Waterloo, World War I
Historical Periods	the Manchu Dynasty, Reconstruction
Documents	the Bill of Rights, the Magna Carta
Days and Months	Monday, June 22, the third week in May
Holidays	Labor Day, Memorial Day, Veterans Day
Religious Holidays	Rosh Hashanah, Christmas, Easter
Special Events	the World Series, the Holiday Antiques Show

Capitalizing Seasons

Do not capitalize seasons unless the name of the season is being used as a proper noun or adjective.

EXAMPLES   We are going to the lake this **s**ummer.

Our town's **S**ummer Festival is held each August.

Capitalize the names of organizations, government bodies, political parties, races, nationalities, languages, and religions.

VARIOUS GROUPS	
Clubs and Organizations	Rotary, Knights of Columbus, the Red Cross, National Organization for Women
Institutions	the Museum of Fine Arts, the Mayo Clinic
Schools	Kennedy High School, University of Texas
Businesses	General Motors, Prentice Hall
Government Bodies	Department of State, Federal Trade Commission, House of Representatives
Political Parties	Republicans, the Democratic party
Nationalities	American, Mexican, Chinese, Israeli, Canadian
Languages	English, Italian, Polish, Swahili
Religions and Religious References	Christianity: God, the Holy Spirit, the Bible Judaism: the Lord, the Prophets, the Torah Islam: Allah, the Prophets, the Qur'an, Mohammed Hinduism: Brahma, the Bhagavad Gita, the Vedas Buddhism: the Buddha, Mahayana, Hinayana

References to Mythological Gods When referring to mythology, do not capitalize the word *god* (the *gods* of Olympus).

Capitalize the names of awards; the names of specific types of air, sea, and spacecraft; and brand names.

EXAMPLES   the **G**andhi **P**eace **P**rize   the **S**ilver **S**tar

Smooth & **C**lean soap   **A**pollo **X**

See Practice 10.2A
See Practice 10.2B

PRACTICE 10.2A > Identifying Proper Nouns

Read each sentence. Then, write the proper noun or nouns in each sentence.

EXAMPLE   Mount Rushmore is located in South Dakota.

ANSWER   *Mount Rushmore, South Dakota*

1. The Oceans Cruise Line travels through the Mediterranean Sea, making stops in Spain, Italy, and Greece.

2. The Republican candidate gave a speech in Little Rock, Arkansas, today.

3. We took a family vacation to the Grand Canyon with Aunt Esther.

4. My friend, Nathan, enjoys playing songs on his Superstar electric guitar.

5. Mr. Gonzalez, the exchange teacher from Spain, also speaks Portuguese.

6. The reporter received a Pulitzer Prize.

7. The Constitution was ratified by most of the states by 1788.

8. Sacagawea guided Lewis and Clark on their westward expedition.

9. In Pompeii, Mount Vesuvius erupted and destroyed the entire city.

10. Governor Fields became a member of the cabinet; he was the head of the Department of Agriculture.

PRACTICE 10.2B > Capitalizing Proper Nouns

Read each sentence. Then, write the word or words in each sentence that should be capitalized.

EXAMPLE   What event caused the start of world war I?

ANSWER   *World War I*

11. The terra-cotta warriors guarded the tomb of shi huangdi, china's first emperor.

12. Write to the board of health if you have some concerns about penelope's restaurant.

13. We mapped marco polo's travels through china.

14. In science class, I learned about the sun, mercury, venus, earth, and mars.

15. Mrs. o'neill gave us the task of planning the girl scouts of america camping trip this year.

16. The renaissance is a period of history with advances in art, science, and literature.

17. Sue marched in the memorial day parade.

18. Many african americans, from the northeast to the southwest, voted in the election.

19. The new comic book store, bookorama, is located on the corner of main street and green avenue.

20. In greek mythology, the goddess artemis was the twin sister of the god apollo.

SPEAKING APPLICATION

Take turns with a partner. Tell about an organization that you belong to or would like to belong to someday. Your partner should identify the proper nouns that you use.

WRITING APPLICATION

Use sentence 17 as a model to write three similar sentences. Replace the proper nouns in sentence 17 with other proper nouns.

Using Capitals for Proper Adjectives

A **proper adjective** is either an adjective formed from a proper
noun or a proper noun used as an adjective.

> Capitalize most **proper adjectives.**

PROPER ADJECTIVES FORMED FROM PROPER NOUNS		
Austrian choir	**I**bsen play
Afghan hound	**N**ordic countries
German ambassador	**R**ussian food

PROPER NOUNS USED AS ADJECTIVES		
the **S**enate floor	the **K**ennedy speeches
Shakespeare festival	a **B**ible class
the **S**miths' house	**S**icilian pizza

Some proper adjectives have become so commonly used that they
are no longer capitalized.

EXAMPLES		
herculean **e**ffort	**f**rench **f**ries
pasteurized **m**ilk	**q**uixotic **h**ope
venetian **b**linds	**t**eddy **b**ear

Brand names are often used as proper adjectives.

> Capitalize a **brand name** when it is used as an adjective, but
> do not capitalize the common noun it modifies.

EXAMPLES	
Timo **w**atches	**S**witzles **c**hewy bars
Super **C**ool **j**eans	**L**onglasting **f**reezers

Multiple Proper Adjectives

When you have two or more proper adjectives used together, do not capitalize the associated common nouns.

> **Do not capitalize a common noun used with two proper adjectives.**

10.2.9 RULE

ONE PROPER ADJECTIVE	TWO PROPER ADJECTIVES
Hudson River	Niagara and Hudson rivers
Wilson Street	Wilson, Main, and Lakewood streets
Shinnecock Canal	Shinnecock and Chemung canals
Banking Act	Banking and Civil Rights acts
Atlantic Ocean	Atlantic and Pacific oceans
Somerset County	Somerset and Camden counties
Galapagos Islands	Galapagos and Solomon islands

Prefixes and Hyphenated Adjectives

Prefixes and hyphenated adjectives cause special problems. Prefixes used with proper adjectives should be capitalized only if they refer to a nationality.

> **Do not capitalize prefixes attached to proper adjectives unless the prefix refers to a nationality. In a hyphenated adjective, capitalize only the proper adjective.**

10.2.10 RULE

EXAMPLES

all-American   Anglo-American

German-speaking   pro-Russian

American Italian-language newspaper

pre-Renaissance   Sino-Japanese

pre-Christian architecture   Indo-Greeks

See Practice 10.2C
See Practice 10.2D

PRACTICE 10.2C **Capitalizing Proper Adjectives**

Read each sentence. Then, write the word or words in each sentence that should be capitalized.

EXAMPLE Nina and David are in the same french class.

ANSWER *French*

1. St. mark's basilica in Venice is an example of byzantine architecture.

2. kenyan long-distance runners have won many olympic medals.

3. We spent a relaxing day along the lake michigan shore.

4. He subscribes to a spanish-language newspaper.

5. Both african elephants and asian elephants are endangered species.

6. Damien exchanged his musicala brand trumpet for a kingly.

7. My house is across from sheila young's house.

8. His family went to the irish festival last month.

9. Bonnie has a french bull dog and a german shepherd.

10. During summer, I attend shakespeare plays performed in davidson's park.

PRACTICE 10.2D **Revising Sentences to Correct Capitalization Errors**

Read each sentence. Then, rewrite each sentence, using the conventions of capitalization.

EXAMPLE My grandparents like to listen to italian operas on the radio.

ANSWER *My grandparents like to listen to Italian operas on the radio.*

11. Meshaun's favorite baseball team is the texas rangers.

12. ulysses s. grant led the union forces during the civil war.

13. The chinatown restaurants serve excellent chinese soups and entrees.

14. I have seen travel express buses all over the country, from miami to seattle.

15. The all-american athletes enjoyed the white house luncheon.

16. I never saw such adorable french poodles as the ones in the park.

17. In russian history, nicholas II was the last tsar, or emperor.

18. Many european immigrants arrived at ellis island in new york harbor.

19. Will you take german or french next year?

20. Last monday was rosh hashanah, the jewish new year.

SPEAKING APPLICATION

Discuss with a partner the importance of capitals. Suggest three ways capitalization makes reading and comprehension easier.

WRITING APPLICATION

Write a brief paragraph that contains proper adjectives and proper nouns. Be sure to use conventions of capitalization.

10.3 Other Uses of Capitals

Even though the purpose of using capital letters is to make writing clearer, some rules for capitalization can be confusing. For example, it may be difficult to remember which words in a letter you write need to start with a capital, which words in a book title should be capitalized, or when a person's title—such as Senator or Reverend—needs to start with a capital. The rules and examples that follow should clear up the confusion.

Using Capitals in Letters

Capitalization is required in parts of personal letters and business letters.

> **Capitalize the first word and all nouns in letter salutations and the first word in letter closings.**

10.3.1 RULE

SALUTATIONS   **D**ear **W**endy,

               Dear **D**octor:

               Dear **M**rs. **P**arson:

               My **D**ear **S**ister,

CLOSINGS   **W**ith **d**eep **r**espect,

               Yours with **m**uch **l**ove,

               Sincerely and **f**orever **y**ours,

               Best **r**egards,

Using Capitals for Titles

Capitals are used for titles of people and titles of literary and artistic works. The charts and rules on the following pages will guide you in capitalizing titles correctly.

Capitalize a person's title only when it is used with the person's name or when it is used as a proper name by itself.

WITH A PROPER NAME
Senator **P**ilter was reelected for a second term.

AS A PROPER NAME
I'm glad you can join us, **G**randfather.

IN A GENERAL REFERENCE
The **c**ongressman followed the results of the election.

The following chart illustrates the correct form for a variety of titles. Study the chart, paying particular attention to compound titles and titles with prefixes or suffixes.

SOCIAL, BUSINESS, RELIGIOUS, MILITARY, AND GOVERNMENT TITLES	
Commonly Used Titles	Sir, Madam, Miss, Professor, Doctor, Reverend, Bishop, Sister, Father, Rabbi, Corporal, Major, Admiral, Mayor, Governor, Ambassador
Abbreviated Titles	*Before names*: Mr., Mrs., Ms., Dr., Hon. *After names*: Jr., Sr., Ph.D., M.D., D.D.S., Esq.
Compound Titles	Vice President, Secretary of State, Lieutenant Governor, Commander in Chief
Titles With Prefixes or Suffixes	ex-Congressman Randolph, Governor-elect Loughman

Some honorary titles are capitalized. These include First Lady of the United States, Speaker of the House of Representatives, Queen Mother of England, and the Prince of Wales.

> Capitalize certain honorary titles even when the titles are not followed by a proper name.

10.3.3 RULE

EXAMPLE   The **p**resident and **F**irst **L**ady visited with the **q**ueen of England.

Occasionally, the titles of other government officials may be capitalized as a sign of respect when referring to a specific person whose name is not given. However, you usually do not capitalize titles when they stand alone.

EXAMPLES   We thank you, **G**overnor, for taking us on this guided tour.

Twelve **s**enators voted to block the bill.

> Relatives are often referred to by titles. These references should be capitalized when used with or as the person's name.

10.3.4 RULE

WITH THE PERSON'S NAME   In the spring, **U**ncle **B**ill would take us hiking.

AS A NAME   Bob said that **G**randmother showed him how to do it.

> Do not capitalize titles showing family relationships when they are preceded by a possessive noun or pronoun.

10.3.5 RULE

EXAMPLES   our **a**unt   his **f**ather   Evan's **m**other

> **Capitalize the first word and all other key words in the titles of books, periodicals, poems, stories, plays, paintings, and other works of art.**

The following chart lists examples to guide you in capitalizing titles and subtitles of various works. Note that the articles (*a, an,* and *the*) are not capitalized unless they are used as the first word of a title or subtitle. Conjunctions and prepositions are also left uncapitalized unless they are the first or last word in a title or subtitle or contain four letters or more. Note also that verbs, no matter how short, are always capitalized.

TITLES OF WORKS	
Books	*The Red Badge of Courage,* *Profiles in Courage,* *All Through the Night,* *John Ford: The Man and His Films* *Heart of Darkness*
Periodicals	*International Wildlife, Allure,* *Better Homes and Gardens*
Poems	"The Raven" "The Rime of the Ancient Mariner" "Flower in the Crannied Wall"
Stories and Articles	"Editha" "The Fall of the House of Usher" "Here Is New York"
Plays and Musicals	*The Tragedy of Macbeth* *Our Town* *West Side Story*
Paintings	*Starry Night* *Mona Lisa* *The Artist's Daughter With a Cat*
Music	*The Unfinished Symphony* "Heartbreak Hotel" "This Land Is Your Land"

> Capitalize titles of educational courses when they are language courses or when they are followed by a number or preceded by a proper noun or adjective. Do not capitalize school subjects discussed in a general manner.

10.3.7 RULE

WITH CAPITALS | **H** onors **B** iology | **M** ath 3
| **H** istory 105 | **E** conomics 313
| **L** atin | **F** rench

WITHOUT CAPITALS | **g** eology | **p** sychology
| **a** lgebra | **b** iology
| **h** istory | **m** ath

EXAMPLES

This year, I will be taking **w** oodworking, **E** nglish, **H** onors **C** hemistry, and **w** orld **h** istory.

Mary's favorite classes are **a** rt **h** istory, **F** rench, and **c** hemistry.

She does not like **m** ath and **p** hysical **e** ducation as much.

After **R** ussian class, I have to rush across the building to **b** iology.

See Practice 10.3A
See Practice 10.3B

Read each sentence. Then, write the word or words in each sentence that should be capitalized.

EXAMPLE   I have never met dr. Branson.

ANSWER   *Dr.*

1. Pardon my saying so, senator, but mayor Harding is right.

2. I agree that mr. Felt is fully recovered.

3. queen Elizabeth I ruled when sir Francis Drake defeated the Spanish Armada.

4. A colonel without a captain is useless according to general Campbell.

5. I voted for congressman Moore because he had more experience than his opponent.

6. In my opinion, *a day apart* is a fantastic title for the book.

7. In the movie *one flew over the cuckoo's nest,* nurse Ratchet plays the antagonist.

8. I noticed sergeant Smithers with the commander this morning.

9. The nurse asked dr. Blithe to clarify his prescription for mr. Bloomberg.

10. When will professor Jackson return our papers on Homer's *the odyssey*?

PRACTICE 10.3B **Using All of the Rules of Capitalization**

Read each sentence. Then, rewrite each sentence, using the conventions of capitalization.

EXAMPLE   Kelly is an american citizen; her father, mr. borge, is danish-born.

ANSWER   *Kelly is an American citizen; her father, Mr. Borge, is Danish-born.*

11. the president of the united states both works and lives in the white house.

12. It is ironic that general "stonewall" jackson was killed by his own troops.

13. The great wall of china impressed mr. cheng so much that he wrote a book about it.

14. robert louis stevenson's book *kidnapped* is an adventure story set in scotland.

15. ms. malone was appointed the new head of the english department at the university.

16. "Her royal majesty queen elizabeth II recently visited the united states," said the british reporter.

17. I think senator McVittie made strong arguments during the debate.

18. *The star-spangled banner* was written in baltimore harbor by francis scott key.

19. mr. and mrs. lane hosted the memorial day picnic.

20. Did you read the latest issue of *stars*?

SPEAKING APPLICATION

Discuss with a partner the importance of capitalization in names and titles. Together, answer the following question: How does capitalizing a title show respect?

WRITING APPLICATION

Choose a personal title, such as "professor" or "mayor" and write four sentences. Two sentences should demonstrate when the title is capitalized, and the other two sentences should demonstrate when it is not capitalized.

PUNCTUATION

Follow the conventions of punctuation to craft clear sentences that readers can follow with ease.

WRITE GUY *Jeff Anderson, M.Ed.*

WHAT DO YOU NOTICE?

Keep track of punctuation as you zoom in on lines from *Beowulf*, translated by Burton Raffel.

MENTOR TEXT

> Now Grendel and I are called
> Together, and I've come. Grant me, then,
> Lord and protector of this noble place,
> A single request!

Now, ask yourself the following questions:

- What purpose does the apostrophe serve in the second line?
- What does the exclamation mark tell you about the request being made?

In the second line, the apostrophe in *I've* shows that the letters *h* and *a* have been deleted from the word *have* to form the contraction. Writers also use apostrophes to show possession, such as in the phrase *Beowulf's request*. The exclamation mark shows that the speaker is making his single request with great emotion.

Grammar for Writers Writers who understand how to correctly use punctuation can be creative while knowing that readers will still understand their ideas. Punctuation serves many purposes, so use it in a variety of ways to make your writing more interesting.

Do you always check your punctuation?

Yes! Of course! Especially the exclamation marks!

11.1 End Marks

End marks tell readers when to pause and for how long. They signal the end or conclusion of a sentence, word, or phrase. There are three end marks: the **period (.)**, the **question mark (?)**, and the **exclamation mark (!)**.

Using Periods

A **period** indicates the end of a declarative or imperative sentence, an indirect question, or an abbreviation. The period is the most common end mark.

> **RULE 11.1.1**
>
> Use a **period** to end a declarative sentence, a mild imperative sentence, and an indirect question.

A **declarative sentence** is a statement of fact or opinion.

DECLARATIVE SENTENCE	This is an interesting painting.

An **imperative sentence** gives a direction or command. Often, the first word of an imperative sentence is a verb.

MILD IMPERATIVE SENTENCE	Finish cooking the meal.

An **indirect question** restates a question in a declarative sentence. It does not give the speaker's exact words.

INDIRECT QUESTION	Bill asked me whether it would rain.

Other Uses of Periods

In addition to signaling the end of a statement, periods can also signal that words have been shortened, or abbreviated.

> **RULE 11.1.2**
>
> Use a period after most abbreviations and after initials.

PERIODS IN ABBREVIATIONS	
Titles	Dr., Sr., Mrs., Mr., Gov., Maj., Rev., Prof.
Place Names	Ave., Bldg., Blvd., Mt., Dr., St., Ter., Rd.
Times and Dates	Sun., Dec., sec., min., hr., yr., A.M.
Initials	E. B. White, Robin F. Brancato, R. Brett

Some abbreviations do not end with periods. Metric measurements, state abbreviations used with ZIP Codes, and most standard measurements do not need periods. The abbreviation for inch, *in.,* is the exception.

EXAMPLES mm, cm, kg, L, C, CA, TX, ft, gal

The following chart lists some abbreviations with and without periods.

ABBREVIATIONS WITH AND WITHOUT END MARKS	
approx. = approximately	misc. = miscellaneous
COD = cash on delivery	mph = miles per hour
dept. = department	No. = number
doz. = dozen(s)	p. or pg. = page; pp. = pages
EST = Eastern Standard Time	POW = prisoner of war
FM = frequency modulation	pub. = published, publisher
gov. or govt. – government	pvt. = private
ht. = height	rpm = revolutions per minute
incl. = including	R.S.V.P. = please reply
ital = italics	sp. = spelling
kt. = karat or carat	SRO = standing room only
meas. = measure	vol. = volume
mfg. = manufacturing	wt. = weight

Sentences Ending With Abbreviations When a sentence ends with an abbreviation that uses a period, do not put a second period at the end. If an end mark other than a period is required, add the end mark.

Please call Bob Fans Sr.

Is that Sam Bents Jr.?   See Practice 11.1A

Do not use periods with acronyms, words formed with the first or first few letters of a series of words.

ACRONYMS   USA (United States of America)

DOB (Date of Birth)

Use a period after numbers and letters in outlines.

EXAMPLE   I. Maintaining your pet's health

A. Diet

1. For a puppy

2. For a mature dog

B. Exercise

Using Question Marks

A **question mark** follows a word, phrase, or sentence that asks a question. A question is often in inverted word order.

Use a question mark to end an interrogative sentence, an incomplete question, or a statement intended as a question.

INTERROGATIVE   Does grass grow from seed?
SENTENCE
What time do you want to meet for brunch?

INCOMPLETE   Many birds fly south for the winter. Why?
QUESTION
I will take you home. When?

Use care, however, in ending statements with question marks. It is better to rephrase the statement as a direct question.

STATEMENT WITH A QUESTION MARK	The puppies haven't been born yet **?**
	We are going home **?**
REVISED INTO A DIRECT QUESTION	Haven't the puppies been born yet **?**
	Are we going home **?**

Use a period instead of a question mark with an **indirect question**—a question that is restated as a declarative sentence.

EXAMPLE	Ken wanted to know when the take-out food he ordered would come **.**
	He wondered if it would be on time **.**

Using Exclamation Marks

An **exclamation mark** signals an exclamatory sentence, an imperative sentence, or an interjection. It indicates strong emotion and should be used sparingly.

> Use an **exclamation mark** to end an exclamatory sentence, a forceful imperative sentence, or an interjection expressing strong emotion.

RULE 11.1.6

EXCLAMATORY SENTENCE	Look at the great weather **!**
FORCEFUL IMPERATIVE SENTENCE	Don't drop the packages **!**

An interjection can be used with a comma or an exclamation mark. An exclamation mark increases the emphasis.

EXAMPLES	Wow **!** The day was wonderful **.**
	Oh **!** The action was great **.**
WITH A COMMA	Wow **,** the day was wonderful **.**

See Practice 11.1B

PRACTICE 11.1A **Using Periods Correctly in Sentences**

Read each sentence. Then, rewrite the sentence, adding periods where needed. If the sentence is correct, write *correct*.

EXAMPLE   Socrates, who was born in 469 BC, was a philosopher.

ANSWER   *Socrates, who was born in 469 B.C., was a philosopher.*

1. I found a 5-kt gold earring on the ground.

2. Mail the letter to Dr Hugo Rivera, 9 Main St, Ft Worth, Tex, before Wednesday.

3. J R R Tolkien wrote the *Lord of the Rings* trilogy.

4. Kylie asked if Thurgood Marshall had been a supreme court judge.

5. Her flight is scheduled for arrival on Tues, Mar 12, at 7:14 PM.

6. Capt Mattson led the parade down Grant Blvd before turning onto Fifth St.

7. It took 6 m of string to tie all the newspapers.

8. Dr Sanchez asked me if I brushed my teeth after every meal

9. Tang finally woke up at 9:50 AM.

10. Franklin M. Martin Jr gave me this book.

PRACTICE 11.1B **Using Question Marks and Exclamation Marks Correctly in Sentences**

Read each item. Then, write the correct end mark for each item.

EXAMPLE   What time does the museum open

ANSWER   *?*

11. What a lovely card

12. Great work

13. How long have I been asleep

14. How often does the train stop at this station

15. Will you help at the car wash

16. Don't slam the door

17. Do you know how to change a flat tire

18. Thank you for these sweet-smelling flowers

19. I'm glad that's over

20. When did Jacinta call

SPEAKING APPLICATION

Take turns with a partner. Say sentences that contain initials and abbreviations for titles, place names, times, and dates. Your partner should tell where periods would be inserted if your sentences were written.

WRITING APPLICATION

Write two sentences that use question marks and two sentences that use exclamation marks. Label each sentence as *interrogative*, *exclamatory*, or *forceful imperative*.

11.2 Commas

A **comma** tells the reader to pause briefly before continuing a sentence. Commas may be used to separate elements in a sentence or to set off part of a sentence.

Commas are used more than any other internal punctuation mark. To check for correct comma use, read a sentence aloud and note where a pause helps you to group your ideas. Commas signal to readers that they should take a short breath.

Using Commas With Compound Sentences

A **compound sentence** consists of two or more main or independent clauses that are joined by a coordinating conjunction, such as *and, but, for, nor, or, so,* or *yet*.

> Use a **comma** before a conjunction to separate two or more independent or main clauses in a **compound sentence.**

11.2.1 RULE

Use a comma before a conjunction only when there are complete sentences on both sides of the conjunction. Do not use a comma if the conjunction joins a compound subject, a compound verb, prepositional phrases, or subordinate clauses.

EXAMPLE

Jane is getting ready to compete **,** but I won't
<small>independent clause</small>

be able to see her perform.
<small>independent clause</small>

In some compound sentences, the main or independent clauses are very brief, and the meaning is clear. When this occurs, the comma before the conjunction may be omitted.

EXAMPLES

Polly read the chapter but she didn't understand it.

Laura would like to come for dinner but she is too busy today.

In other sentences, conjunctions are used to join compound subjects or verbs, prepositional phrases, or subordinate clauses. Because these sentences have only one independent clause, they do not take a comma before the conjunction.

CONJUNCTIONS WITHOUT COMMAS	
Compound Subject	Tim and Mike met at camp for the hike.
Compound Verb	The team laughed and reminisced as they remembered their season.
Two Prepositional Phrases	The player ran down the field and past the goalie.
Two Subordinate Clauses	I enjoy hiking trips only if they are short and if we camp outside.

A **nominative absolute** is a noun or pronoun followed by a participle or participial phrase that functions independently of the rest of the sentence.

RULE 11.2.2

Use a comma after a nominative absolute.

The following example shows a comma with a nominative absolute.

EXAMPLE   Important people being present, I decided to dress appropriately.

Avoiding Comma Splices

Remember to use both a comma and a coordinating conjunction in a compound sentence. Using only a comma can result in a **run-on sentence** or a **comma splice**. A **comma splice** occurs when two or more complete sentences have been joined with only a comma. Either punctuate separate sentences with an end mark or a semicolon, or find a way to join the sentences. (See Section 11.3 for more information on semicolons.)

RULE 11.2.3

Avoid comma splices.

INCORRECT   The snow clumped on the house, some of the gutters snapped under the weight.

CORRECT   The snow clumped on the house. Some of the gutters snapped under the weight.

Using Commas in a Series

A **series** consists of three or more words, phrases, or subordinate clauses of a similar kind. A series can occur in any part of a sentence.

> Use commas to separate three or more words, phrases, or clauses in a series.

11.2.4 RULE

Notice that a comma follows each of the items except the last one in these series. The conjunction *and* or *or* is added after the last comma.

SERIES OF WORDS
The pet store sold birds, cats, dogs, fish, and pet products.

SERIES OF PREPOSITIONAL PHRASES
The sign showed the way through the city, over the bridge, and past the river.

SUBORDINATE CLAUSES IN A SERIES
The critic wrote that the food was great, the atmosphere was exceptional, and the music was beautiful.

If each item (except for the last one) in a series is followed by a conjunction, do not use commas.

EXAMPLE
I rented comedies and romances and horror movies.

A second exception to this rule concerns items such as *salt and pepper*, which are paired so often that they are considered a single item.

EXAMPLES
On the platter were peanut butter and jelly, ham and cheese, and turkey and cheese sandwiches.

Tim's favorite breakfast foods are toast and juice, oatmeal and raisins, and bacon and eggs.

Using Commas Between Adjectives

Sometimes, two or more adjectives are placed before the noun they describe.

> Use commas to separate **coordinate adjectives,** also called **independent modifiers,** or adjectives of equal rank.

EXAMPLES   a dark, long tunnel

a long, tiring, challenging race

An adjective is equal in rank to another if the word *and* can be inserted between them without changing the meaning of the sentence. Another way to test whether or not adjectives are equal is to reverse their order. If the sentence still sounds correct, they are of equal rank. In the first example, *a long, dark tunnel* still makes sense.

If you cannot place the word *and* between adjectives or reverse their order without changing the meaning of the sentence, they are called **cumulative adjectives.**

> Do not use a comma between cumulative adjectives.

EXAMPLES   a new life jacket
(*a life new jacket* does not make sense)

many long days
(*long many days* does not make sense)

> Do not use a comma to separate the last adjective in a series from the noun it modifies.

INCORRECT   The bright, sunny, day felt wonderful.

CORRECT   The bright, sunny day felt wonderful.

See Practice 11.2A
See Practice 11.2B

PRACTICE 11.2A Using Commas Correctly in Sentences

Read each sentence. Then, rewrite each sentence, adding commas where needed. Write the reason(s) for the comma usage.

EXAMPLE We requested the change months ago yet it hasn't happened.

ANSWER *We requested the change months ago, yet it hasn't happened.—compound sentence*

1. The camping trip was fun but it rained a lot.
2. Chili the mockingbird the pecan tree and the rodeo are all symbols of Texas.
3. The soft cushiony chair is so comfortable.
4. Sam is a sweet mild-tempered dog.
5. She took her jacket but she forgot her gloves.
6. His arm tired and sore the pitcher retired to the dugout.
7. Smiles cheers and thunderous clapping welcomed the new team to the field.
8. George flipped his hat into the air caught it and then put it on his head.
9. Dark green vegetables red meat beans and nuts are excellent sources of iron.
10. Their hands up in the air the thieves surrendered to the police.

PRACTICE 11.2B Revising to Correct Errors in Comma Use

Read each sentence. Then, rewrite each sentence, adding or deleting commas as necessary.

EXAMPLE I wanted to play, basketball, but the ball was deflated.

ANSWER *I wanted to play basketball, but the ball was deflated.*

11. Our clients, enjoyed the presentation, but didn't like the lunch.
12. During the flight I read my book.
13. Join us for the rally because, it's going to be a wild exciting gathering!
14. Mrs. Ramos has a collection of fancy, teapots.
15. No one is better than Leslie at buying designer-like expensive-looking outfits.
16. Frowns on their faces the audience, protested the delay.
17. The ski instructor, was a young energetic teenager.
18. Mr. Harper took great care, with planning his garden, and selecting plants for it.
19. We took the boat out to go fishing, water-skiing and swimming.
20. Elizabeth took many pictures of the city, and the country, and the people she met.

SPEAKING APPLICATION

With a partner, read sentences 2 and 7 aloud. Discuss why commas are needed in those sentences.

WRITING APPLICATION

Write four sentences that use commas incorrectly. Exchange papers with a partner. Your partner should correct your sentences.

Using Commas After Introductory Material

Most material that introduces a sentence should be set off with a comma.

> **Use a comma after an introductory word, phrase, or clause.**

KINDS OF INTRODUCTORY MATERIAL	
Introductory Words	Yes, we do expect to meet with them soon. No, there has not been a time set to meet. Well, I was definitely surprised by his remark.
Nouns of Direct Address	Mia, will you answer the phone?
Introductory Adverbs	Hurriedly, they collected the money for the pizza. Patiently, the coach explained the play again.
Participial Phrases	Moving quickly, she avoided a potential disaster. Working next to each other in the office, we introduced ourselves and started to chat.
Prepositional Phrases	On the snowy mountain, the family went skiing together. After the lengthy flight, we were all exhausted.
Infinitive Phrases	To choose the right gift, I reviewed their housewarming list. To finish her test on time, Addie will have to use fewer details.
Adverbial Clauses	When he asked for a permit for the house, he was sure it would be denied. If you play baseball, you may be interested in going to a game.

Commas and Prepositional Phrases Only one comma should be used after two prepositional phrases or a compound participial or infinitive phrase.

EXAMPLES   In a pocket in the backpack, he found
his cellphone.

Wandering in the crowd and to avoid getting lost,
the children asked a firefighter for help.

It is not necessary to set off short prepositional phrases. However,
a comma can help avoid confusion.

CONFUSING   In the rain puddles covered the road.

CLEAR   In the rain, puddles covered the road.

Using Commas With Parenthetical Expressions

A **parenthetical expression** is a word or phrase that interrupts
the flow of the sentence.

> **Use commas to set off parenthetical expressions from the rest
> of the sentence.**

11.2.9 RULE

Parenthetical expressions may come in the middle or at the end
of a sentence. A parenthetical expression in the middle of a
sentence needs two commas—one on each side; it needs only one
comma if it appears at the end of a sentence.

KINDS OF PARENTHETICAL EXPRESSIONS	
Nouns of Direct Address	Will you have breakfast with us, Cathy? I wonder, Mr. Colette, where they'll go for breakfast.
Conjunctive Adverbs	Someone had already bought them glasses, however. We could not, therefore, buy them.
Common Expressions	I listened to Ellie's report as carefully as everyone else did, I think.
Contrasting Expressions	Dena is twenty, not nineteen. Eva's personality, not her beauty, won Frank's heart.

Using Commas With Nonessential Expressions

To determine when a phrase or clause should be set off with commas, decide whether the phrase or clause is *essential* or *nonessential* to the meaning of the sentence. The terms *restrictive* and *nonrestrictive* may also be used.

An **essential,** or **restrictive, phrase** or **clause** is necessary to the meaning of the sentence. **Nonessential,** or **nonrestrictive, expressions** can be left out without changing the meaning of the sentence. Although the nonessential material may be interesting, the sentence can be read without it and still make sense. Depending on their importance in a sentence, appositives, participial phrases, and adjectival clauses can be either essential or nonessential. Only nonessential expressions should be set off with commas.

NONESSENTIAL APPOSITIVE	The meal was prepared by Christopher, the newest young chef.
NONESSENTIAL PARTICIPIAL PHRASE	The mountain, one that few have climbed, is the largest in the state.
NONESSENTIAL ADJECTIVAL CLAUSE	The river, which freezes in the winter, is popular with canoers in the summer.

Do not use commas to set off essential expressions.

ESSENTIAL APPOSITIVE	The part was played by the famous actress Katharine Hepburn.
ESSENTIAL PARTICIPIAL PHRASE	The man wearing the coat is my father.
ESSENTIAL ADJECTIVAL CLAUSE	The article that Laura suggested would change my conclusions.

See Practice 11.2C
See Practice 11.2D

PRACTICE 11.2C **Placing Commas Correctly in Sentences**

Read each sentence. Then, rewrite each sentence, adding commas where they are needed.

EXAMPLE   Before Monica could react the dishes had fallen to the floor.

ANSWER   *Before Monica could react, the dishes had fallen to the floor.*

1. Once the storm was over the snow melted quickly in the sun.

2. To win at chess I usually take my opponent's queen first.

3. Janice not Fernando will take the girls to the mall.

4. In addition the city has many accessible walking tours.

5. I am without a doubt the tallest person in the room.

6. Molly please make your bed.

7. Growing up we never had a treehouse.

8. Laura Ingalls Wilder who had three sisters wrote nine books in the *Little House* series.

9. Tomatoes are in fact fruits not vegetables.

10. To prevent a fire check that the toaster is unplugged.

PRACTICE 11.2D **Revising Sentences for Proper Comma Use**

Read each sentence. Then, rewrite each sentence, adding or deleting commas as necessary.

EXAMPLE   To ensure accuracy we counted the ballots, three times.

ANSWER   *To ensure accuracy, we counted the ballots three times.*

11. Warned by the radio announcer Mom took that alternate route, to avoid the accident not, because she was lost.

12. Please return this book to the library, for me Pru.

13. If you think you're going to sneeze, have a tissue, ready.

14. The meat, was overcooked, and too salty.

15. Moving much more slowly, than usual, Caleb showed us the dance steps.

16. Mr. Bailey who used to be a member of the Coast Guard, took in the lost kitten.

17. He must nevertheless, take the exam before Wednesday.

18. The keys, will turn up soon we hope.

19. I always use yellow mustard, not, ketchup on my hot dogs.

20. Happily she took the project home, with her.

SPEAKING APPLICATION

Take turns with a partner. Say sentences with appositives, participial phrases, and adverbial clauses. Your partner should tell where commas would be inserted if your sentences were written.

WRITING APPLICATION

Write a short story that includes at least six different ways to use commas, including introductory material, parenthetical expressions, and nonessential expressions.

Using Commas With Dates, Geographical Names, and Titles

Dates usually have several parts, including months, days, and years. Commas separate these elements for easier reading.

RULE 11.2.10

When a date is made up of two or more parts, use a comma after each item, except in the case of a month followed by a day.

EXAMPLES   The engagement took place on February 10, 2009, and they were married on June 6, 2010.

Our vacation started on April 15 and ended eight days later.
(no comma needed after the day of the month)

Commas are also used when the month and the day are used as an appositive to rename a day of the week.

EXAMPLES   Friday, June 12, was the first trial flight of our new plane.

Beth will arrive on Monday, December 5, and will stay until Friday.

When a date contains only a month and a year, commas are unnecessary.

EXAMPLES   I will run for office in November 2012.

Tom will visit South Africa in April 2011.

If the parts of a date have already been joined by prepositions, no comma is needed.

EXAMPLE   The city's new street lighting was first turned on in May of 1935.

> **When a geographical name is made up of two or more parts, use a comma after each item.**
> 11.2.11 RULE

EXAMPLES My parents, who moved to Dallas, Texas, missed their old friends but like their new friends.

They're going to Ottawa, Ontario, Canada, for their spring choir trip.

See Practice 11.2E

> **When a name is followed by one or more titles, use a comma after the name and after each title.**
> 11.2.12 RULE

EXAMPLE John Chang, P.T., works with the football team.

A similar rule applies with some business abbreviations.

EXAMPLE BookQual, Inc., publishes books about travel.

Using Commas in Numbers

Commas make large numbers easier to read by grouping them.

> **With large numbers of more than three digits, use a comma after every third digit starting from the right.**
> 11.2.13 RULE

EXAMPLES 1,000,000 dollars, 2,500 cars, 1,400 cups

> **Do not use a comma in ZIP Codes, telephone numbers, page numbers, years, serial numbers, or house numbers.**
> 11.2.14 RULE

ZIP CODE	07481	YEAR NUMBER	2010
TELEPHONE NUMBER	(201) 555-0748	SERIAL NUMBER	603-528-919
PAGE NUMBER	Page 2343	HOUSE NUMBER	12581 Rivers Road

See Practice 11.2F

PRACTICE 11.2E ▷ **Using Commas With Dates and Geographical Names**

Read each sentence. Then, rewrite each sentence to show where to correctly place commas in dates and geographical names.

EXAMPLE His golf vacation is in Yona Guam.

ANSWER *His golf vacation is in Yona, Guam.*

1. The Declaration of Independence was not actually signed on July 4 1776.

2. On September 17 1998, we visited our friends in Helena Montana.

3. Tuesday February is a holiday in China.

4. Anika was born in Brisbane Queensland Australia.

5. Many students in Anne Arundel County Maryland apply to the Naval Academy in Annapolis.

6. February 29 2000 was a leap day.

7. Terrance graduated at the top of his class on June 3 2004 in Alexandria Virginia.

8. We left for Santa Fe New Mexico on November 15 2005.

9. Abraham Lincoln was born on February 12 1809 and died on April 15 1865.

10. He is a doctor in Pago Pago American Samoa.

PRACTICE 11.2F ▷ **Editing Sentences for Proper Comma Usage**

Read each sentence. Then, rewrite each sentence, adding or deleting commas where needed.

EXAMPLE Did Jane Carrie and Jean go to Lincoln Nebraska last summer?

ANSWER *Did Jane, Carrie, and Jean go to Lincoln, Nebraska, last summer?*

11. Taylor Paul Ph.D. will be teaching this class, and Ms. Tiffany Lloyd will assist.

12. My favorite beaches were in Santa Monica California and Cape Cod Massachusetts.

13. Each box contains 185000 plastic cups.

14. My neighbor bought the house on, Saturday April 20 and he built that fence on April 25.

15. Edgar Allan Poe was born in 1,809.

16. Lionel Blaire M.D. lives in Boise Idaho during the summer and Dallas Texas in the winter.

17. Despite the traffic, we made it to Wilmington Delaware by Saturday July 9.

18. Neville Ward Sr. opened Kiddie Toys Ltd. in March 2002.

19. Karen lives at 1,394, Livingston Street.

20. If my printer breaks, I won't be able to finish the assignment by Friday October 9.

SPEAKING APPLICATION

Reread sentences 4 and 10. Discuss with a partner the necessity of commas in geographical names, especially in the names of foreign locations.

WRITING APPLICATION

Write six sentences with misused commas in dates, geographical names, titles, and numbers. Exchange papers with a partner. Your partner should correct your sentences.

Using Commas With Addresses and in Letters

Commas are also used in addresses, salutations of friendly letters, and closings of friendly or business letters.

> **Use a comma after each item in an address made up of two or more parts.**

11.2.15 RULE

Commas are placed after the name, street, and city. No comma separates the state from the ZIP Code. Instead, insert an extra space between them.

EXAMPLE   Send a card to the Santana family, 350 Ocean
           Lane, Brooklyn, New York 11201.

Fewer commas are needed when an address is written in a letter or on an envelope.

EXAMPLE   Ms. Wanda Smith

           85 Tribute Street

           Scranton, PA 18501

> **Use a comma after the salutation in a personal letter and after the closing in all letters.**

11.2.16 RULE

SALUTATIONS	Dear Aunt Sarah,	Dear Will,
CLOSINGS	Your friend,	Cordially,

See Practice 11.2G

Using Commas in Elliptical Sentences

In **elliptical sentences,** words that are understood are left out. Commas make these sentences easier to read.

> **Use a comma to indicate the words left out of an elliptical sentence.**

11.2.17 RULE

EXAMPLE   The Brinks celebrate their holidays formally;
          the Blanes **,** casually.

The words *celebrate their holidays* have been omitted from the
second clause of the sentence. The comma has been inserted in
their place so the meaning is still clear. The sentence could be
restated in this way: *The Brinks celebrate their holidays formally;
The Blanes celebrate their holidays casually.*

Using Commas With Direct Quotations

Commas are also used to indicate where **direct quotations** begin
and end. (See Section 11.4 for more information on punctuating
quotations.)

RULE 11.2.18

> **Use commas to set off a direct quotation from the rest of a
> sentence.**

EXAMPLES   "You're here late **,** " commented Jake's brother.

           She said **,** "The orientation ran longer than
           expected **.** "

           "I hope **,** " Anna's mother said **,** "the professor
           doesn't forget the test **.** "

Using Commas for Clarity

Commas help you group words that belong together.

RULE 11.2.19

> **Use a comma to prevent a sentence from being misunderstood.**

UNCLEAR   Near the auditorium builders were constructing
          new dorms.

CLEAR   Near the auditorium **,** builders were constructing
          new dorms.

Misuses of Commas

Because commas appear so frequently in writing, some people are tempted to use them where they are not needed. Before you insert a comma, think about how your ideas relate to one another.

MISUSED WITH AN ADJECTIVE AND A NOUN	After a walk, I enjoy a hot, hearty, snack.
CORRECT	After a walk, I enjoy a hot, hearty snack.
MISUSED WITH A COMPOUND SUBJECT	After their vacation, my friend John, and his friend Steve, were invited to the reunion.
CORRECT	After their vacation, my friend John and his friend Steve were invited to the reunion.
MISUSED WITH A COMPOUND VERB	He peeked over the wall, and found his book.
CORRECT	He peeked over the wall and found his book.
MISUSED WITH A COMPOUND OBJECT	He chose a jacket with pockets, and a hood.
CORRECT	He chose a jacket with pockets and a hood.
MISUSED WITH PHRASES	Reading the book, and wondering about the author, she read the back cover.
CORRECT	Reading the book and wondering about the author, she read the back cover.
MISUSED WITH CLAUSES	She discussed what sources are useful in writing an essay, and which sources are reliable.
CORRECT	She discussed what sources are useful in writing an essay and which sources are reliable.

See Practice 11.2H

PRACTICE 11.2G ▷ Adding Commas to Addresses and Letters

Read each item. Then, add commas where needed.

EXAMPLE   Dear Uncle Steve

ANSWER   *Dear Uncle Steve,*

1. Dear Cousin Debbie

2. Send an invitation to Theodore Keyes 112 Jackson Lane Miami Florida 33126.

3. Yours truly
   Mason West

4. My best friend moved to Fort Meyers Texas.

5. All the best
   Aunt Tilda

6. Dear Lynn Sharyn and Andrew

7. Douglas Frey
   4 Main Street
   Hastings-on-Hudson NY 10706

8. Sincerely
   Uncle Cory

9. With love
   Mom and Dad

10. My penpal lives at 135 E. River Street Lake Winnipesaukee New Hampshire 03245.

PRACTICE 11.2H ▷ Revising Sentences With Misused Commas

Read each sentence. Then, if a sentence contains a misused comma(s), rewrite the sentence with the comma(s) placed correctly. If the sentence is correct, write *correct*.

EXAMPLE   Last year I traveled, to Montevideo Uruguay for my job.

ANSWER   *Last year, I traveled to Montevideo, Uruguay, for my job.*

11. As of November, 16 2008, the district no longer served juice with school lunches.

12. I enjoy, ice cold, sweet yet sour lemonade.

13. Kemau, and his sister, ski every weekend.

14. Nobel prizes are presented in Stockholm Sweden every December, 10th.

15. Marlene, the spelling bee winner, is a good writer, too.

16. Austin Texas, and Salem Oregon are state capitals.

17. On February, 14 a special day to many people, I always give my mother a dozen roses.

18. Thinking about his next vacation, and where it would be, Mike drank his sweet herbal tea.

19. Greta shook my hand, and thanked me.

20. The inventor's notebook filled with diagrams, and illustrations, showed his innovative ideas.

SPEAKING APPLICATION

After correcting the items in Practice 11.2G, discuss with a partner the use of the comma or commas in each item.

WRITING APPLICATION

Write three compound-complex sentences, using as many commas as you can.

11.3 Semicolons and Colons

The **semicolon (;)** is used to join related independent clauses. Semicolons can also help you avoid confusion in sentences with other internal punctuation. The **colon (:)** is used to introduce lists of items and in other special situations.

Using Semicolons to Join Independent Clauses

Semicolons establish relationships between two independent clauses that are closely connected in thought and structure. A semicolon can also be used to separate independent clauses or items in a series that already contain a number of commas.

> Use a semicolon to join related independent clauses that are not already joined by the conjunctions *and, but, for, nor, or, so,* or *yet.*

EXAMPLE   We explored the country together; we were amazed at all the different kinds of people we met.

Do not use a semicolon to join two unrelated independent clauses. If the clauses are not related, they should be written as separate sentences with a period or another end mark to separate them.

Note that when a sentence contains three or more related independent clauses, they may still be separated with semicolons.

EXAMPLE   The sky grew dark; the wind picked up; the storm rolled in.

Semicolons Join Clauses Separated by Conjunctive Adverbs or Transitional Expressions

Conjunctive adverbs are adverbs that are used as conjunctions to join independent clauses. **Transitional expressions** are expressions that connect one independent clause with another one.

> Use a semicolon to join independent clauses separated by either a **conjunctive adverb** or a **transitional expression.**

CONJUNCTIVE ADVERBS	*also, besides, consequently, first, furthermore, however, indeed, instead, moreover, nevertheless, otherwise, second, then, therefore, thus*
TRANSITIONAL EXPRESSIONS	*as a result, at this time, for instance, in fact, on the other hand, that is*

Place a semicolon *before* a conjunctive adverb or a transitional expression, and place a comma *after* a conjunctive adverb or transitional expression. The comma sets off the conjunctive adverb or transitional expression, which introduces the second clause.

EXAMPLE   He always wins; in fact, he runs faster than everyone.

Because words used as conjunctive adverbs and transitions can also interrupt one continuous sentence, use a semicolon only when there is an independent clause on each side of the conjunctive adverb or transitional expression.

EXAMPLES   He visited army bases in four states in only one week; consequently, he had no time to say good-bye.

We were very impressed, however, with Amy's knowledge of English history.

Using Semicolons to Avoid Confusion

Sometimes, semicolons are used to separate items in a series.

RULE 11.3.3 > **Use semicolons to avoid confusion when independent clauses or items in a series already contain commas.**

When the items in a series already contain several commas, semicolons can be used to group items that belong together. Semicolons are placed at the end of all but the last complete item in the series.

INDEPENDENT CLAUSES

The city, supposedly filled with food, was a fable; and the hungry, tired explorers would only find it in their dreams.

ITEMS IN A SERIES

On their holiday, my cousins visited their older brother, who lives in New Mexico; my sister, who lives in Texas; and my friend, Bill, who lives in California.

Semicolons appear most commonly in a series that contains either nonessential appositives, participial phrases, or adjectival clauses. Commas should separate the nonessential material from the word or words they modify; semicolons should separate the complete items in the series.

APPOSITIVES

I went to the offices of Mr. Wills, the dean; Mrs. Monegro, the admissions director; and William Dee, the president.

PARTICIPIAL PHRASES

I acquired a love for cooking from television, watching live cooking shows; from home, watching my mother cook; and from magazines, reading about famous chefs.

ADJECTIVAL CLAUSES

The large truck that I bought has headlamps, which are very bright; a spot light, which has just been installed; and a powerful engine, which has been newly rebuilt.

Using Colons

The **colon (:)** is used to introduce lists of items and in certain special situations.

> Use a colon after an independent clause to introduce a list of items. Use commas to separate three or more items.

Independent clauses that appear before a colon often include the words *the following*, *as follows*, *these*, or *those*.

EXAMPLES   For my presentation, I had to interview the following experts: a senator, an assemblyperson, and a mayor.

> Do not use a colon after a verb or a preposition.

INCORRECT   Terry always orders: books, tapes, and DVDs.

CORRECT   Terry always orders books, tapes, and DVDs.

> Use a colon to introduce a quotation that is formal or lengthy or a quotation that does not contain a "he said/she said" expression.

EXAMPLE   Oliver Wendell Holmes Jr. wrote this about freedom: "It is only through free debate and free exchange of ideas that government remains responsive to the will of the people and peaceful change is effected."

Even if it is lengthy, dialogue or a casual remark should be introduced by a comma. Use the colon if the quotation is formal or has no tagline.

A colon may also be used to introduce a sentence that explains the sentence that precedes it.

> **Use a colon to introduce a sentence that summarizes or explains the sentence before it.**

EXAMPLE Her explanation for being late was believable : She got lost and had to stop to ask for directions.

Notice that the complete sentence introduced by the colon starts with a capital letter.

> **Use a colon to introduce a formal appositive that follows an independent clause.**

EXAMPLE I had finally decided on a sport : running.

The colon is a stronger punctuation mark than a comma. Using the colon gives more emphasis to the appositive it introduces.

> **Use a colon in a number of special writing situations.**

SPECIAL SITUATIONS REQUIRING COLONS	
Numerals Giving the Time	10 : 30 A.M. 7 : 15 P.M.
References to Periodicals (Volume Number: Page Number)	*Scientific American* 32 : 16 *Time* 24 : 19
Biblical References (Chapter Number: Verse Number)	Esther 4 : 14
Subtitles for Books and Magazines	*A Field Guide for Aquatic Life* : *Sea Creatures and Their Habitats*
Salutations in Business Letters	Dear Mr. Jones : Dear Madam :
Labels Used to Signal Important Ideas	**Warning** : NO Trespassing

See Practice 11.3A
See Practice 11.3B

PRACTICE 11.3A **Adding Semicolons and Colons to Sentences**

Read each item. Then, rewrite each item, adding a semicolon or colon as needed.

EXAMPLE   It would seem like sound advice however, I must consider the source.

ANSWER   *It would seem like sound advice; however, I must consider the source.*

1. The following animals are marsupials kangaroos, koalas, and opossums.

2. The judge ordered "Court is adjourned."

3. Nora lost her compass as a result, she'll have to borrow one.

4. The answer is clear Lower ticket prices.

5. Spiro works days Mindy works nights.

6. Calvin disagreed with the council's decision nevertheless, he supported the council.

7. Janet had written a list of groceries lettuce, tomatoes, cereal, and bread.

8. Dear Ms. Mayor

9. Fred's trip went through several cities Atlanta, New York, Boston, and Chicago.

10. Don't forget the bus leaves at 800 A.M. sharp.

PRACTICE 11.3B **Using Semicolons and Colons**

Read each sentence. Then, rewrite each sentence, replacing the incorrect comma with a semicolon or a colon.

EXAMPLE   The movie starred a famous actor, Paul Newman.

ANSWER   *The movie starred a famous actor: Paul Newman.*

11. Due to the foggy conditions, visibility was low, therefore, traffic was slow.

12. The departing time is 4,30 P.M.

13. Joan brought all the decorations, streamers, lights, posters, and confetti.

14. The elephants ran to higher ground, the monkeys climbed back up their trees.

15. The book was written by a prolific writer, Isaac Asimov.

16. Substituting olive oil for butter is beneficial, The olive oil has no cholesterol.

17. The host welcomed his guests, "Please come in and make yourselves at home."

18. The air was cold, in fact, snow was falling.

19. We stopped in Cheyenne, Wyoming, Louisville, Kentucky, and Savannah, Georgia.

20. Guyana is in South America, Ghana is in Africa.

SPEAKING APPLICATION

With a partner, read aloud the sentences in Practice 11.3A. Then, read your corrected sentences aloud. Discuss whether it is easier or harder to read the sentences that have the semicolons and colons. Explain your answer.

WRITING APPLICATION

Write a short story about a kid who finds a good-luck piece. Use colons and semicolons to combine sentences in your story.

11.4 Quotation Marks, Underlining, and Italics

Quotation marks (" ") set off direct quotations, dialogue, and certain types of titles. Other titles are <u>underlined</u> or set in *italics,* a slanted type style.

Using Quotation Marks With Quotations

Quotation marks identify spoken or written words that you are including in your writing. A **direct quotation** represents a person's exact speech or thoughts. An **indirect quotation** reports the general meaning of what a person said or thought.

> A **direct quotation** is enclosed in quotation marks.

RULE 11.4.1

DIRECT
QUOTATION
"When I learn to play piano," said the girl, "I'm going to practice every day."

> An **indirect quotation** does not require quotation marks.

RULE 11.4.2

INDIRECT
QUOTATION
The girl said that when she learns to play the piano, she'll practice every day.

Both types of quotations are acceptable when you write. Direct quotations, however, generally result in a livelier writing style.

Using Direct Quotations With Introductory, Concluding, and Interrupting Expressions

A writer will generally identify a speaker by using words such as *he asked* or *she said* with a quotation. These expressions, called **conversational taglines** or **tags,** can introduce, conclude, or interrupt a quotation.

Direct Quotations With Introductory Expressions
Commas help you set off introductory information so that your reader understands who is speaking.

Use a comma after short introductory expressions that precede direct quotations.

EXAMPLE   My neighbor cautioned, "If you use the pool, you'll be liable for your safety."

If the introductory conversational tagline is very long or formal in tone, set it off with a colon instead of a comma.

EXAMPLE   At the end of the week, Bill talked about his idea: "My desire is to advance the cause of feeding hungry children."

Direct Quotations With Concluding Expressions
Conversational taglines may also act as concluding expressions.

Use a comma, question mark, or exclamation mark after a direct quotation followed by a concluding expression.

EXAMPLE   "When you received the ticket, you were responsible for paying it on time," the judge stated.

Concluding expressions are not complete sentences; therefore, they do not begin with capital letters. Closing quotation marks are always placed outside the punctuation at the end of direct quotations. Concluding expressions generally end with a period.

Divided Quotations With Interrupting Expressions
You may use a conversational tagline to interrupt the words of a direct quotation, which is also called a **divided quotation.**

> Use a comma after the part of a quoted sentence followed by an interrupting conversational tagline. Use another comma after the tagline. Do not capitalize the first word of the rest of the sentence. Use quotation marks to enclose the quotation. End punctuation should be inside the last quotation mark.

11.4.5 RULE

EXAMPLE "When you received the ticket**,** " the judge stated**,** "you were responsible for paying it on time**.** "

> Use a comma, question mark, or exclamation mark after a quoted sentence that comes before an interrupting conversational tagline. Use a period after the tagline.

11.4.6 RULE

EXAMPLE "You received the ticket**,** " stated the judge**.** "You are responsible for paying it on time**.** "

Quotation Marks With Other Punctuation Marks

Quotation marks are used with commas, semicolons, colons, and all of the end marks. However, the location of the quotation marks in relation to the punctuation marks varies.

> Place a comma or a period *inside* the final quotation mark. Place a semicolon or colon *outside* the final quotation mark.

11.4.7 RULE

EXAMPLES "Georginna was a great monkey**,** " sighed Father.

We just learned about his "archaeological find"**;** we are very excited.

> Place a question mark or an exclamation mark inside the final quotation mark if the end mark is part of the quotation. Do not use an additional end mark.

11.4.8 RULE

EXAMPLE Mike wondered**,** "How could I lose the race**?** "

RULE 11.4.9 Place a question mark or exclamation mark outside the final quotation mark if the end mark is part of the entire sentence, not part of the quotation.

EXAMPLE I was stunned when I heard, "Leave the room"!

Using Single Quotation Marks for Quotations Within Quotations

As you have learned, double quotation marks (" ") should enclose the main quotation in a sentence. The rules for using commas and end marks with double quotation marks also apply to **single quotation marks.**

RULE 11.4.10 Use **single quotation marks (' ')** to set off a quotation within a quotation.

EXAMPLES "I remember Shane quoting Tanya, 'If summer comes, can fall be far behind?'," Ken said.

"The instructor said, 'You may begin'," the student explained.

Punctuating Explanatory Material Within Quotations

Explanatory material within quotations should be placed in brackets. (See Section 11.7 for more information on brackets.)

RULE 11.4.11 Use brackets to enclose an explanation located within a quotation. The brackets show that the explanation is not part of the original quotation.

EXAMPLE The council person said, "This law is a link between two generations [young and old]."

See Practice 11.4A
See Practice 11.4B

PRACTICE 11.4A **Using Quotation Marks**

Read each sentence. Then, rewrite each sentence, inserting quotation marks where they are needed.

EXAMPLE   He said, I may not remember a name, but I never forget a face.

ANSWER   *He said, "I may not remember a name, but I never forget a face."*

1. Sure, said Fareed. I'll get it for you.

2. Pam interjected, Pick me!

3. How many songs are on the CD? asked Mike.

4. The reporter said, The grateful mother repeated, Thank you, several times.

5. Shyly, Sarah asked, Can I help?

6. Keri thought that Jill said, I can't make it; so Keri went to the library alone.

7. The machine answered, Record your message at the beep.

8. Winnie answered the phone, but no one responded when she said, Hello.

9. Taylor groaned, Not again!

10. Please don't turn off the computer, Miss Patel, the librarian requested.

PRACTICE 11.4B **Revising for the Correct Use of Quotation Marks**

Read each sentence. Then, rewrite each sentence, correcting the misuse of quotation marks.

EXAMPLE   "The river, said Virginia, is rising fast."

ANSWER   *"The river," said Virginia, "is rising fast."*

11. "The principal addressed the students: Stay in your classes until the bell rings."

12. When Ed says, "I'll be there," I believe him, I explained.

13. "Dan continued, Then, the horse jumped the fence and galloped across the field."

14. Ellen said, "I'll be right back," Marcos claimed.

15. "The article stated, The recent news leaked to the press [about the new train station] is false."

16. Oh well! said Robert, "That's the end."

17. "How much time is left to complete the exam? Myra asked."

18. "That's the best I can do, the salesman said." It is my final offer.

19. "You know, my mother said, you should really wear a coat. It is cold outside."

20. "The dessert," said Nina, is too sweet for me."

SPEAKING APPLICATION

Take turns with a partner. Say sentences that are direct quotations. Your partner should indicate where quotation marks would be needed if your sentences were written.

WRITING APPLICATION

Write five additional sentences that contain misused quotation marks. Exchange papers with a partner. Your partner should correct the misuse of the quotation marks.

Using Quotation Marks for Dialogue

A conversation between two or more people is called a **dialogue.**

When writing a dialogue, begin a new paragraph with each change of speaker.

The sun slowly set over the western edge of the ski resort, as the people watched the sky turn pink.

Beth looked at the heavy snow and talked with her sister about her plans.

"I'm going south," said Beth. "I think I'll like the sunny weather better; you know I don't like the snow."

"Have you packed yet?" asked Meg. "Can I have your blue snow jacket?"

"It's all yours," said Beth. "It is fine with me if I never see it again."

For quotations longer than a paragraph, put quotation marks at the beginning of each paragraph and at the end of the final paragraph.

John McPhee wrote an essay about a canoe trip on the St. John River in northern Maine. He introduces his readers to the river in the following way:

"We have been out here four days now and rain has been falling three. The rain appears to be ending. Breaks of blue are opening in the sky. Sunlight is coming through, and a wind is rising.

"I was not prepared for the St. John River, did not anticipate its size. I saw it as a narrow trail flowing north, twisting through balsam and spruce—a small and intimate forest river, something like the Allagash . . . ."

Using Quotation Marks in Titles

Generally, quotation marks are used around the titles of shorter works.

> **Use quotation marks to enclose the titles of short written works.**

WRITTEN WORKS THAT USE QUOTATION MARKS	
Title of a Short Story	"Through the Looking Glass" by Lewis Carroll "The Fairy Box" by Louisa May Alcott
Chapter From a Book	"The Boy Who Lived" in *Harry Potter and the Sorcerer's Stone*
Title of a Short Poem	"Mending Wall" by Robert Frost
Essay Title	"Nature" by Ralph Waldo Emerson
Title of an Article	"Tear Down This Wall" by Patrick Symmes

> **Use quotation marks around the titles of episodes in a television or radio series, songs, and parts of a long musical composition.**

ARTISTIC WORK TITLES THAT USE QUOTATION MARKS	
Episode	"The Loneliest People" from *60 Minutes*
Song Title	"What's Love Got to Do With It" Tina Turner
Part of a Long Musical Composition	"Spring" from *The Four Seasons* "E.T. Phone Home" from *E.T. The Extra-Terrestrial* soundtrack

> **Use quotation marks around the title of a work that is mentioned as part of a collection.**

The title *Plato* would normally be underlined or italicized. In the example below, however, the title is placed in quotation marks because it is cited as part of a larger work.

EXAMPLE   "Plato" from *Great Books of the Western World*

Using Underlining and Italics in Titles and Other Special Words

Underlining and **italics** help make titles and other special words and names stand out in your writing. Underlining is used only in handwritten or typewritten material. In printed material, italic (slanted) print is generally used instead of underlining.

> Underline or italicize the titles of long written works and the titles of publications that are published as a single work.

WRITTEN WORKS THAT ARE UNDERLINED OR ITALICIZED	
Title of a Book	*Harry Potter and the Sorcerer's Stone*
Title of a Newspaper	*The Boston Globe*
Title of a Play	*Death of a Salesman* *Hamlet*
Title of a Long Poem	*On Time*
Title of a Magazine	*Time*

The portion of a newspaper title that should be italicized or underlined will vary from newspaper to newspaper. *The New York Times* should always be fully capitalized and italicized or underlined. Other papers, however, can be treated in one of two ways: the *Los Angeles Times* or the Los Angeles *Times*. You may want to check the paper's Web site for correct formatting.

> Underline or italicize the titles of movies, television and radio series, long works of music, and works of art.

ARTISTIC WORKS THAT ARE UNDERLINED OR ITALICIZED	
Title of a Movie	*Jaws, E.T. The Extra-Terrestrial*
Title of a Television Series	*Seinfeld, The Simpsons*
Title of a Long Work of Music	*Jupiter in C Major*
Title of an Album (on any media)	*Yellow Submarine*
Title of a Painting	*Flying Machine, Battle*
Title of a Sculpture	*Crouching Woman* *Young Mother with Child*

> Do not underline, italicize, or place in quotation marks the name of the Bible, its books and divisions, or other holy scriptures, such as the Torah and the Qu'ran.

11.4.19 RULE

EXAMPLE   Betty read from James in the New Testament?

Government documents should also not be underlined or enclosed in quotation marks.

> Do not underline, italicize, or place in quotation marks the titles of government charters, alliances, treaties, acts, statutes, speeches, or reports.

11.4.20 RULE

EXAMPLE   The Taft-Hartley Labor Act was passed in 1947.

> Underline or italicize the names of air, sea, and space craft.

11.4.21 RULE

EXAMPLE   My aunt sailed on the *Queen Mary II*.

> Underline or italicize words, letters, or numbers (figures) used as names for themselves.

11.4.22 RULE

EXAMPLES   Her *i's* and her *I's* look too much like *1's*.

Avoid sprinkling your speech with *like*.

> Underline or italicize foreign words and phrases not yet accepted into English.

11.4.23 RULE

See Practice 11.4C
See Practice 11.4D

EXAMPLE   "*Buenos dias*," she said, meaning "good day" in Spanish.

PRACTICE 11.4C Using Punctuation in Titles and Dialogue

Read each sentence. Then, rewrite each sentence, adding the correct punctuation where needed. If any words need to be italicized, underline those words.

EXAMPLE   I just finished reading The Grapes of Wrath, said Oscar.

ANSWER   *"I just finished reading The Grapes of Wrath," said Oscar.*

1. Let's go to the movies, Diane suggested.

2. I can't said Tony. I have to pick up my uncle at the train station. Want to come along?

3. Diana replied immediately, Sure.

4. It's going to be cold. Bring a warm sweater. Tony told Diane.

5. Whoever thought said Diego that the race would end in a tie?

6. Joe replied, Yeah, that's really unusual.

7. Kelly asked Who wrote the book Emma?

8. Trina answered, Jane Austen wrote that book; she also wrote Sense and Sensibility.

9. Julian asked, Who are the main characters in the short story The Gift of the Magi?

10. I think they're James and Della Young, said Jerome.

PRACTICE 11.4D Revising Punctuation in Titles and Dialogue

Read each sentence. Then, rewrite each sentence, revising the use of quotation marks. If any words need to be italicized, underline those words.

EXAMPLE   "My book report is on Frankenstein by Mary Shelley, said Louise"

ANSWER   *"My book report is on Frankenstein by Mary Shelley," said Louise.*

11. "My report Carl said is on The Canterbury Tales."

12. Isn't that about a group of people telling stories while on a trip? "asked Carmen."

13. "Yes. My favorite character is the clerk, replied Carl."

14. "Joanna chimed in I wrote my report on the Odyssey."

15. "Me, too, said Wayne" .

16. "Who was your favorite character?" Joanna asked. Mine is Odysseus.

17. "Wayne replied, I liked Circe, the siren."

18. "Louise added, "I felt sorry for the Cyclops."

19. "What's a cyclops? Carmen asked"

20. "A creature with one eye," Wayne answered. Odysseus outsmarted him."

SPEAKING APPLICATION

Take turns with a partner. Say sentences that contain both dialogue and titles. For each sentence, your partner should indicate which words would be put into quotation marks and/ or italicized if the sentences were written.

WRITING APPLICATION

Write a short dialogue in which two characters discuss their favorite works of literature. Use at least three titles and five lines of dialogue.

11.5 Hyphens

The **hyphen** (-) is used to combine words, spell some numbers and words, and show a connection between the syllables of words that are broken at the ends of lines.

Using Hyphens in Numbers

Hyphens are used to join compound numbers and fractions.

> Use a hyphen when you spell out two-word numbers from twenty-one through ninety-nine.

 RULE 11.5.1

EXAMPLES fifty-five centimeters   sixty-eight meters

> Use a hyphen when you use a fraction as an adjective but not when you use a fraction as a noun.

 RULE 11.5.2

ADJECTIVE   The recipe calls for one-half cup of milk.

NOUN   Three quarters of the convention is over.

> Use a hyphen between a number and a word when they are combined as modifiers. Do not use a hyphen if the word in the modifier is possessive.

 RULE 11.5.3

EXAMPLES   The members took a 20-minute break.

The team put twelve weeks' work into the report.

> If a series of consecutive, hyphenated modifiers ends with the same word, do not repeat the modified word each time. Instead, use a suspended hyphen (also called a dangling hyphen) and the modified word only at the end of the series.

RULE 11.5.4

EXAMPLE   The eleventh- and twelfth-grade students came.

Using Hyphens With Prefixes and Suffixes

Hyphens help your reader easily see the parts of a long word.

RULE 11.5.5 Use a hyphen after a prefix that is followed by a proper noun or proper adjective.

The following prefixes are often used before proper nouns: *ante-*, *anti-*, *mid-*, *post-*, *pre-*, *pro-*, and *un-*.

EXAMPLES post-Renaissance   mid-March

RULE 11.5.6 Use a hyphen in words with the prefixes *all-*, *ex-*, and *self-* and words with the suffix *-elect*.

EXAMPLES self-employed   mayor-elect

Many words with common prefixes are no longer hyphenated. Check a dictionary if you are unsure whether to use a hyphen.

Using Hyphens With Compound Words

Hyphens help preserve the units of meaning in compound words.

RULE 11.5.7 Use a hyphen to connect two or more words that are used as one compound word, unless your dictionary gives a different spelling.

EXAMPLES over-react   on-site

father-in-law   five-year-old

RULE 11.5.8 Use a hyphen to connect a compound modifier that appears before a noun. The exceptions to this rule include adverbs ending in *-ly* and compound proper adjectives or compound proper nouns that are acting as an adjective.

EXAMPLES WITH HYPHENS	EXAMPLES WITHOUT HYPHENS
a well-made pair of gloves	class worksheet
the bright-eyed hikers	doctor's waiting room
an up-to-date map	Eastern European languages

When compound modifiers follow a noun, they generally do not require the use of hyphens.

EXAMPLE   The backpacks were **well made.**

However, if a dictionary spells a word with a hyphen, the word must always be hyphenated, even when it follows a noun.

EXAMPLE   The message was up-to-date.

Using Hyphens for Clarity

Some words or group of words can be misread if a hyphen is not used.

> Use a hyphen within a word when a combination of letters might otherwise be confusing.

11.5.9 RULE

EXAMPLES   hi-fi, high-tech, re-elect

> Use a hyphen between words to keep readers from combining them incorrectly.

11.5.10 RULE

See Practice 11.5A   INCORRECT   the well known-actress
See Practice 11.5B   CORRECT   the well-known actress

Hyphens   287

PRACTICE 11.5A **Using Hyphens Correctly**

Read each item. If an item needs a hyphen or hyphens, add them. If an item does not need hyphenation, write *correct*.

EXAMPLE   editor in chief

ANSWER   *editor-in-chief*

1. happy go lucky

2. easy going nature

3. outgoing person

4. twenty first passenger

5. sister in law

6. bright young lady

7. never say never attitude

8. post Civil War

9. ever quickening pace

10. 2 liter bottle

PRACTICE 11.5B **Revising Sentences With Hyphens**

Read each sentence. Then, rewrite each sentence, correcting any error in hyphenation as needed.

EXAMPLE   She likes wearing old-fashioned-clothes.

ANSWER   *She likes wearing old-fashioned clothes.*

11. There is an exhibit on man eating sharks at the city-aquarium.

12. Charlotte stared-longingly at the blue green sports car.

13. The forest is full of three hundred-year-old trees.

14. Happy Housing is a Detroit-based-organization.

15. The salesman was trying his best-to-sell me his state of the art product.

16. Jillian's mother is a board-certified-physician.

17. A government issued photo-ID is needed to enter the Pentagon.

18. My literature professor assigned us an award winning novel to read for-next-week.

19. This-is-a-time sensitive issue.

20. The meeting was for Native-American people to tell about their experiences with self employment.

SPEAKING APPLICATION

Take turns with a partner. Say words or phrases that may or may not need to be hyphenated. Your partner should indicate where the hyphens would occur in the words or phrases if they were written.

WRITING APPLICATION

Write ten sentences that include words that should be hyphenated. Exchange sentences with a partner. Your partner should correct your sentences by adding hyphens where needed.

Using Hyphens at the Ends of Lines

Hyphens help you keep the lines in your paragraphs more even, making your work easier to read.

Dividing Words at the End of a Line

Although you should try to avoid dividing a word at the end of a line, if a word must be broken, use a hyphen to show the division.

> **If a word must be divided at the end of a line, always divide it between syllables.**

RULE 11.5.11

EXAMPLE   In the middle of the day, we antici-
pated having dinner at five P.M.

> **A hyphen used to divide a word should never be placed at the beginning of the second line. It must be placed at the end of the first line.**

RULE 11.5.12

INCORRECT   The teachers and students plan to sup
-port this principal as long as he is here.

CORRECT   The teachers and students plan to support this principal as long as he is here.

Using Hyphens Correctly to Divide Words

One-syllable words cannot be divided.

> **Do not divide one-syllable words even if they seem long or sound like words with two syllables.**

RULE 11.5.13

INCORRECT   mo-ose   clo-wn   thro-ugh
CORRECT   moose   clown   through

Do not divide a word so that a single letter or the letters *-ed* stand alone.

INCORRECT	a-lert	bus-y	e-rode	accept-ed
CORRECT	alert	busy	erode	accepted

Avoid dividing proper nouns and proper adjectives.

INCORRECT	Ste-wart	Span-ish
CORRECT	Stewart	Spanish

Divide a hyphenated word only after the hyphen.

INCORRECT   I saw the ocean with my best friend and her sis-
ter-in-law last year.

CORRECT   I saw the ocean with my best friend and her sister-
in-law last year.

Avoid dividing a word so that part of the word is on one page and the remainder is on the next page.

Often, chopping up a word in this way will confuse your readers or cause them to lose their train of thought. If this happens, rewrite the sentence or move the entire word to the next page.

See Practice 11.5C
See Practice 11.5D

PRACTICE 11.5C **Using Hyphens to Divide Words**

Read each word. If a word has been divided incorrectly, rewrite the word, putting the hyphen(s) in the correct place. If a word has been divided correctly, write *correct*.

EXAMPLE   butt-on

ANSWER   *but-ton*

1. gigg-le
2. mon-itor
3. spac-ious
4. destin-y
5. spark-le
6. Jes-sica
7. demo-cratic
8. let-hal
9. semi-tran-sparent
10. fo-reign

PRACTICE 11.5D **Correcting Divided Words at the End of Lines**

Read each sentence. Then, rewrite the incorrectly divided word at the end of each sentence so that it is divided correctly.

EXAMPLE   Flowers are brightly color-
ed to attract insects and birds.

ANSWER   *Flowers are brightly col-*
ored to attract insects and birds.

11. Hybrid cars, wind turbines, and solar-po-wered house are environmentally friendly.
12. Lulu had to show a valid driver's lice-nse when she went to buy the tickets.
13. Yesterday, I spent the entire day reorgani-zing the garage by myself.
14. Because her father was a diplomat, she li-ved in many different countries.
15. After hitting the game-winning run, Ty-ler celebrated with his teammates.
16. On a hot summer day, jumping into a swimm-ing pool is a great idea.
17. Rain, snow, sleet, and hail are forms of prec-ipitation.
18. Dan, a tennis champion, serves more a-ces than any other player that I know.
19. Mr. Potts recited lines from William Shakes-peare's *Romeo and Juliet*.
20. At the close of the ceremony, fireworks brigh-tened the sky.

SPEAKING APPLICATION

Take turns with a partner. Say six words not found in Practice 11.5C. Your partner should tell where each word can be divided.

WRITING APPLICATION

Write a paragraph, using at least four correctly divided words at the end of four lines.

11.6 Apostrophes

The **apostrophe** (') is used to form possessives, contractions, and a few special plurals.

Using Apostrophes to Form Possessive Nouns

Apostrophes are used with nouns to show ownership or possession.

Add an apostrophe and -s to show the possessive case of most singular nouns.

EXAMPLES   the scales of the alligator   the alligator's scales

the hat of the boy   the boy's hat

Even when a singular noun already ends in -s, you can usually add an apostrophe and -s to show possession. However, names that end in the *eez* sound get an apostrophe, but no -s.

EXAMPLE   The Ganges' source is in the Himalayas.

For classical references that end in -s, only an apostrophe is used.

EXAMPLES   Hercules' strength   Zeus' crown

Add an apostrophe to show the possessive case of plural nouns ending in -s or -es.

EXAMPLE   the color of the leaves   the leaves' color

Add an apostrophe and an -s to show the possessive case of plural nouns that do not end in -s or -es.

EXAMPLE   the suits of the men

the men's suits

> Add an apostrophe and *-s* (or just an apostrophe if the word is a plural ending in *-s*) to the last word of a compound noun to form the possessive.

APOSTROPHES THAT SHOW POSSESSION	
Names of Businesses and Organizations	the Central High School's main office the Washington Monument's spotlight the Wong and Associates' office
Titles of Rulers or Leaders	Catherine the Great's victories Louis XVI's palace the head of the department's decision
Hyphenated Compound Nouns Used to Describe People	my brother-in-law's skis the secretary-treasurer's chair the physician-assistant's patient

> To form possessives involving time, amounts, or the word *sake,* use an apostrophe and an *-s* or just an apostrophe if the possessive is plural.

APOSTROPHES WITH POSSESSIVES	
Time	a year's vacation five days' vacation a half-hour's walk
Amount	one quarter's worth ten cents' worth
Sake	for Luke's sake for goodness' sake

To show joint ownership, make the final noun possessive.
To show individual ownership, make each noun possessive.

JOINT
OWNERSHIP
I enjoyed Patricia and Tom**'**s dinner party.

INDIVIDUAL
OWNERSHIP
Liz**'**s and Meg**'**s coats are hanging here.

Use the owner's complete name before the apostrophe to form the possessive case.

INCORRECT
SINGULAR
Jame**'**s phone number

CORRECT
SINGULAR
James**'**s phone number

INCORRECT
PLURAL
two girl**'**s dresses

CORRECT
PLURAL
two girls**'** dresses

Using Apostrophes With Pronouns

Both indefinite and personal pronouns can show possession.

Use an apostrophe and -s with indefinite pronouns to show possession.

EXAMPLES
somebody**'**s rain coat

each other**'**s houses

Do not use an apostrophe with possessive personal pronouns; their form already shows ownership.

EXAMPLES
her shoes   our pool   his red sports car

its doors   their house   whose report

Be careful not to confuse the contractions *who's*, *it's*, and *they're* with possessive pronouns. They are contractions for *who is*, *it is* or *it has*, and *they are*. Remember also that *whose*, *its*, and *their* show possession.

PRONOUNS	CONTRACTIONS
Whose homework is this?	*Who's* answering the phone?
Its tires were all flat.	*It's* going to be cold and windy.
Their dinner is ready.	*They're* going swimming today.

Using Apostrophes to Form Contractions

Contractions are used in informal speech and writing. You can often find contractions in the dialogue of stories and plays; they often create the sound of real speech.

> Use an apostrophe in a **contraction** to show the position of the missing letter or letters.

11.6.9 RULE

COMMON CONTRACTIONS			
Verb + *not*	cannot could not	can't couldn't	are not will not	aren't won't
Pronoun + *will*	he will you will she will	he'll you'll she'll	I will we will they will	I'll we'll they'll
Pronoun + *would*	she would he would you would	she'd he'd you'd	I would we would they would	I'd we'd they'd
Noun or Pronoun + *be*	you are she is they are	you're she's they're	I am Jane is dog is	I'm Jane's dog's

Still another type of contraction is found in poetry.

EXAMPLES   e'en *(even)*   o'er *(over)*

Other contractions represent the abbreviated form of *of the* and *the* as they are written in several different languages. These letters are most often combined with surnames.

EXAMPLES   O'Hare

d'Italia

o'clock

l'Abbé

Using Contractions to Represent Speaking Styles
A final use of contractions is for representing individual speaking styles in dialogue. As noted previously, you will often want to use contractions with verbs in dialogue. You may also want to approximate a regional dialect or a foreign accent, which may include nonstandard pronunciations of words or omitted letters. However, you should avoid overusing contractions in dialogue. Overuse reduces the effectiveness of the apostrophe.

EXAMPLES   "Hey, ol' buddy. How you feelin'?"

"Don' you be foolin' me."

Using Apostrophes to Create Special Plurals

Apostrophes can help avoid confusion with special plurals.

> Use an apostrophe and *-s* to create the plural form of a letter, numeral, symbol, or a word that is used as a name for itself.

EXAMPLES   *A*'s and *an*'s cause confusion.

There are five *3*'s in that number.

I don't like to hear *if*'s or *maybe*'s.

Form groups of *5*'s and *6*'s.

We have two *?*'s in a row.

See Practice 11.6A
See Practice 11.6B

PRACTICE 11.6A › Identifying the Use of Apostrophes

Read each sentence. Then, tell if each apostrophe is used to form a *possessive*, a *contraction*, or a *special plural*.

EXAMPLE   Randy always crosses his *t's* and dots his *i's*.

ANSWER   *special plurals*

1. The fabric and buttons on my mother's old wedding dress have turned yellow.

2. There's the book of stamps from the 1920s.

3. With Paul and Donovan's help, this year's fundraiser will raise the most money yet.

4. Elijah got straight *B*'s in music class last year.

5. I can't leave until eight o'clock.

6. The chair's legs were cracked and warped.

7. Cindy's daughter told us that she'd meet us for lunch.

8. Count by *2*'s.

9. The girl's dress's skirt had ribbon trim.

10. In a month's time, we'll be traveling to Aunt Vanessa's house.

PRACTICE 11.6B › Revising to Add Apostrophes

Read the sentence. Then, rewrite each sentence, adding apostrophes as necessary.

EXAMPLE   Julians jacket was too small for him this year.

ANSWER   *Julian's jacket was too small for him this year.*

11. Gus birthplace is Lockhart, Texas.

12. Johns and Petes lockers are around the corner from mine.

13. The childrens boots were jumbled in a big mess by my sister Susans front door.

14. Mrs. Robinsons student teacher said I use too many !s in my writing.

15. The Department of the Interiors budget wasnt cut in half this year.

16. The mens hockey team couldve won second place at the state championship.

17. Carol Anns mothers brother is Carol Anns uncle.

18. This sweatshirt could be anyones.

19. Its so funny to see a dog chase its own tail.

20. Rufus made a point to say "No *ifs*, *ands*, or *buts* are acceptable."

SPEAKING APPLICATION

Take turns with a partner. Say different sentences with words that indicate possession, contractions, and special plurals. Your partner should tell how each word uses an apostrophe.

WRITING APPLICATION

Write a paragraph, using at least six words with apostrophes. Not all of the words with apostrophes should be contractions.

11.7 Parentheses and Brackets

Parentheses enclose explanations or other information that may be omitted from the rest of the sentence without changing its basic meaning or construction. Using parentheses is a stronger, more noticeable way to set off a parenthetical expression than using commas. **Brackets** are used to enclose a word or phrase added by a writer to the words of another.

Parentheses

Parentheses help you group material within a sentence.

> Use parentheses to set off information when the material is not essential or when it consists of one or more sentences.

EXAMPLE   The test of driving the car (as he learned from his friends) did require great skill and knowledge.

> Use parentheses to set off numerical explanations such as dates of a person's birth and death and around numbers and letters marking a series.

EXAMPLES   Jose Sanchez invented a version of water tag with the help of his father, Juan Sanchez (1825–1900).

Go to the store and pick up these items for dinner: (1) sauce, (2) pasta, (3) bread.

Which team won the Super Bowl you saw: (a) Giants, (b) Steelers, or (c) Cowboys?

Although material enclosed in parentheses is not essential to the meaning of the sentence, a writer indicates that the material is important and calls attention to it by using parentheses.

RULE 11.7.3

When a phrase or declarative sentence interrupts another sentence, do not use an initial capital letter or end mark inside the parentheses.

EXAMPLE   Steve took the furniture (it was beautiful) and delivered it as promised.

RULE 11.7.4

When a question or exclamation interrupts another sentence, use both an initial capital letter and an end mark inside the parentheses.

EXAMPLE   Jack (He is one strong man!) lifted the box on his shoulder.

RULE 11.7.5

When you place a sentence in parentheses between two other sentences, use both an initial capital letter and an end mark inside the parentheses.

EXAMPLE   Italy is known for its incredible art and artists. (See the Sistine Chapel as an example.) Italian art is staggering to behold.

RULE 11.7.6

In a sentence that includes parentheses, place any punctuation belonging to the main sentence after the final parenthesis.

EXAMPLE   The school board approved the construction (after some debate), and they explained the new parking rules to the students (with some doubts about how the changes will be followed).

Special Uses of Parentheses

Parentheses are also used to set off numerical explanations such as dates of a person's birth and death and numbers or letters marking a series.

EXAMPLES   William Shakespeare (1564-1616) was an English poet and playwright.

Chelsea's phone number is (919) 777-1532.

His research will take him to (1) China, (2) Korea, and (3) Thailand.

Brackets

Brackets are used to enclose a word or phrase added by a writer to the words of another writer.

> **Use brackets to enclose words you insert in quotations when quoting someone else.**

EXAMPLES   Cooper noted: "And with [E.T.'s] success, 'Phone home' is certain to become one of the most often repeated phrases of the year [1982]."

"The results of this vote [35–5] indicate overwhelming support by the board," she stated.

The Latin expression *sic* (meaning "thus") is sometimes enclosed in brackets to show that the author of the quoted material has misspelled or mispronounced a word or phrase.

EXAMPLE   Michaelson, citing Dorothy's signature line from *The Wizard of Oz,* wrote, "Theirs [sic] no place like home."

See Practice 11.7A
See Practice 11.7B

PRACTICE 11.7A> **Using Parentheses and Brackets Correctly**

Read each item. Then, write a sentence in which you enclose the item in either parentheses or brackets.

EXAMPLE   the protagonist

ANSWER   *In the novel Pride and Prejudice, Elizabeth Bennett (the protagonist) is an intelligent, good-natured young woman.*

1. the youngest son
2. a bright, sunny day
3. sic
4. in the next three weeks
5. the former state senator
6. where it was lost
7. I couldn't believe my eyes
8. my best friend
9. a friendly dog
10. in the morning

PRACTICE 11.7B> **Revising to Add Parentheses or Brackets**

Read each sentence. Then, add parentheses or brackets wherever they are appropriate.

EXAMPLE   We took the early bus 7:45 A.M. into the city.

ANSWER   *We took the early bus (7:45 A.M.) into the city.*

11. Water is a compound made from different atoms hydrogen and oxygen.
12. Benjamin Franklin 1706–1790 did not invent electricity, but he did invent the lightning rod.
13. Cecilia calls her grandmother *"Abuela"* which means "grandmother" in Spanish.
14. The mayor said, "The building will be renamed in honor of Mr. Byrd the retired post master."
15. During our trip, we went fishing for trout.
16. Baby dolphins calves stay with their mothers for five to seven years.
17. Mozart's first symphony written at age eight is *Symphony No. 1* in E-flat major.
18. A low-pressure system a storm is forecasted.
19. The trees obscured our view from the terrace.
20. The report stated, "The brige sic is in need of repairs."

SPEAKING APPLICATION

Take turns with a partner. Say four phrases. Your partner should use the phrases in sentences, indicating if the phrases would be appropriate in parentheses or brackets.

WRITING APPLICATION

Write two paragraphs in the form of a newspaper article about any topic of your choice. Include sentences that contain parentheses and brackets.

11.8 Ellipses, Dashes, and Slashes

An **ellipsis** (...) shows where words have been omitted from a quoted passage. It can also mark a pause or interruption in dialogue. A **dash** (—) shows a strong, sudden break in thought or speech. A **slash** (/) separates numbers in dates and fractions, shows line breaks in quoted poetry, and represents *or*. A slash is also used to separate the parts of a Web address.

Using the Ellipsis

An **ellipsis** is three evenly spaced periods, or ellipsis points, in a row. Always include a space before the first ellipsis point, between ellipsis points, and after the last ellipsis point. (The plural of *ellipsis* is *ellipses*.)

RULE 11.8.1 | Use an **ellipsis** to show where words have been omitted from a quoted passage.

ELLIPSES IN QUOTATIONS	
The Entire Quotation	"The Black River, which cuts a winding course through southern Missouri's rugged Ozark highlands, lends its name to an area of great natural beauty. Within this expanse are old mines and quarries to explore, fast-running waters to canoe, and wooded trails to ride."—Suzanne Charle
At the Beginning	Suzanne Charle described the Black River area in Missouri as having " . . . old mines and quarries to explore, fast-running waters to canoe, and wooded trails to ride."
In the Middle	Suzanne Charle wrote, "The Black River . . . lends its name to an area of great natural beauty. Within this expanse are old mines and quarries to explore, fast-running waters to canoe, and wooded trails to ride."
At the End	Suzanne Charle wrote, "The Black River, which cuts a winding course through southern Missouri's rugged Ozark highlands, lends its name to an area of great natural beauty . . ."

Use an ellipsis to mark a pause in a dialogue or speech.

EXAMPLE   The director shouted, "scene...and...cut!"

Dashes

A **dash** signals a stronger, more sudden interruption in thought or speech than commas or parentheses. A dash may also take the place of certain words before an explanation. Overuse of the dash diminishes its effectiveness. Consider the proper use of the dash in the rule below.

Use **dashes** to indicate an abrupt change of thought, a dramatic interrupting idea, or a summary statement.

USING DASHES IN WRITING	
To indicate an abrupt change of thought	The book doesn't provide much information on Europe—by the way, where did you find the book? I cannot believe how many free throws the players missed—oh, I don't even want to think about it.
To set off interrupting ideas dramatically	The house was built—you may find this hard to believe—in two weeks. The house was built—Where did they get the money?—in two weeks.
To set off a summary statement	A lifetime of practice, ambition, and excellent teachers—if you have these, you may be able to get a job as a professional musician. To see her name on her diploma after four years—this was her greatest dream.

> Use **dashes** to set off a **nonessential appositive** or modifier when it is long, when it is already punctuated, or when you want to be dramatic.

APPOSITIVE   The cause of the damage to the antique paint and the chrome—a rare form of rust—went undiscovered for weeks.

MODIFIER   The garden book editor—bored with writing about flowers and vegetables—quit after her last book.

Dashes may be used to set off one other special type of sentence interrupter—the parenthetical expression.

> Use **dashes** to set off a **parenthetical expression** when it is long, already punctuated, or especially dramatic.

EXAMPLE   Today, we visited a gourmet restaurant—what a delicious meal!—set in the city.

Slashes

A **slash** is used to separate numbers in dates and fractions, lines of quoted poetry, or options. Slashes are also used to separate parts of a Web address.

> Use slashes to separate the day, month, and year in dates and to separate the numerator and denominator in numerical fractions.

DATES   The date listed on the tickets was 11/05/10.

           Randy left for Chicago on 4/17/08.

FRACTIONS   3/4   2/5   1/3

Use slashes to indicate line breaks in up to three lines of quoted poetry in continuous text. Insert a space on each side of the slash.

EXAMPLE   I used a quote from William Blake, "Tyger! Tyger! burning bright. **/** In the forests of the night," to begin my paper.

Use slashes to separate choices or options and to represent the words *and* and *or*.

EXAMPLES   Choose your color: pink **/** aqua **/** yellow.

Each lifeguard should bring a board and whistle **/** binoculars.

You can bat and **/** or bunt the next throw from the pitcher.

Use slashes to separate parts of a Web address.

EXAMPLES   http: **//** www.fafsa.ed.gov **/**
(for financial aid for students)

http: **//** www.whitehouse.gov **/**
(the White House)

http: **//** www.si.edu **/**
(the Smithsonian Institution)

See Practice 11.8A
See Practice 11.8B

PRACTICE 11.8A Using Ellipses, Dashes, and Slashes Correctly

Read each sentence. Then, rewrite each sentence, adding ellipses, dashes, and slashes where they are needed.

EXAMPLE   Jed yelled, "On your mark, get set, go!"

ANSWER   *Jed yelled, "On your mark . . . get set . . . go!"*

1. Yarn crafts including knitting and crocheting are becoming a popular hobby again.

2. The paintings have been cleaned restored and are ready to be exhibited.

3. We saw a flock of flamingos they really are pink at the botanical gardens.

4. The Gettysburg Address begins "Four score and seven years ago."

5. The waiter entertainer at the new restaurant sings while he serves food.

6. My mother adds a secret ingredient to her prize-winning chili peanut butter.

7. The vase made of red clay is a historic find.

8. The recipe lists 1 2 cup of vegetable oil.

9. The game-show host took forever to say, "And the winner is Alex Bailey!"

10. A positive attitude and friendliness these things will help you make friends.

PRACTICE 11.8B Revising Sentences With Ellipses, Dashes, and Slashes

Read each sentence. Then, correct the misused punctuation in each sentence to show the correct use of ellipses, dashes, and slashes.

EXAMPLE   Cody said, "I bought tomatoes, rice, eggs wait, I forgot the eggs!"

ANSWER   *Cody said, "I bought tomatoes, rice, eggs — wait, I forgot the eggs!"*

11. During archery class, I think to myself, "ready/aim/shoot."

12. The recipe calls for 2 — 3 cup milk.

13. Shannon ate soup, salad, a sandwich, and fruit. / I would burst if I ate that much for lunch.

14. The best part of the movie/ actually the entire film was good... was the opening scene.

15. Leah timidly replied, "I um — can't make it."

16. The next meeting is on 3 — 12/10.

17. The oboe is part of the woodwind family / by the way, Mrs. Dixon is giving oboe lessons.

18. You may read a book — magazine while you wait.

19. Your resume, cover letter, and referrals/these are the items you need/to apply for the job.

20. The book began with, "I couldn't wait to see."

SPEAKING APPLICATION

With a partner, reread the sentences in Practice 11.8A and your corrections for the sentences. Discuss how adding ellipses, dashes, and slashes changes each sentence.

WRITING APPLICATION

Write a paragraph. Your paragraph should include sentences that contain ellipses, dashes, and slashes. Use each of these types of punctuation at least two times.

PRACTICE 1 ▷ Using Periods, Question Marks, and Exclamation Marks

Read the sentences. Then, rewrite each sentence, adding question marks, periods, and exclamation marks where needed.

1. Push the table to the other side of the room, so we have more space

2. Are you responsible for the grocery shopping

3. That was the most delicious and lavish meal I have ever eaten

4. How remarkable that he was able to complete all of those arduous tasks in one day

5. She budgeted her time well and finished the exam with a few minutes to spare

6. Yen wanted to attend both parties

7. Did you collect all of the water samples that you will need for your project

8. Wow That goal was amazing

9. So as not to get him confused with his father, we simply called Thomas, Jr, Tommy

10. Write an article for the school paper on the dangers of polluting our environment

PRACTICE 2 ▷ Using Commas Correctly

Read the sentences. Then, rewrite each sentence, adding commas where needed. If a sentence is already correct, write correct.

1. Struggling with the homework assignment Ted signed up for a tutoring session.

2. Emma gathered her books pens and notebooks together and headed home.

3. "The next holiday is on October 10 2009" Rebecca told us.

4. He and I waited patiently for the bus and discussed where we wanted to eat.

5. Who wrote, "To be, or not to be?"

6. She lives at 45 East Main Street Apartment B Brookfield New York 12345.

7. The conversation was a stimulating interesting break from our usual talk.

8. I needed to cancel this appointment yesterday, not today.

9. Robert made a gregarious speech at every luncheon and this one would be no exception.

10. He responded "Yes I will review those figures."

PRACTICE 3 ▷ Using Colons, Semicolons, and Quotation Marks

Read the sentences. Then, rewrite each sentence, adding colons, semicolons, and quotation marks where needed. If a sentence is already correct, write correct.

1. It didn't occur to him to notice the new paint in fact, he never noticed it!

2. For his project, Dan reviewed Mowing by Robert Frost Dan considered it a classic work of poetry.

3. Val told us to bring the following items to rehearsal: instruments, music, and pencils.

4. Caution Floors are slippery when wet.

5. The tickets were expensive however, we got a discount.

6. I was late for class, Shauna said, because my alarm was set for 1000.

7. The curry was hot I love Indian food.

8. We surveyed the destruction after the storm the wind had toppled our boat.

Continued on next page ▶

9. Marjorie announced the decision, Resolved The vote stands, there will be revote.

10. Jack claimed that he had everything under control, so we all believed him.

 Using Apostrophes

Read the sentences. Then, rewrite each sentence, adding apostrophes where needed. If a sentence is already correct, write *correct*.

1. Deirdres new apartment is located just south of the train station.

2. Oh, for goodness sake, just take Kevins keys.

3. The politician was described as the peoples choice; he couldnt let them down.

4. I went to Mel and Randys house yesterday.

5. We usually carried each others books when we didnt have that many of our own.

6. His first year of college, he read many of John Keatss works.

7. The vice-chancellors order was to reduce the budget by one-third.

8. James's doctor told him to get more sleep.

9. Whos going to come? Isnt it late?

10. Its time to have a talk; lets meet at 4 oclock.

 Using Underlining (or Italics), Hyphens, Dashes, Slashes, Parentheses, Brackets, and Ellipses

Read the sentences. Then, rewrite each sentence, adding underlining (or italics), hyphens, dashes, slashes, parentheses, brackets, and ellipses where needed.

1. Reading War and Peace was difficult, but in the end, it was very rewarding.

2. Duncan he is president of the student body always comes to meetings well prepared.

3. She read that 700 page book if you can believe it in three days.

4. The film is set during World War II 1939–1945.

5. In her address, she told the people, "It the economy can no longer be ignored."

6. The recipe called for 1 2 cup of flour and 1 3 cup of sugar.

7. The twelfth graders all the seniors had to take the exit exam.

8. The runners took their positions, and the referee yelled, "On your mark get set go!"

9. They needed fifty thousand dollars $50,000 to launch the project.

10. Each member of the committee the committee leaders as well as the regular members should attend.

PRACTICE 6 **Using Capital Letters Correctly**

Read the sentences. Then, rewrite each sentence, using capital letters where needed.

1. isis is the egyptian goddess of motherhood.

2. the mcteagues took a yearly trip to puerto rico, and last year they visited san juan hill.

3. jen inquired, "in which language are you most fluent—french, swedish, or german?"

4. buckingham palace is in london, england.

5. the department of the treasury is headquartered in washington, d.c.

Modes
of Writing

Writing is a process that begins with the exploration of ideas and ends with the presentation of a final piece of writing. Often, the types of writing we do are grouped into modes according to their form and purpose.

Narration

Whenever writers tell any type of story, they are using narration. Most narratives share certain elements, such as characters, a setting, a sequence of events, and, often, a theme. The following are some types of narration:

● **Autobiographical Writing** Autobiographical writing tells a true story about an important period, experience, or relationship in the writer's life.

Effective autobiographical writing includes:
- *A series of events that involve the writer as the main character*
- *Details, thoughts, feelings, and insights from the writer's perspective*
- *A conflict or an event that affects the writer*
- *A logical organization that tells the story clearly*

Types of autobiographical writing include personal narratives, autobiographical sketches, reflective essays, eyewitness accounts, and memoirs.

● **Short Story** A short story is a brief, creative narrative.

Most short stories contain:
- *Details that establish the setting in time and place*
- *A main character who undergoes a change or learns something during the course of the story*
- *A conflict or a problem to be introduced, developed, and resolved*
- *A plot—the series of events that make up the action of the story*
- *A theme or message about life*

Types of short stories include realistic stories, fantasies, historical narratives, mysteries, thrillers, science fiction, and adventure stories.

Description

Descriptive writing is writing that creates a vivid picture of a person, place, thing, or event.

Most descriptive writing includes:
- *Sensory details—sights, sounds, smells, tastes, and physical sensations*
- *Vivid, precise language*
- *Figurative language or comparisons*
- *Adjectives and adverbs that help to paint a word picture*
- *An organization suited to the subject*

Types of descriptive writing include description of ideas, observations, travel brochures, physical descriptions, functional descriptions, remembrances, and character sketches.

Persuasion

Persuasion is writing or speaking that attempts to convince people to accept a position or take a desired action. The following are some types of persuasion:

● **Persuasive Essay**
A persuasive essay presents a position on an issue, urges readers to accept that position, and may encourage a specific action.

An effective persuasive essay:
- *Explores an issue of importance to the writer*
- *Addresses an arguable issue*
- *Is supported by facts, examples, statistics, or personal experiences*
- *Tries to influence the audience through appeals to the readers' knowledge, experiences, or emotions*
- *Uses clear organization to present a logical argument*

Forms of persuasion include editorials, position papers, persuasive speeches, grant proposals, advertisements, and debates.

● **Advertisements**
An advertisement is a planned communication that is meant to be seen, heard, or read. It attempts to persuade an audience to buy or use a product or service. Advertisements may appear in print or broadcast form.

An effective advertisement includes:
- *A concept, or central theme*
- *A device, such as a memorable slogan, that catches people's attention*
- *Language that conveys a certain view of a product or issue*

Common types of advertisements include public service announcements, billboards, merchandise ads, service ads, and public campaign literature.

Exposition

Exposition is writing that relies on facts to inform or explain. Effective expository writing reflects an organization that is well planned—one that includes a clear introduction, body, and conclusion. The following are some types of exposition:

● **Comparison-and-Contrast Essay**
A comparison-and-contrast essay analyzes similarities and differences between or among two or more things.

An effective comparison-and-contrast essay:
- *Identifies a purpose for comparing and contrasting*
- *Identifies similarities and differences between or among two or more things, people, places, or ideas*
- *Gives factual details about the subjects*
- *Uses an organizational plan suited to the topic and purpose*

● **Cause-and-Effect Essay** A cause-and-effect essay examines the relationship between events, explaining how one event or situation causes another.

A successful cause-and-effect essay includes:
- *A discussion of a cause, event, or condition that produces a specific result*
- *An explanation of an effect or result*
- *Evidence and examples to support the relationship between cause and effect*
- *A logical organization that makes the relationship between events clear*

● **Problem-and-Solution Essay** A problem-and-solution essay describes a problem and offers one or more solutions. It describes a clear set of steps to achieve a result.

An effective problem-and-solution essay includes:
- *A clear statement of the problem, with its causes and effects summarized*
- *A proposal of at least one realistic solution*
- *Facts, statistics, data, or expert testimony to support the solution*
- *A clear organization that makes the relationship between problem and solution obvious*

Research Writing

Research writing is based on information gathered from outside sources.

An effective research paper:
- *Focuses on a specific, narrow topic*
- *Presents relevant information from a variety of sources*
- *Is clearly organized and includes an introduction, body, and conclusion*
- *Includes a bibliography or works-cited list*

In addition to traditional research reports, types of research writing include statistical reports and experiment journals.

Response to Literature

When you write a response to literature, you can discover how a piece of writing affected you.

An effective response:
- *Reacts to a work of literature*
- *Analyzes the content of a literary work*
- *Focuses on a single aspect or gives a general overview*
- *Supports opinion with evidence from the text*

You might respond to a literary work in reader's response journals, literary letters, and literary analyses.

Writing for Assessment

Essays are commonly part of school tests.

An effective essay includes:
- *A clearly stated and well-supported thesis*
- *Specific information about the topic derived from your reading or from class discussion*
- *A clear organization with an introduction, body, and conclusion*

In addition to writing essays for tests, you might write essays to apply to schools or special programs, or to enter a contest.

Workplace Writing

Workplace writing communicates information in a structured format.

Effective workplace writing:
- *Communicates information concisely*
- *Includes details that provide necessary information and anticipate potential questions*

Common types of workplace writing include business letters, memorandums, résumés, forms, and applications.

Writing Effective
Paragraphs

A paragraph is a group of sentences that share a common topic or purpose. Most paragraphs have a main idea or thought.

Stating the Main Idea in a Topic Sentence

The main idea of a paragraph is directly stated in a single sentence called the topic sentence. The rest of the sentences in the paragraph support or explain the topic sentence, providing support through facts and details.

Sometimes the main idea of a paragraph is implied rather than stated. The sentences work together to present the details and facts that allow the reader to infer the main idea.

WRITING MODELS

from *The Secret Language of Snow*
Terry Tempest Williams and Ted Major

Many types of animal behavior are designed to reduce heat loss. Birds fluff their feathers, enlarging the "dead air" space around their bodies. Quails roost in compact circles, in the same manner as musk oxen, to keep warmth in and cold out. Grouse and ptarmigan dive into the snow, using it as an insulating blanket.

In this passage, the stated topic sentence is highlighted.

from **"The Old Demon"**
Pearl S. Buck

The baker's shop, like everything else, was in ruins. No one was there. At first she saw nothing but the mass of crumpled earthen walls. But then she remembered that the oven was just inside the door, and the door frame still stood erect, supporting one end of the roof. She stood in this frame, and, running her hands in underneath the fallen roof inside, she felt the wooden cover of the iron cauldron. Under this there might be steamed bread. She worked her arm delicately and carefully in. It took quite a long time, but even so, clouds of lime and dust almost choked her. Nevertheless she was right. She squeezed her hand under the cover and felt the first smooth skin of the big steamed bread rolls, and one by one she drew out four.

In this passage, all the sentences work together to illustrate the implied main idea of the paragraph: The woman searches persistently until she finds food.

Writing a Topic Sentence

When you outline a topic or plan an essay, you identify the main points you want to address. Each of these points can be written as a topic sentence—a statement of the main idea of a topical paragraph. You can organize your paragraph around the topic sentence.

A good topic sentence tells readers what the paragraph is about and the point the writer wants to make about the subject matter. Here are some tips for writing a strong topic sentence.

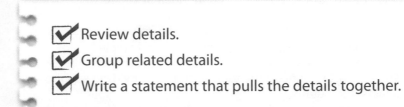

☑ Review details.

☑ Group related details.

☑ Write a statement that pulls the details together.

Writing Supporting Sentences

Whether your topic sentence is stated or implied, it guides the rest of the paragraph. The rest of the sentences in the paragraph will either develop, explain, or support that topic sentence.

You can support or develop the idea by using one or more of the following strategies:

Use Facts

Facts are statements that can be proved. They support your key idea by providing proof.

- **Topic Sentence:** Our football team is tough to beat.
- **Supporting Fact:** It wins almost all of its games.

Use Statistics

A statistic is a fact, usually stated using numbers.

- **Topic Sentence:** Our football team is tough to beat.
- **Supporting Statistic:** The football team's record is 10–1.

Use Examples, Illustrations, or Instances

An example, illustration, or instance is a specific thing, person, or event that demonstrates a point.

- **Topic Sentence:** Our football team is tough to beat.
- **Illustration:** Last week, the team beat the previously undefeated Tigers in an exciting upset game.

Use Details

Details are the specifics—the parts of the whole. They make your point or main idea clear by showing how all the pieces fit together.

- **Topic Sentence:** Our footbal team is tough to beat.
- **Detail:** There were only seconds left in last week's game, when the quarterback threw the winning pass.

Placing Your Topic Sentence

Frequently, the topic sentence appears at the beginning of a paragraph. Topic sentences can, however, be placed at the beginning, middle, or end of the paragraph. Place your topic sentence at the beginning of a paragraph to focus readers' attention. Place your topic sentence in the middle of a paragraph when you must lead into your main idea. Place your topic sentence at the end of a paragraph to emphasize your main idea.

Paragraph Patterns

Sentences in a paragraph can be arranged in several different patterns, depending on where you place your topic sentence. One common pattern is the TRI pattern (Topic, Restatement, Illustration).

- **T**opic sentence (State your main idea.)
- **R**estatement (Interpret your main idea; use different wording.)
- **I**llustration (Support your main idea with facts and examples.)

T	Participating in after-school clubs is one of the ways you can meet new people. Getting involved in extracurricular activities brings you in contact with a wide range of individuals. The drama club, for example, brings together students from several different grades.
R	
I	

Variations on the TRI pattern include sentence arrangements such as TIR, TII, IIT, or ITR.

I	This month alone the service club at our high school delivered meals to thirty shut-ins. In addition, members beautified the neighborhood with new plantings. If any school-sponsored club deserves increased support, the service club does.
I	
T	

Paragraphs
in Essays
and Other Compositions

To compose means "to put the parts together, to create." Most often, composing refers to the creation of a musical or literary work—a composition. You may not think of the reports, essays, and test answers you write as literary works, but they are compositions. To write an effective composition, you must understand the parts.

The Introduction

The introduction does what its name suggests. It introduces the topic of the composition. An effective introduction begins with a strong lead, a first sentence that captures readers' interest. The lead is followed by the thesis statement, the key point of the composition. Usually, the thesis statement is followed by a few sentences that outline how the writer will make the key point.

The Body

The body of a composition consists of several paragraphs that develop, explain, and support the key idea expressed in the thesis statement. The body of a composition should be unified and coherent. The paragraphs in a composition should work together to support the thesis statement. The topic of each paragraph should relate directly to the thesis statement and be arranged in a logical organization.

The Conclusion

The conclusion is the final paragraph of the composition. The conclusion restates the thesis and sums up the support. Often, the conclusion includes the writer's reflection or observation on the topic. An effective conclusion ends on a memorable note, for example, with a quotation or call to action.

Recognizing Types of Paragraphs

There are several types of paragraphs you can use in your writing.

Topical Paragraphs

A topical paragraph is a group of sentences that contain one key sentence or idea and several sentences that support or develop that key idea or topic sentence.

Functional Paragraphs

Functional paragraphs serve a specific purpose. They may not have a topic sentence, but they are unified and coherent because the sentences (if there is more than one) are clearly connected and follow a logical order. Functional paragraphs can be used for the following purposes:

- **To create emphasis** A very short paragraph of one or two sentences focuses the reader on what is being said because it breaks the reader's rhythm.

- **To indicate dialogue** One of the conventions of written dialogue is that a new paragraph begins each time the speaker changes.

- **To make a transition** A short paragraph can help readers move between the main ideas in two topical paragraphs.

WRITING MODEL

from **"The Hatchling Turtles"**

by Jean Craighead George

One morning each small turtle fought for freedom within its shell.

They hatched two feet down in the sand, all of them on the same day. As they broke out, their shells collapsed, leaving a small room of air for them to breathe. It wasn't much of a room, just big enough for them to wiggle in and move toward the sky. As they wiggled they pulled the sand down from the ceiling and crawled up on it. In this manner the buried room began to rise, slowly, inch by inch.

The highlighted functional paragraph emphasizes the struggle of the turtles to emerge from their shells.

Paragraph Blocks

Sometimes, you may have so much information to support or develop a main idea that it "outgrows" a single paragraph. When a topic sentence or main idea requires an extensive explanation or support, you can develop the idea in a paragraph block—several paragraphs that work together and function as a unit. Each paragraph in the block supports the key idea or topic sentence. By breaking the development of the idea into separate paragraphs, you make your ideas clearer.

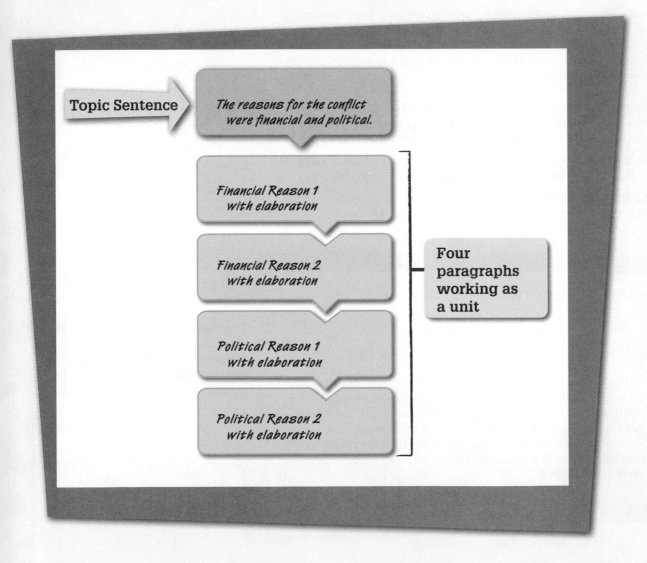

Topic Sentence → *The reasons for the conflict were financial and political.*

Financial Reason 1 with elaboration

Financial Reason 2 with elaboration

Political Reason 1 with elaboration

Political Reason 2 with elaboration

Four paragraphs working as a unit

Qualities
of Good Writing

The quality of your writing depends on how well you develop six important traits: ideas, organization, voice, word choice, sentence fluency, and conventions.

Ideas

Good writing begins with interesting ideas. Explore topics that you find interesting and that you think will interest others. Focus on presenting information that will be new and fresh to readers.

Organization

Organization refers to the way in which the ideas and details are arranged in a piece of writing. To enable readers to follow your ideas, choose an organization that makes sense for your topic, and stick with that organization throughout the piece of writing.

Voice

Just as you have a distinctive way of expressing yourself when you speak, you can develop a distinctive voice as a writer. Your voice consists of the topics you choose, the attitude you express toward those topics, the words you use, and the rhythm of your sentences. By developing your own voice, you let your personality come through in your writing.

Conventions

Conventions refer to the grammatical correctness of a piece of writing. Don't let errors in grammar, usage, mechanics, and spelling interfere with your message.

Sentence Fluency

In a piece of writing, it is important that sentences flow well from one to another. By using a variety of sentences—different lengths and different structures—and using transitions to connect them, you will create smooth rhythm in your writing.

Word Choice

Words are the building blocks of a piece of writing. By choosing precise and vivid words, you will add strength to your writing and enable readers to follow your ideas and picture the things that you describe.

Stages of the
Writing Process

Writing is called a process because it goes through a series of changes or stages. These five stages are:

- In **prewriting**, you explore an idea by using various prewriting techniques, such as brainstorming and questioning.

- In **drafting**, you get your ideas down on paper or on the computer in roughly the format you intend.

- Once you finish your first draft, you decide on the changes, or **revisions**, you want to make.

- Finally, when you are happy with your work, you **edit** it, checking the accuracy of facts and for errors in spelling, grammar, usage, and mechanics.

- You then make a final copy and **publish** it, or share it with an audience.

You will not always progress through these stages in a straight line. You can backtrack to a previous stage, repeat a stage many times, or put the stages in a different sequence to fit your needs. To get an idea of what the writing process is like, study the following diagram. Notice that the arrows in the drafting and revising sections can lead you back to prewriting.

Prewriting
- Using prewriting techniques to gather ideas
- Choosing a purpose and an audience
- Ordering ideas

Drafting
- Putting ideas down on paper
- Exploring new ideas as you write

Publishing
- Producing a final polished copy of your writing
- Sharing your writing

Revising
- Consulting with peer readers
- Evaluating suggested changes
- Making revisions

Editing
- Checking the accuracy of facts
- Correcting errors in spelling, grammar, usage, and mechanics

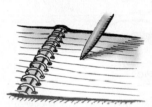

Prewriting
- Using prewriting techniques to gather ideas
- Choosing a purpose and an audience
- Ordering ideas

Prewriting

No matter what kind of writing assignment you are given, you can use prewriting techniques to find and develop a topic. Some prewriting techniques will work better than others for certain kinds of assignments.

Choosing a Topic

Try some of the following ways to find topics that fit your assignment.

● **Look Through Newspapers and Magazines** In the library or at home, flip through recent magazines or newspapers. Jot down each interesting person, place, event, or topic you come across. Review your notes and choose a topic that you find especially interesting and would like to learn more about.

● **Keep an Events Log** Every day you probably encounter many situations about which you have opinions. One way to remember these irksome issues is to keep an events log. For a set period of time—a day or a week—take a small notebook with you wherever you go. Whenever you come across something you feel strongly about, write it down. After the specified time period, review your journal and select a topic.

● **Create a Personal Experience Timeline** Choose a memorable period in your life and map out the events that occurred during that period. Create a timeline in which you enter events in the order they occurred. Then, review your timeline and choose the event or events that would make the most interesting topic.

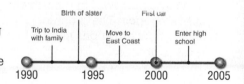

	Birth of sister		First car	
Trip to India with family		Move to East Coast		Enter high school
1990	1995		2000	2005

Narrowing Your Topic

Note that narrowing a topic is not an exact science. It is part of the creative process of writing, which involves experimentation and leads to discovery. Here are some specific techniques you can use.

● **Questioning** Asking questions often helps narrow your topic to fit the time and space you have available. Try asking some of the six questions that journalists use when writing news stories: *Who? What? When? Why? Where?* and *How?* Then, based on your answers, refocus on a narrow aspect of your topic.

Who?
What?
When?
Why?
Where?
How?

● **Using Reference Materials** The reference materials you use to find information can also help you narrow a broad topic. Look up your subject in an encyclopedia, or find a book on it at the library. Scan the resource, looking for specific, narrow topics. Sometimes a resource will be divided into sections or chapters that each deal with a specific topic.

● **Using Graphic Devices** Another way to narrow a topic is to combine questioning with a graphic device, such as a cluster or inverted pyramid. Draw one in your notebook or journal, and write your broad topics across the top of the upside-down pyramid. Then, as the pyramid narrows to a point, break down your broad topic into narrower and narrower subcategories. The graphic shows how questions can be used to do this.

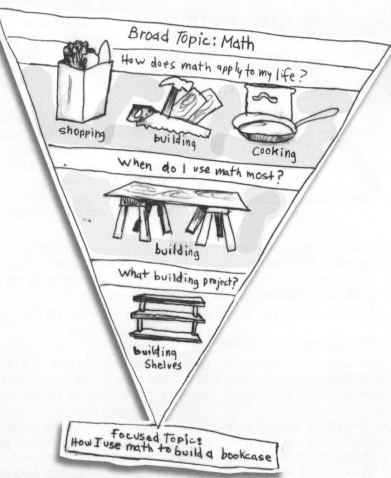

Broad Topic: Math
How does math apply to my life?
shopping
building
cooking
When do I use math most?
building
What building project?
building Shelves
Focused Topic:
How I use math to build a bookcase

Purpose and Audience

Every piece of writing is written for an audience. Even when you write a secret in your journal, you are writing for an audience of one—yourself. To succeed in any writing task, you have to understand what your audience wants and needs to know.

Pinpointing your purpose is also essential when you write. Sometimes you write to fulfill an assignment; at other times you decide to whom you will write and why. For example, you might decide to write a letter to your sister about your bunkmates at camp. Your purpose might be to describe your bunkmates' looks and personalities. Another time you might write a letter to your principal about cellphones. Your purpose might be to convince her to ban cellphones inside your school.

- **Defining Your Purpose and Audience** Answering certain questions can help you define your purpose for writing and identify your audience.

  - *What is my topic?*
  - *What is my purpose for writing?*
  - *Who is my audience?*
  - *What does my audience already know about this topic?*
  - *What does my audience need or want to know?*
  - *What type of language will suit my audience and purpose?*

Gathering Details

After finding a topic to write about, you will want to explore and develop your ideas. You can do this on your own or with classmates. The following techniques may help you.

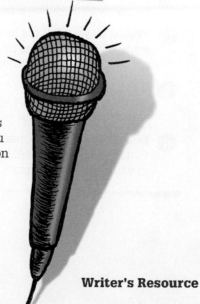

- **Interview a Classmate** Questioning a classmate can help both of you develop your topics. You can interview a friend who has a special skill. Find out how she or he developed that skill. You could also find an interview partner and question each other on an acceptable topic.

- **Fill In an Observation Chart** To come up with details to develop a piece of descriptive writing or to help you create the setting and characters for a narrative, you can fill in an observation chart. A writer created the chart that follows while wondering how to describe the school cafeteria at lunch time.

Once you have completed your own observation chart, circle the details you want to include in your piece of writing.

SUBJECT: CAFETERIA AT LUNCHTIME

See	Hear	Touch	Smell	Taste
swirl of motion	kids' voices	hot melted cheese	stuff they wash the floors with	tart juice
fluorescent lights	thuds and clunks of chairs and trays	wet plastic trays	delicious aroma of pizza	pepperoni
colors of plastic trays	scraping of chairs	cold, wet milk cartons	apple crisp baking	mild cheese

- **Do a Focused Freewriting** Freewriting can be used to either find or develop a topic. When it is used to develop a topic, it is called focused freewriting. Follow these four steps as you use focused freewriting to develop a topic:

1 Set a time limit. (Until you get used to freewriting, write for no more than five minutes at a time.)

2 Repeat to yourself the key words of your topic, and then write whatever comes to mind about them. Do not stop; do not read or correct what you write.

3 If you get stuck, repeat a word (even the word *stuck*), or write the last word you wrote until new ideas come. You can be sure they will.

4 When the time is up, read what you wrote. Underline parts that you like best. Decide which of these parts you will use in your piece of writing.

Drafting

Drafting
- Putting ideas down on paper
- Exploring new ideas as you write

In writing, an **organizational plan** is an outline or map that shows the key ideas and details that you want to include in the order that you want to include them. Following such a plan can help you structure your writing so that it makes a clearer and stronger impression on your audience.

Organizing Your Ideas

Often, a piece of writing lends itself to a particular order. For instance, if you are describing a scene so that readers can visualize it, spatial order may be your best option. However, if you are describing a person, you might compare and contrast the person with someone else you and your readers know, or you might reveal the person's character by describing a series of past incidents in chronological order.

ORGANIZATIONAL PLANS

Chronological Order	Events or details are arranged in the order in which they occur. Words showing **chronological order** include *first, next,* and *finally.*
Spatial Order	Details are given by location so that readers can visualize the scene, object, or person. Expressions showing **spatial order** include *to the right (or left), in the middle, nearby, in front of, on, beside, behind,* and *next to.*
Order of Importance	Events and details are arranged from the least to the most significant, or vice versa. Expressions showing **order of importance** include *most important, above all,* and *also.*
Logical Order	Each point that is made builds on previous information, and ideas are clearly linked. Expressions showing **logical order** include *it follows that, for example,* and *therefore.*

Introductions

The introduction to your paper should include a **thesis statement**, a sentence about your central purpose or what you plan to "show" in your paper. Here is a thesis statement for a paper on the ancient Kingdom of Ghana:

> Ghana was one of the strongest, richest kingdoms of its time.

An effective written introduction draws your readers into your paper and interests them in the subject. The way you introduce your paper depends on the goal you want to achieve and the type of writing you are doing. The following are some possibilities.

GOAL	TYPE OF INTRODUCTION	COULD BE USED FOR
Be clear and direct	a statement of the main point	• an informative paper • a research report • an editorial
Appeal to readers' senses	a vivid description	• a description of a scene • an observation report • a character sketch
Get readers' attention	a startling fact or statistic	• an informative paper • a persuasive essay • a research report
Lure readers into the story quickly	dialogue	• a story • a personal narrative
Make readers wonder	a question	• an informative paper • a persuasive essay • a research report
Give your writing authority	a quotation	• a persuasive essay • an informative paper • a research report • a book review or report

Elaboration

Sometimes what you write seems to be only the bare bones of a composition. In order to flesh out your work, you must add the right details. This process is called **elaboration**.

Certain types of elaboration are more effective for certain forms of writing, but there are no hard-and-fast rules about which type of elaboration to use. You can use facts and statistics in a poem if you want to! Some types of elaboration include the following:

Facts and Statistics	Facts are statements that can be proved true. Statistics are facts that you express as numbers.
Sensory Details	Sensory details are details that appeal to the five senses—sight, hearing, touch, smell, and taste.
Anecdotes	An anecdote is a short account of an interesting or funny incident.
Examples	An example is an instance of something.
Quotations	A quotation is someone's words—often those of an expert or public figure.
Personal Feelings	Personal feelings are thoughts and emotions that are yours alone.
Memories	Memories are recollections from the past.
Observations	Observations are things you have seen or noticed firsthand.
Reasons	Reasons are explanations of why something is true.

- **Uses of Elaboration** Here is a chart showing the types of elaboration you can use and what each is used for.

TYPE OF ELABORATION	USED FOR	
facts and statistics	essays news stories feature articles business letters	advertisements reviews research reports
sensory details	observations poems personal essays advertisements	stories plays descriptions
anecdotes	journal entries personal letters news stories	personal essays feature articles
examples	essays news stories business letters editorials advertisements poems	responses to literature book reports research reports feature articles reviews
quotations	news stories feature articles essays	responses to literature book reports
personal feelings	journal entries personal letters personal essays poems	editorials observations responses to literature persuasive essays
memories	journal entries personal letters personal essays poems	descriptions observations stories
observations	journal entries personal letters personal essays poems	reviews feature articles stories plays
reasons	essays business letters reviews book reports news stories feature articles	editorials advertisements research reports responses to literature personal essays

Conclusions

The type of conclusion you will use depends on your subject and on your purpose. Here are some ways to end a paper effectively, with suggestions on what type of writing might best suit each type of conclusion.

● **Summarize Your Main Points** Review the most important ideas you have discussed and what you have said about them. Instead of just listing them, try to present them in a creative way. This will help you remember your key ideas.

This is a great way to conclude the following types of writing:
- *observation report*
- *personal essay*
- *research report*
- *informative essay*
- *comparison-and-contrast essay*

● **Resolve Conflicts and Problems** Bring your narrative to a close by addessing unanswered questions. Did the main character survive the battle? Did the enemies become friends?

This is especially important when you are writing the following:
- *personal narrative or autobiographical incident*
- *story or fable*
- *play*

● **Recommend an Action or Solution** You have presented your readers with an issue or problem. Now tell them what they can do about it. This will enable them to do something constructive after reading.

This is a great way to conclude these writing pieces:
- *persuasive essay*
- *letter to the editor*
- *problem-and-solution essay*

● **Offer a Final Comment or Ask a Question** Talk directly to your readers. You can do this by sharing your personal feelings, asking questions, or both. This will make your readers feel more involved.

This is a great way to conclude the following:
- *personal letter*
- *persuasive essay*
- *response to literature*
- *review*

Revising

Revising
- Consulting with peer readers
- Evaluating suggested changes
- Making revisions

When you have included all your ideas and finished your first draft, you are ready to revise it. Few writers produce perfect drafts the first time around. You can almost always improve your paper by reworking it. Here are some hints to help you revise your work.

● **Take a Break** Do not begin to revise right after you finish a draft. In a few hours or days you will be better able to see the strengths and weaknesses of your work.

● **Look It Over** When you reread your draft, look for ways to improve it. Use a pencil to mark places where an idea is unclear or the writing is jumpy or disjointed. Also, remember to let yourself know when you have written an effective image or provided a wonderful example. Write Good! next to the parts that work well.

● **Read Aloud** Your ear is a wonderful editor. Read your work aloud and listen for dull, unnecessary, or awkward parts that you did not notice when you read your work silently. Are there any passages that you stumble over as you read aloud? Try different wordings and then read them aloud with expression, emphasizing certain words. Listen and identify which wording sounds best.

● **Share Your Work** Your friends or family members can help you by telling you how your work affects them. Ask them whether your ideas are clear. What is interesting? What is boring?

When it is time to revise a draft, many writers are tempted to just correct a few spelling mistakes and combine a sentence or two. Eliminating surface errors, however, is only a small part of revising. After all, what good is a neat and perfectly spelled paper if it does not make sense or prove a point? The word *revise* means "to see again" or "to see from a new perspective." In order to revise your work, you need to rethink your basic ideas.

Revising by Rethinking

Taking a close look at the ideas in your draft is the most important part of revising. Usually, you will spot some "idea" problems. When you do, it is time to get to work. Here are some strategies to help you rethink your draft.

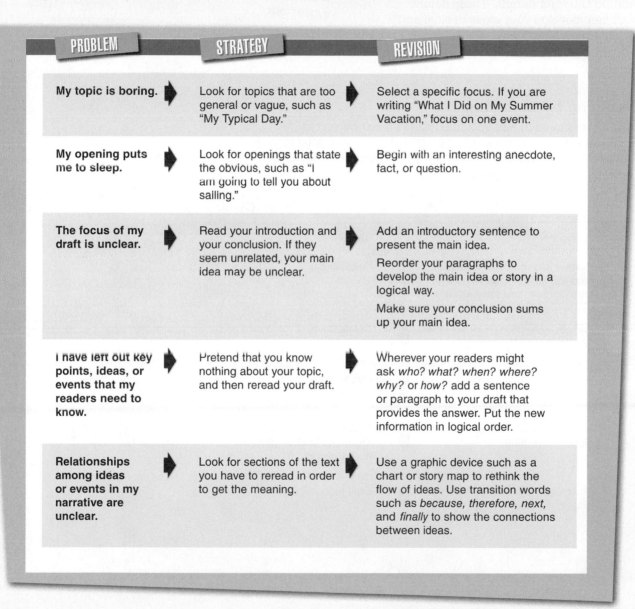

PROBLEM	STRATEGY	REVISION
My topic is boring.	Look for topics that are too general or vague, such as "My Typical Day."	Select a specific focus. If you are writing "What I Did on My Summer Vacation," focus on one event.
My opening puts me to sleep.	Look for openings that state the obvious, such as "I am going to tell you about sailing."	Begin with an interesting anecdote, fact, or question.
The focus of my draft is unclear.	Read your introduction and your conclusion. If they seem unrelated, your main idea may be unclear.	Add an introductory sentence to present the main idea. Reorder your paragraphs to develop the main idea or story in a logical way. Make sure your conclusion sums up your main idea.
I have left out key points, ideas, or events that my readers need to know.	Pretend that you know nothing about your topic, and then reread your draft.	Wherever your readers might ask *who? what? when? where? why?* or *how?* add a sentence or paragraph to your draft that provides the answer. Put the new information in logical order.
Relationships among ideas or events in my narrative are unclear.	Look for sections of the text you have to reread in order to get the meaning.	Use a graphic device such as a chart or story map to rethink the flow of ideas. Use transition words such as *because, therefore, next,* and *finally* to show the connections between ideas.

Revising by Elaborating

When you are sure your ideas are clear and in order, it is time to judge whether you have provided enough appropriate details. Remember, elaborating means developing and expanding on ideas by adding the right details. These details will help develop your ideas in clear and interesting ways.

You might choose any of the following types of details explained on page 327:

- *facts and statistics*
- *sensory details*
- *anecdotes*
- *examples*
- *quotations*
- *personal feelings*
- *memories*
- *observations*
- *reasons*

Revising by Reducing

Just as you need to add specific details when you revise your draft, you sometimes need to get rid of material that is unnecessary. Following are some ways you can solve revision problems by removing unneeded words.

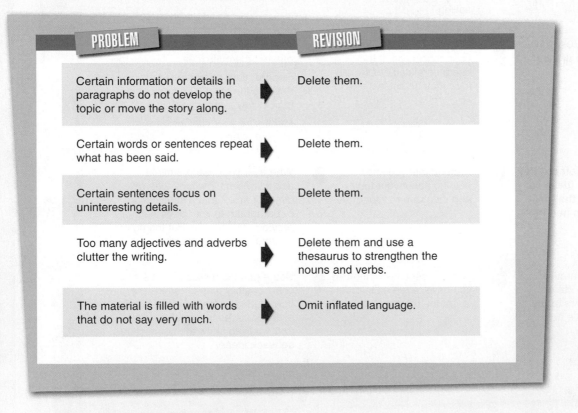

PROBLEM	REVISION
Certain information or details in paragraphs do not develop the topic or move the story along.	Delete them.
Certain words or sentences repeat what has been said.	Delete them.
Certain sentences focus on uninteresting details.	Delete them.
Too many adjectives and adverbs clutter the writing.	Delete them and use a thesaurus to strengthen the nouns and verbs.
The material is filled with words that do not say very much.	Omit inflated language.

Revising by Rewording

Choosing the right words is essential to good writing. As a final step in revising, improve your choice of words. At times, a better word will spring to mind. At other times, use a thesaurus to find words. As you rework your draft, you will reveal your own style.

The following chart can help you find the right word.

PROBLEM

Have I used the most effective word possible?

REVISION ACTIVITIES:

Choose specific nouns.
General: I wish I had some food.
Specific: I wish I had some pizza.

Choose active, colorful verbs.
General: The sick man walked to his bed.
Specific: The sick man hobbled to his bed.

Avoid the word _be_.
General: My horse is a good jumper.
Specific: My horse easily jumps four feet.

Choose the active voice.
General: Chocolate should never be fed to dogs.
Specific: Never feed dogs chocolate.

Editing

Editing
- Checking the accuracy of facts
- Correcting errors in spelling, grammar, usage, and mechanics

Here are some specific editing strategies that may help you.

Editing is the process of finding and correcting errors in grammar, usage, and mechanics. When you have finished drafting and revising your paper, here is how to edit your work.

General Tips
- Look first for mistakes that you typically make.
- Proofread your paper for one type of error at a time.
- Read your work aloud word for word.
- When in doubt, use reference sources to help you.

SPECIFIC TASKS	STRATEGY
Check Your Grammar Have you written any run-on sentences or fragments? Do your subjects and verbs agree?	Check that each sentence has a subject and verb. Use a comma and conjunction to connect main clauses. Make sure that singular subjects have singular verbs and plural subjects have plural verbs.
Check Your Usage Have you used the past forms of irregular verbs correctly? Have you used subject and object pronouns correctly?	Watch out for irregular verb forms such as *seen, done, gone,* and *taken.* Check that the pronouns *me, him, her, us,* and *them* are used only after verbs or prepositions.
Check Your Punctuation Does each sentence have the correct end mark? Have you used apostrophes in nouns, but not in pronouns, to show possession? Have you used quotation marks around words from another source?	Look for inverted word order that may signal a question. Use a phrase with *of* to check for possession. Avoid plagiarism by checking your notecards to be sure.
Check Your Capitalization Did you begin each sentence or direct quotation with a capital letter? Have you capitalized proper nouns?	Look for an end mark and then check the next letter. Look for the name of specific people and places.
Check Your Spelling Did you correctly spell all words?	Use a dictionary. Look for your common errors.

Publishing

Publishing
- Producing a final polished copy of your writing
- Sharing your writing

Once you have made a final, clean copy of a piece of writing that pleases you, you may want to share it with others. What you have to say might be important or meaningful to someone else. Here are some ways you can publish your writing—that is, bring it to the public eye.

- Submit your work to a school newspaper or magazine.

- Have a public reading of your work. Perform it in one of the following ways:
  - Over the school P.A. or radio system
  - In a school assembly or talent show
  - In a group in which members take turns reading their work
  - At your local library or community center

- If your work is a play or skit, have a group of classmates or the drama club present it.

- Work with classmates to put together a class collection of written work. You can have it copied and bound at a copy shop.

- Submit your piece to a local or national writing contest.

- Send your writing to a local newspaper or area magazine.

- Publish your own work and the writings of classmates by using a computer with a desktop publishing program.

Reflecting

Your writing can help you learn about your subject or the writing process—or even yourself. Once you have completed a writing assignment, sit back and think about the experience for a few minutes.

Ask yourself questions such as the following:

- What did I learn about my subject through my writing?

- Did I experiment with writing techniques and forms? If so, were my experiments successful? If not, what held me back?

- Am I pleased with what I wrote? Why or why not?

- Did I have difficulty with any part of the writing process? If so, which part gave me trouble? What strategies did I use to overcome my difficulties?

This resource section contains tips on writing in English and information on grammar topics that are sometimes challenging for English learners.

The numbered arrows in the side margins also appear on other pages of the Grammar Handbook that provide information on writing or instruction in these same grammar topics.

EL1

Understand the Demands of Writing in a Second Language

Talk with other writers.

When you write in an unfamiliar situation, it may be helpful to find a few examples of the type of writing you are trying to produce. For example, if you are writing a letter of application to accompany a résumé, ask your friends to share similar letters of application with you and look for the various ways your friends presented themselves in writing in that situation.

Use your native language as a resource.

You can also use your native language to develop your texts. Many people, when they cannot find an appropriate word in English, write down a word, a phrase, or even a sentence in their native language and consult a dictionary later. Incorporating key terms from your native language is also a possible strategy.

A Japanese term adds perspective to this sentence.

"Some political leaders need to have *wakimae*—a realistic idea of one's own place in the world."

Use dictionaries.

Bilingual dictionaries are especially useful when you want to check your understanding of an English word or find equivalent words for culture-specific concepts and technical terms. Some bilingual dictionaries also provide sample sentences.

Learner's dictionaries, such as the *Longman Dictionary of American English,* include information about count/non-count nouns and transitive/intransitive verbs. Many of them also provide sample sentences.

Understand English idioms.

Some English idioms function like proverbs. In the United States, for example, if someone has to "eat crow," they have been forced to admit they were wrong about something. But simpler examples of idiomatic usage—word order, word choice, and combinations that don't follow any obvious set of rules—are common in even the plainest English. If you are unsure about idioms, use Google or another search engine to find out how to use them.

INCORRECT IDIOM — Here is the answer **of** your question.

ACCEPTED IDIOM — Here is the answer **to** your question.

INCORRECT IDIOM — I had jet **legs** after flying across the Pacific.

ACCEPTED IDIOM — I had jet **lag** after flying across the Pacific.

Understand Nouns in English

Perhaps the most troublesome conventions for nonnative speakers are those that guide usage of the common articles *the, a,* and *an.* To understand how articles work in English, you must first understand how the language uses **nouns.**

Proper nouns and common nouns

EL2

There are two basic kinds of nouns. A **proper noun** begins with a capital letter and names a unique person, place, or thing: *Elvis Presley, Russia, Eiffel Tower.*

The other basic kind of noun is called a **common noun.** Common nouns such as *man, country* and *tower,* do not name a unique person, place, or thing. Common nouns are not names and are not capitalized unless they are the first word in a sentence.

PROPER NOUNS
Beethoven   Michael Jordan   Honda
South Korea   Africa
Empire State Building

COMMON NOUNS
composer   athlete   vehicle   country
continent   building

Count and non-count nouns

EL3

Common nouns can be classified as either **count** or **non-count.** Count nouns can be made plural, usually by adding the letter *s* (*finger, fingers*) or by using their plural forms (*person, people; datum, data*).

Non-count nouns cannot be counted directly and cannot take the plural form (*information,* but not *informations; garbage,* but not *garbages*). Some nouns can be either count or non-count, depending on how they are used. *Hair* can refer to either a strand of hair, when it serves as a count noun, or a mass of hair, when it becomes a non-count noun.

Count nouns usually take both singular and plural forms, while non-count nouns usually do not take plural forms and are not counted directly. A count noun can have a number before it (as in *two books, three oranges*) and can be qualified with adjectives such as *many* (as in *many books*), *some* (as in *some schools*), and *few* (as in *few people volunteered*).

Non-count nouns can be counted or quantified in only two ways: either by general adjectives that treat the noun as a mass (*much* information, *some* news) or by placing another noun between the quantifying word and the non-count noun (two *kinds* of information, a *piece* of news).

CORRECT USE OF HAIR *AS A COUNT NOUN*
Three blonde hairs were in the sink.

CORRECT USE OF HAIR *AS A NON-COUNT NOUN*
My roommate spent an hour combing his hair.

| INCORRECT | five horse   many accident |
| CORRECT | five horses
many accidents |

| INCORRECT | three breads
I would like a mustard on my hot dog. |
| CORRECT | three loaves of bread
I would like some mustard on my hot dog. |

Understand Articles in English

Articles indicate that a noun is about to appear, and they clarify what the noun refers to. There are only two kinds of articles in English, definite and indefinite.

1. **the:** *The* is a **definite article,** meaning that it refers to (1) a specific object already known to the reader, (2) one about to be made known to the reader, or (3) a unique object.

2. **a, an:** The **indefinite articles** *a* and *an* refer to an object whose specific identity is not known to the reader. The only difference between *a* and *an* is that *a* is used before a consonant sound (*a man, a friend, a yellow toy*), while *an* is used before a vowel sound (*an orange, an old shoe*).

Look at these sentences, which are identical except for their articles, and imagine that each is taken from a different newspaper story.

Rescue workers lifted **the** man to safety.

Rescue workers lifted **a** man to safety.

By using the definite article *the*, the first sentence indicates that the reader already knows something about the identity of this man. The news story has already referred to him.

The indefinite article *a* in the second sentence indicates that the reader does not know anything about this man. Either this is the first time the news story has referred to him, or there are other men in need of rescue.

RULES FOR USING ARTICLES

1. *A* or *an* is not used with non-count nouns.

   INCORRECT The crowd hummed with **an** excitement.

   CORRECT The crowd hummed with excitement.

2. *A* or *an* is used with singular count nouns whose identity is unknown to the reader or writer.

   INCORRECT Detective Johnson was reading book.

   CORRECT Detective Johnson was reading **a** book.

3. *The* is used with most count and non-count nouns whose particular identity is known to readers.

   CORRECT I bought a book yesterday. **The** book is about kayaking.

4. *The* is used when the noun is accompanied by a superlative form of a modifier: for example, *best, worst, highest, lowest, most expensive, least interesting.*

   CORRECT **The** most interesting book about climbing Mount Everest is Jon Krakauer's *Into Thin Air.*

Understand Verbs and Modifiers in English

Verbs, verb phrases, and helping verbs

EL5

Verbs in English can be divided between one-word verbs like *run, speak,* and *look,* and verb phrases like *may have run, have spoken,* and *will be looking.* The words that appear before the main verbs—*may, have, will, do,* and *be*—are called **auxiliary (or helping) verbs**. Auxiliary verbs help express something about the action of main verbs: for example, when the action occurs, whether the subject acted or was acted upon, or whether or not an action occurred.

Indicating tense with *be* verbs

EL6

Like the auxiliary verbs *have* and *do, be* changes form to signal tense. In addition to *be* itself, the **be verbs** are *is, am, are, was, were,* and *been.*

To show ongoing action, *be* verbs are followed by the present participle, which is a verb ending in *-ing.*

INCORRECT	I **am think** of all the things I'd rather **be do**.
CORRECT	I **am thinking** of all the things I'd rather **be doing**.

To show that an action is being done to the subject rather than by the subject, follow *be* verbs with the past participle (a verb usually ending in *-ed, -en,* or *-t*).

INCORRECT	The movie **was direct** by John Woo.
CORRECT	The movie **was directed** by John Woo.

Auxiliary verbs that express certain conditions

EL7

The auxiliary verbs *will, would, can, could, may, might, shall, must,* and *should* express conditions like possibility, permission, speculation, expectation, and necessity. Unlike the auxiliary verbs *be, have,* and *do,* the auxiliary verbs listed above do not change form based on the grammatical subject of the sentence (*I, you, she, he, it, we, they*).

Two basic rules apply to all uses of these auxiliary verbs. First, these auxiliary verbs are always followed by the simple form of the verb. The simple form is the verb by itself, in the present tense, such as *talk* but not *talked, talking,* or *to talk.*

INCORRECT	She **should studies** harder to pass the exam.
CORRECT	She **should study** harder to pass the exam.

The second rule is that you should not use these auxiliary verbs consecutively.

INCORRECT	If you work harder at writing, you **might could** improve.
CORRECT	If you work harder at writing, you **might** improve.

1. **Speculation:** If you had flown, you **would** have arrived yesterday.

2. **Ability:** She **can** run faster than Jennifer.

3. **Necessity:** You **must** know what you want to do.

4. **Intention:** He **will** wash his own clothes.

5. **Permission:** You **may** leave now.

6. **Advice:** You **should** wash behind your ears.

7. **Possibility:** It **might** be possible to go home early.

8. **Assumption:** You **must** have stayed up late last night.

9. **Expectation:** You **should** enjoy the movie.

10. **Order:** You **must** leave the building.

EL8

Placement of Modifiers

Modifiers will be unclear if your reader can't connect them to the words to which they refer. How close a modifier is to the noun or verb it modifies provides an important clue to their relationship.

Clarity should be your first goal when using a modifier.

UNCLEAR	Many pedestrians are killed each year by motorists **not using sidewalks**.
CLEAR	Many pedestrians **not using sidewalks** are killed each year by motorists.

An **adverb**—a word or group of words that modifies a verb, adjective, or another adverb—should not come between a verb and its direct object.

AWKWARD	The hurricane destroyed **completely** the city's tallest building.
BETTER	The hurricane **completely** destroyed the city's tallest building.

Try to avoid placing an adverb between *to* and its verb. This construction is called a **split infinitive**.

AWKWARD	The water level was predicted **to not rise**.
BETTER	The water level was predicted **not to rise**.

Understand English Sentence Structure

Words derive much of their meaning from how they function in a sentence.

With the exception of **imperatives** (commands such as *Watch out!*), sentences in English usually contain a *subject* and a *predicate*. A subject names who or what the sentence is about; the predicate tells what the subject is or does.

The Lion	is asleep.
subject	predicate

A predicate consists of at least one main verb. If the verb is **intransitive,** like *exist*, it does not take a direct object. Some verbs are **transitive,** which means they require a **direct object** to complete their meaning.

INCORRECT The bird saw.
CORRECT The bird saw a cat.

Some verbs (*write, learn, read,* and others) can be both transitive and intransitive, depending on how they are used.

INTRANSITIVE Pilots fly.
TRANSITIVE Pilots fly airplanes.

Formal written English requires that each sentence includes a subject and a verb, even when the meaning of the sentence would be clear without it. In some cases you must supply an expletive, such as *it* and *there*.

INCORRECT Is snowing in Alaska.
CORRECT It is snowing in Alaska.

INDEX

Reread and read aloud, 330

Research writing, 312

Response to literature, 312

Restatement, 315

Restrictive phrases or clauses
adjectival, 79, *80*
appositive, **64**
commas with, **260**
participial, 69–70, *71*

Rethinking, 331

Revising, **320**, 330–333

Rewording, 333

Run-ons, 105, **108**, *109*, 254

S —————————————————

Seacraft names, 236, 283

Seasons, names of, 236

Second person, **7**, 8, 183

Semicolons, **269**, *274*
to correct run-ons, 108
to join independent clauses, 90, 98, 269–271
parentheses and, 299
quotation marks with, 277
to separate series, 270–271

Sensory details, **327**, 328

Sentence fluency in writing, 319

Sentences, **42**, 95
adverbial clauses in, 83
adverbs in, 27
appositive phrases in, 65
basic parts, 41
complements, **53–57**, *58*
hard-to-find subjects, 49–51, *52*
subjects and predicates, **42–43**, *44*
beginning with *here* or *there*, **49**, *52*
capitalizing, 230–231, *232*, 240, *246*
colons introducing, 273
combining, 98–99, *100–101*
with adjectival clauses, 79

with appositives/appositive phrases, 66, *67*
to form compound/complex sentences, 92
with gerund phrases, *76*
with participial phrases, 70
with prepositional phrases, *67*
with compound subjects/verbs, **47**
elliptical, **45**, 265–266
ending with abbreviations, 249–250
faulty coordination, 116–117, *118*
faulty parallelism, 113–115, *118*
fragmented, **45–46**, *48*, 105–107, *109*
functions, **96**, *97*
fused, **108**, *109*
inverted. *See* Word order, inverted
locating subjects and verbs in, 46, *48*
negative, 208–210, *211*
in parentheses, 299
pronoun usage in, 165–166, *168*
run-on, 105, **108**, *109*, 254
simple, **90**, *92*
structures, **90–91**, *92*, **341**
supporting, 314
tense sequence in, 142–145, *146*
topic, **313**, 314, 315, 318
varying, 102–103, *104*
word order. *See* Word order, inverted
See also Complex sentences; Compound sentences; Declarative sentences; Exclamatory sentences; Imperative sentences; Interrogative sentences

Sequential events, expressing, 142–145, *146*

Series
commas in, **255**, 256, 272
fragmented, 105, 107
hyphens in, 285
nonparallel items in, 114–115, *118*
numbers/letters marking, 298, 300
semicolons in, 269, 270–271

Sharing your work, 330

Short story, 244, 281, **309**

Simple predicates, **43**, *44*

Simple sentences, **90**, *92*

Simple subjects, **43**, *44*, 48

Simultaneous events, expressing, 142–145, *146*

Single quotation marks, 278

Slashes, **302**, 304–305, *306*

Solution or action, recommending, 329

Spacecraft names, 236, 283

Spatial order, 325

Special events/times, names of, 235

Speech, pause in, 303. *See also* Dialogue

Spelling, 334

Split infinitives, 340

Statements with question mark, 250, 251

Statistics, 314, **327**, 328

Stringy sentences, 116, 117

Subject and verb agreement, 169
compound subjects and, 175–176, *177*
confusing subjects and, 178–181, *182*
in number, **170–171**, *173*
singular/plural subjects and, 172, *173*, 174–175, *177*

Subject complements, **56–57**, *58*

Subjects, 42, 341
adjectival phrases modifying, 61, *63*
appositive phrases and, 65
complete, **42**, *44*
confusing, 178–181, *182*
fragments with, 106
gerunds as, 72
hard-to-find, 49–51, *52*
in independent clause, 91
of infinitive, 162